Paradigm SHIFT

TRANSFORMATIONAL LIFE TEACHINGS *of the* LUBAVITCHER REBBE

Authors
Rabbi Mordechai Dinerman
Rabbi Naftali Silberberg

Curriculum Development
Rabbi Eli Raksin
Rabbi Yanky Raskin
Mrs. Rachel Holzkenner

Printed in the United States of America

The Rohr Jewish Learning Institute
822 Eastern Parkway, Brooklyn, NY 11213

(888) YOUR-JLI/718-221-6900
www.myJLI.com

The **Rohr Jewish Learning Institute**
gratefully acknowledges
the pioneering support of

George and Pamela Rohr

SINCE ITS INCEPTION,
the **Rohr JLI** has been
a beneficiary of the vision, generosity,
care, and concern
of the **Rohr family**

In the merit of
the tens of thousands of hours of Torah study
by **JLI** students worldwide,
may they be blessed with health,
Yiddishe nachas from all their loved ones,
and extraordinary success
in all their endeavors

Paradigm Shift

IS DEDICATED

in loving memory of

מרים בת נתנאל ושרה ע"ה

Miriam bat Netanel and Sara

and in the merit of

יצחק בן לאה

רבקה ויקה בת רחל

מיכאל בן רבקה ויקה

רות בת רבקה ויקה

Yitzchak ben Leah

Rivka Vika bat Rachel

Michael ben Rivka Vika

Ruth bat Rivka Vika

The Rebbe often blessed those who dedicate themselves to Jewish education and continuity that they should be showered with boundless spiritual and material goodness.

May this be realized to the fullest extent, accompanying their family in all of their endeavors, and may they be blessed with health, nachas from all their loved ones, and extraordinary success.

The Rebbe

Rabbi Menachem Mendel Schneerson

of righteous memory

1902-1994

Known widely as "the Rebbe," Rabbi Menachem M. Schneerson, of righteous memory, assumed leadership of the Chabad Lubavitch movement in 1950, establishing a worldwide network of educational, social, and religious institutions which transformed the post-Holocaust Jewish landscape. One of the foremost religious leaders of our time, the Rebbe touched the lives of countless individuals and continues to live on through his visionary teachings, and in the work of his emissaries whom he charged with bringing the light of Judaism to every corner of the globe.

THIS COURSE IS OFFERED IN COMMEMORATION OF THE 20TH ANNIVERSARY OF THE REBBE'S PASSING.

THE REBBE: A BRIEF BIOGRAPHY

by Rabbi Shmuel Klatzkin, PhD

Rabbi Menachem Mendel Schneerson, the seventh leader of the Chabad-Lubavitch movement, was born in Nikolaev, Ukraine, on the 11th of Nisan, 5662 (April 18, 1902). The Rebbe's father, Rabbi Levi Yitzchak Schneerson, was a fourth-generation descendant of the third leader of Chabad, after whom the child was named. The Rebbe's mother, Chana Schneerson, was the daughter of the rabbi of Nikolaev, Rabbi Meir Shlomo Yanovski. The Rebbe had two younger siblings, Dovber (murdered by the Nazis) and Yisrael Aryeh Leib (d. 1952). In 1909, the Rebbe's family relocated to Yekatrinoslav, now known as Dnepropetrovsk, Ukraine, where Rabbi Levi Yitzchak was appointed as the city's rabbi.

At a very young age, the Rebbe's teachers informed his parents that his scholastic abilities and knowledge far surpassed that of his peers. From that point onward, the Rebbe's education was almost entirely a private program of study with his father and with tutors, which enabled him to proceed at his own pace.

In 1923, the Rebbe first met the man he considered his own Rebbe, Rabbi Yosef Yitzchak Schneersohn, the sixth Lubavitcher Rebbe. There was mutual admiration, and the Rebbe was soon engaged to marry Rabbi Yosef Yitzchak's second daughter, Rebbetzin Chaya Mushka. In 1927, the Rebbe left the Soviet Union together with his future wife and father-in-law. One year later, the Rebbe's wedding was celebrated in Warsaw, Poland.

The young couple moved to Berlin, where the Rebbe attended the University of Berlin and studied math, physics, and philosophy. As the Nazis rose to power, the Rebbe relocated to Paris, where he continued his higher education, studying mechanics, electrical engineering, and mathematics. Throughout this period, the Rebbe continued his intensive Judaic studies regimen; many decades later, notebooks filled with scholarly writings penned during this period were published. During this period, the Rebbe also edited a journal of rabbinic and Chasidic thought, *Hatamim*, and served as his father-in-law's right-hand man in many areas of his communal activism.

When World War II erupted, both the Rebbe and his father-in-law were overtaken by the German conquests; both overcame many difficulties and made their ways, separately, to America. The Rebbe arrived in 1941, settled in the Crown Heights neighborhood of Brooklyn, and immediately assumed a senior administrative role in the Chabad movement, being appointed by Rabbi Yosef Yitzchak to chair the three organizations that conducted Chabad's educational, social service, and publishing activities. During these years, the Rebbe published a commentary, with extensive scholarly citations, on the Passover *Haggadah*. He also compiled *Hayom Yom*, a work of brief teachings from his father-in-law, which were to be studied each day. For a brief period, the Rebbe also joined the war effort by employing his electrical engineering skills at the Brooklyn Navy Yard.

In the winter of 1950, Rabbi Yosef Yitzchak passed away. At first, the Rebbe was highly reluctant to accept the mantle of leadership; but on the first anniversary of Rabbi Yosef Yitzchak's passing, the Rebbe acceded to the pleas of Chabad Chasidim worldwide and assumed the leadership of the movement. Immediately, the Rebbe set for himself the task of continuing and exponentially expanding the work his father-in-law had begun, that of fostering Jewish identity, Torah study, and mitzvah observance. The Rebbe pointed young couples outward, challenging them to go even to places with little Jewish infrastructure and to build Jewish life there, if necessary, from the ground up. Within ten days after the passing of Rabbi Yosef Yitzchak, the Rebbe sent a *shliach* (emissary) to Morocco.

It took time for Chasidim to grasp the scope of the Rebbe's plan. Starting in the late Fifties, the Rebbe would often cite the verse (Genesis 28:14), "And and you shall burst forth westward, eastward, northward, and southward," and adopted this as Chabad's motto. It was at this time that a significant number of emissaries started to establish "Chabad Houses" in various cities around the world. The Rebbe also set up and managed a covert network of aid for the Jews who remained behind the Iron Curtain.

In 1964, the Rebbe's mother passed away. She had immigrated to the United States in 1947 (her husband, the Rebbe's father, had passed away in the USSR in 1944), from which time on the Rebbe would unfailingly visit her every day. In the wake of her passing, the Rebbe began a new initiative: at every Shabbat gathering, the Rebbe would address a passage of Rashi—the most famous biblical exegete—and deliver a sophisticated analysis of its content. The result was an altogether novel method of studying Rashi.

In response to the 1967 attempt by Arab nations to destroy Israel, the Rebbe initiated the first of his mitzvah campaigns. He encouraged all Jewish men, especially Israeli soldiers, to perform the mitzvah of *tefilin,* thereby eliciting divine protection and strength. Within a few years, the Rebbe began other mitzvah campaigns: women and young girls should light Shabbat candles, Jewish homes should be equipped with valid *mezuzot,* and numerous others.

The Rebbe kept himself deeply informed on all matters affecting Israel, and Israelis of all stripes increasingly sought his counsel. Yitzchak Rabin, Zalman Shazar, Menachem Begin, Ariel Sharon, and many others from all parts of Israeli society came to his study to talk and exchanged correspondence. The Rebbe constantly sought Israel's integrity, safety, and peace. After the miraculous victory of the Six-Day War, the Rebbe often spoke publically about many Israeli issues, and the Israeli press was always attentive.

In 1972 when the Rebbe turned seventy and was urged by Chasidim to slow down and rest, he delivered a public address in which he stated that he would not decelerate but, to the contrary, would augment his activities. He asked that his emissaries establish during his seventy-first year seventy-one additional Jewish institutions.

On the holiday of Shemini Atzeret 1977, the Rebbe suffered a severe heart attack. While he did recover, he was eventually forced to cut certain routines out of his schedule. Most notably, the Rebbe ceased to hold regular private meetings with people, something he had done for more than thirty years, two or three nights a week.

Throughout his leadership, the Rebbe focused on children's education, emblemized by his presiding over the Lag Ba'omer parade. The Rebbe initiated these parades in the 1940s, and they seem to have been the first Jewish public parades in the United States. In the early 1980s, the Rebbe established *Tzivos Hashem* ("God's Army"), a worldwide organization serving the physical and spiritual needs of Jewish children.

Also in the early Eighties, the Rebbe pointed out that Jewish acceptance in the Western world raised a new possibility barely imaginable in preceding centuries: active engagement with the non-Jewish world. It is fundamental to Judaism, the Rebbe taught, that all humanity is created, sustained, and governed by God. By teaching the outer and inner meanings of the Seven Noahide Laws, the Rebbe taught, Jews could teach the world that it is meant to be a place of peace and of blessing. The Rebbe also emphasized that education must be centered on virtue and holiness, and to this end he strongly encouraged that a "moment of silence" be established in the American public schools.

The Rebbe's wife, Chaya Mushka, passed away in 1988. After her passing, the Rebbe often spoke about the need for "the living to take to heart" her legacy and derive personal positive life lessons.

Starting in 1986, the Rebbe would spend hours every Sunday standing and greeting people, one by one, distributing dollars for them to give to charity. During these brief encounters, the Rebbe would also respond to people's requests for blessing and advice.

In 1991, the Rebbe reassured the Jewish people that Israel would not be harmed by the Iraqi threats associated with the Gulf War. During this period, the Rebbe spoke about the bloodless fall of the Iron Curtain and considered it a sign that the world was ready for complete redemption. In May 1991, the Rebbe spoke with great directness to his Chasidim and told them that he had done all he could do and that now the work of bringing Mashiach was in their hands.

In the winter of 1992, the Rebbe suffered a stroke that took away his speech. On the 3rd of Tamuz 5754 (June 12, 1994), the Rebbe passed away. He was interred next to his father-in-law in Montefiore Cemetery in Queens, New York.

Thus far, more than two hundred volumes of the Rebbe's teachings—talks, essays, and letters—have been published. And in the two decades following his passing, more and more men and women were inspired by the Rebbe's call. Today there are more than four thousand couples stationed in over one thousand communities in some eighty countries who have dedicated themselves to be the Rebbe's emissaries.

TABLE OF CONTENTS

1 Lesson 1
Seeing a Beautiful Garden

37 Lesson 2
Realizing Your Potential

73 Lesson 3
Eliminating the Divide

101 Lesson 4
Synching with the Divine

127 Lesson 5
Redefining Failure

155 Lesson 6
Opening Our Eyes

185 Additional Readings

264 Glossary

LESSON 1

Seeing a Beautiful Garden

Many a scientific study has concluded that people who tend to view things through a positive prism lead happier and more successful lives. But is it possible to see goodness in everything? Even if feasible, is it a naïve and unrealistic approach to life? A sophisticated understanding of reality uncovers a world in which opportunity, positivity, and goodness abound.

Lesson Introduction

Half Full or Half Empty?

LEARNING EXERCISE 1

In the charts below, choose your most and least likely responses to the situations described. (Ignore the numbers on the right side of the charts.)

A. Your child is not conforming to classroom rules and also instigates others to disrupt class.

most / least	Every child has ups and downs.	1 2 3 4 5
most / least	I'm not a good parent.	1 2 3 4 5
most / least	I wish he were like his sister.	1 2 3 4 5
most / least	He has lots of energy that needs to be channeled.	1 2 3 4 5
most / least	Kids are not as well mannered as they used to be.	1 2 3 4 5
most / least	He has leadership qualities.	1 2 3 4 5

B. A newcomer opens a competing business within a mile of your own.

most / least	I'm not good at my job.	1 2 3 4 5
most / least	I'm going to have to work harder.	1 2 3 4 5
most / least	This can bankrupt me.	1 2 3 4 5
most / least	The demand for my goods/services has risen recently.	1 2 3 4 5
most / least	I can't believe there isn't a law that forbids this.	1 2 3 4 5
most / least	This will compel me to improve the quality of my product and service.	1 2 3 4 5

C. You are approaching your seventieth birthday.

most / least	Older is wiser.	1 2 3 4 5
most / least	My best years are behind me.	1 2 3 4 5
most / least	I'm unable to be very productive anymore.	1 2 3 4 5
most / least	I need to retire.	1 2 3 4 5
most / least	I look forward to many more happy years.	1 2 3 4 5
most / least	The younger generation does not "get it."	1 2 3 4 5

LEARNING EXERCISE 2

Where on this continuum would you put the realist?

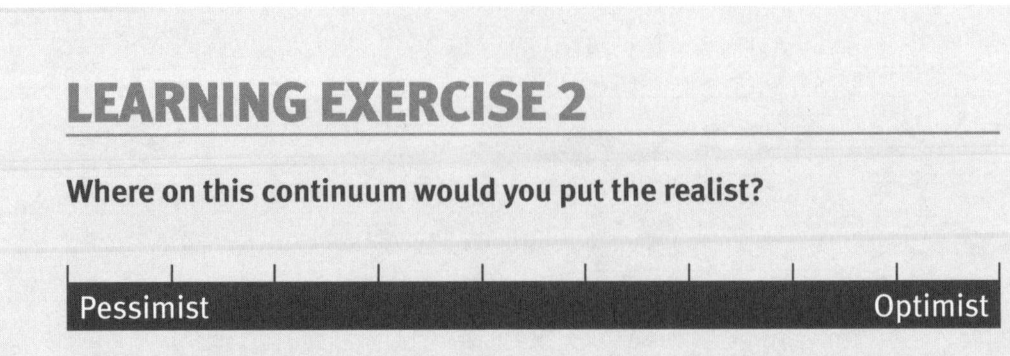

I Have Come to My Garden

LEARNING EXERCISE 3

Match up each entity on the left with the most suitable metaphor on the right. (You may use the same metaphor multiple times.)

You	**Desert**
Your family	**Farm**
Your social circle	**Field**
Your job	**Forest**
Your daily schedule	**Garden**
Human beings	**Jungle**
Your synagogue	**Park**
The political arena	**Yard**
Planet Earth	**Zoo**

Text 1

The Rebbe, *Sichot Kodesh* 5732, 1:361–362

אז מ'הייבט זיך אן ארום קוקן בעיני בשר, מיט פליישיגע אויגן, זעהט מען דאן די "פלייש" און די גשמיות שבכל דבר, ווערט מען דערשראקן: וואס טוט זיך אין דער וועלט? וואס מדור לדור ומשנה לשנה איז "אכשור דרא בתמי"'. אז מ'גיט א קוק, איז ניט דער חלק הטוב איז גובה, און ניט דער סדר ווערט אלץ שטארקער, און ניט קדושה ורוחניות איז מושל ושולט, נאר לכאורה להיפך. ובפרט אין ענינים וואס זיינען פארבונדן מיט אידן. אידן זיינען דאך אלעמאל "אתם המעט מכל העמים" (דברים ז,ז), על אחת כמה וכמה איצטער. לויט דעם חשבון קאן איינפאלן על פי טבע, לויט דעם חשבון פון עיני בשר, אז דאס איז אן ענין פון א יער וואו עס געוועלטיגן חיות רעות, ניט א גארטן וואס גיט פירות מאכל אדם . . .

מ'קאן דאך ווערן ביי זיך אראפגעפאלן, ווי קאן מען האבן א האפענונג אויפטאן מיט דער וועלט און איבערמאכן וועלט ווען מיר זעהען אז מדור לדור ומשנה לשנה איז הולך ופוחת, "אכשור דרא בתמי"'? אפילו אז ער וועט דאס טאן מיט קבלת עול . . . ביי אים ווייזט זיך אויס אז ער וועט זיכער ניט מצליח זיין, ווארום די וועלט איז א יער וואו עס געוועלטיגן חיות רעות, איז טוט ער טאקע כל עניניו, אבער ניט מיט דעם חיות, על אחת כמה וכמה ניט מיט שמחה ווי ס'דארף זיין בעבודת ה'.

When we look about with physical eyes, we only perceive the physical aspects in all that we see and we naturally wonder: what is happening with the world? The situation is steadily deteriorating, from one generation to the next and even from one year to the next. Goodness does not prevail, conditions are not improving, holy and spiritual values do not dominate. This is especially true with regard to Jewish concerns. Our nation has always been a small minority among the world's inhabitants, and this is certainly the case today.

Sichot Kodesh

Transcripts (mostly in Yiddish) of most of the Rebbe's public addresses (*farbrengens*) between 1950 and 1981, published in 50 volumes. For the talks that the Rebbe delivered on Shabbat and holidays, when audio recordings and taking notes are proscribed, a team of trained memorizers (*chozrim*) would reconstruct and transcribe the Rebbe's talk from memory. The Rebbe did not edit or review these transcripts for accuracy.

Such thoughts easily lead to the conclusion that this world is but a jungle dominated by vicious animals, and that it certainly does not remotely resemble a garden that yields edible fruit. . . . Such thoughts also lead to dejection and despair. How can we hope to affect and change the world for the better if the situation is consistently degenerating?

If we reach this conclusion, even if we dutifully obey [and continue to study Torah and do good deeds] . . . we will lack the zest and happiness that is necessary in order to fulfill our mission and properly serve God, inasmuch as it appears that we will certainly fail, for the world is no more than a wild jungle ruled by vicious beasts.

Text 2

Song of Songs 5:1

בָּאתִי לְגַנִּי אֲחֹתִי כַלָּה.

I have come to my garden, my sister, [my] bride.

Text 3

The Rebbe, *Sichot Kodesh* 5732, 1:362–363

מיר זאלן וויסן זיין אז די וועלט . . . איז א "גן". דאס הייסט, ניט סתם א שדה עושה תבואה, נאר דאס איז א גן עושה פירות. און דאס איז ניט סתם א גן פון אבי וועמען, במילא איז דאס בערך לבעל הפרדס והגן, איז פאר עם געננוג אז די פירות האבן די און די חשיבות וואס זיי האבן. זאגט מען גלייך מלכתחילה אז דער פסוק זאגט: "באתי לגני". דאס איז א זאך אין וועלט וואס דער אויבערשטער זאגט אז דאס איז זיין פרדס.

We must know that the world . . . is a garden. Not just a field that yields grain [which is necessary in order to subsist], but a garden that yields luxurious fruits [that provide enjoyment and pleasure]. Moreover, the pleasure provided by a given entity is subjective, its extent determined by the needs and taste of its owner. This world is not just anyone's garden; it is *God's* garden, as the verse states, "I have come to *My* garden." [Its goodness is therefore measured according to His infinite terms.]

QUESTION FOR DISCUSSION

What philosophical concept(s) underlies the assertion that our world is a beautiful garden?

Text 4

Sidur Tehilat Hashem, Morning Prayer, p. 41

המחדש בטובו בכל יום תמיד מעשה בראשית. כאמור:
"לעושה אורים גדולים כי לעולם חסדו" (תהלים קלו,ז).

Sidur Tehilat Hashem

One of the prayer books that follow the tradition of the Arizal, as established by Rabbi Shne'ur Zalman of Liadi. It was first published in New York in 1945.

In His goodness, God renews each day, continuously, the work of Creation, as it is said (Psalms 136:7): "[Give thanks] to Him Who makes great luminaries, for His kindness is eternal."

LEARNING EXERCISE 4

List phenomena that challenge the notion that this world is God's garden:

1. ______________________________

____

____

2. ______________________________

____

____

3. ______________________________

____

____

Text 5

The Rebbe, *Sichot Kodesh* 5732, 1:363–364

דעמולט, קוקט ער אויף וועלט אנדערש. און אז ער קוקט אנדערש, דערזעהט ער אז דאס וואס בעיני בשר, בשטחיות, אויף דעם ערשטן קוק, באמערקט מען ניט, איז אבער ווען ער דארף זוכן, און ער זוכט, און זוכט אין דער ריכטונג - אויסצוגעפינען וואס ס'געפינט זיך אונטער דער קליפה, אונטער דער אויסוויינינגסטע שאלעכץ, די פירות פון דעם גן, איז בשעת ער זוכט אין דער ריכטונג - איז צום אלעם ערשטן איז ער זיכער אז ער וועט דאס זיכער געפינען, ווארום תורת אמת זאגט עם אז ס'איז דא, און ווייסנדיק אז ער וועט זיכער געפינען א אוצר יקר מכל יקר - פירות וואס דער אויבערשטער איז אויף זיי מעיד אז דאס איז פירות פון זיין פרדס אין וועלכען ער געפינט זיך, "עיקר שכינה בתחתונים היתה" - איז לפי ערך פון יוקר הפירות וועט עס אים ניט אפשרעקן און ניט אפשטעלן פון קיין השתדלות און קיין יגיעה און ער וועט זיך ניט לאזן אפציען, אפרעדן און פארנעמען זיך מיט זייטיגע זאכן ווייסנדיק אז אויף אים ווארט א אוצר יקר מכל יקר ער זאל עס מגלה זיין אין וועלט . . .

מ'זאל וויסן אז מ'געפינט זיך אין א טייערע וועלט, נאר דער יצר הרע איז זיך משתדל בכל האופנים אויף צודעקן די טייערקייט וואס געפינט זין אין וועלט, כדי מיר זאלן זיך מייאש זיין חס ושלום, אדער על כל פנים טאן מער ניט ווי אויף יוצא געווען וכו' . . . און דורך דער התבוננות, גייט ער לבטח דרכו . . . ווייסנדיק א זיכערע זאך אז מ'וועט צוקומען און געפינען די פירות פון דעם גן.

With this perspective, we view the world differently; and when we do so, we begin to notice things that we missed upon first glance. When we realize that it is our responsibility to constantly be on the search, we endeavor to look around us and perceive that which is beneath the shell, the fruit that is under the peel. We are confident that we will successfully uncover the garden that is latent in creation because the Torah tells us that it is indeed there, waiting to be discovered. The knowledge that we will surely find precious fruit, fruit that God says are a part of the garden in which He dwells, infuses us with supreme confidence and enthusiasm. Knowing that a precious treasure awaits discovery, we remain focused on our task and do not allow ourselves to be sidetracked by other endeavors. . . .

We must know that we inhabit a wonderful world. The evil inclination endeavors in every way possible to obscure the world's preciousness, in the hope that we lose all hope, God forbid, or at least, to lull us into doing the bare required minimum. . . . Through contemplating the above, however, we assuredly traverse through life . . . secure in the knowledge that we will find the fruits of God's garden.

QUESTION FOR DISCUSSION

Look back at your answers in Learning Exercise 4. How might we construe such phenomena as part of God's garden?

A Quest for the Garden

No Place Like Home

Text 6

Midrash, *Kohelet Rabah* 3:15

"והנה טוב" (בראשית א,לא) - זה יצר טוב. "מאד" (שם) - זה יצר הרע.

"It is good" (Genesis 1:31) refers to the human inclination to do good. "It is *very* good" (ibid.) refers to the human's evil inclination.

Kohelet Rabah

A Midrashic text on the Book of Ecclesiastes. Midrash is the designation of a particular genre of rabbinic literature. The term "Midrash" is derived from the root *d-r-sh,* which means "to search," "to examine," and "to investigate." This particular Midrash provides textual exegeses and develops and illustrates moral principles. It was first published in Pesaro, Italy, in 1519, together with four other Midrashic works on the other four biblical *megilot*.

QUESTION FOR DISCUSSION

Why is the evil inclination "very good"?

Rabbi Shne'ur Zalman of Liadi
(Alter Rebbe)
1745–1812

Chasidic rebbe, halachic authority, and founder of the Chabad movement. The Alter Rebbe was born in Liozna, Belarus, and was among the principal students of the Magid of Mezeritch. His numerous works include the *Tanya*, an early classic containing the fundamentals of Chabad Chasidism, and *Shulchan Aruch HaRav*, an expanded code of Jewish law.

Text 7

Rabbi Shne'ur Zalman of Liadi, *Tanya*, ch. 36

והנה מודעת זאת מאמר רז"ל שתכלית בריאת עולם הזה הוא
שנתאוה הקדוש ברוך הוא להיות לו דירה בתחתונים.

The purpose of this world's Creation, a renowned rabbinic statement asserts, is God's desire to have a home in the lowest world.

QUESTION FOR DISCUSSION

What does it mean that God has a desire to have a "home" in the lowest world?

Singing through the Night

Text 8a

The Rebbe, *Likutei Sichot* 20:126

די ירידה פון יעקב אבינו לבית לבן איז געווען בשביל העלי׳, עס זאל זיין "ויפרוץ האיש מאד מאד" (בראשית ל,מג). און וויבאלד יעקב האט **געזען** דעם תכלית המכוון פון זיין ירידה (די עלי׳ וואס וועט דערפון ארויסקומען), דעריבער האט ער זייענדיק בבית לבן געזאגט "**שיר** המעלות".

Jacob's challenging stay in the house of Laban was for the purpose of great gain—in order that he should become [as Genesis 30:43 states] "exceedingly wealthy." Jacob perceived the purpose of the challenge—the profit it would subsequently bring him—and was therefore able to sing, whilst in the house of Laban, the "Song of Ascents."

Likutei Sichot

Widely considered the Rebbe's magnum opus, the 39 volumes of *Likutei Sichot* feature scholarly essays relating to themes in the weekly Torah portions and the Jewish holidays. The Rebbe initially conveyed these concepts in his public talks and subsequently reworked them for publication. In some volumes, the essays appear in Yiddish, while in others they are in Hebrew. Most volumes also present a collection of the Rebbe's correspondence.

Text 8b

The Rebbe, ibid., p. 127

מצד דעם עילוי וואס ווערט דוקא דורך מלחמה ונסיונות,
מאכט לפעמים דער אויבערשטער אז . . . זאלן זיין אזוינע
וואס קומען לוחם זיין און שטערן פון עבודת ה'.

און אויף דעם זאגט ער "שיר המעלות": ניט נאר זיינען די נסיונות אים
ניט מונע פון עבודת ה' און פועל'ן ניט קיין חלישות בעבודתו, נאר
אדרבא, זיי רופן ביי אים ארויס א תוספת כח ואומץ ביתר שאת ויתר
עז, און דאס ברייגנט אים אז ער שטייט אין א מצב פון "שיר".

Because of the advantages that ensue from struggles and challenges, at times, God orchestrates . . . opponents that attempt to battle us and disturb our divine service.

Upon experiencing such adversity, we respond by singing "A Song of Ascents." The difficulties do not impede our service or cause it to flag; to the contrary, they evoke extra energy and courage. They cause us to sing.

LEARNING EXERCISE 5

An example of a recent instance when I encountered adversity:

Possible ways the adversity might beget me an advantage:

When Bad Happens to Good People

Text 9a (Optional)

Maimonides, *Guide to the Perplexed* 3:12

Rabbi Moshe ben Maimon
(Maimonides/Rambam)
1135–1204

Halachist, philosopher, author, and physician. Maimonides was born in Cordoba, Spain. After the conquest of Cordoba by the Almohads, he fled Spain and eventually settled in Cairo, Egypt. There, he became the leader of the Jewish community and served as court physician to the vizier of Egypt. He is most noted for authoring the *Mishneh Torah,* an encyclopedic arrangement of Jewish law, and for his philosophical work, *Guide for the Perplexed.* His rulings on Jewish law are integral to the formation of halachic consensus.

הרבה פעמים יעלה בלב ההמון שהרעות בעולם יהיו יותר מן הטובות, עד שבהרבה מחידות רוב האומות ובשיריהם יכללו זה הענין, ויאמרו כי מן הפלא שימצא בזמן דבר טוב אמנם רעותיו רבות ומתמידות. ואין זה הטעות אצל ההמון לבד, רק עם מי שיחשוב שהוא חכם גם כן. ולאלראז"י ספר מפורסם, קראהו ספר אלהות, כלל בו משגעונותיו וסכלותיו הרבה, ומכללם ענין בדאו והוא שהרע במציאות יותר מן הטוב, שאתה כשתקיש בין מנוחות האדם ועונגו בעת מנוחתו עם מה שיקרהו מן המכאובים והחבלים הקשים והמומים ובטול האברים והמהומות והדאגות והצרות, תמצא שבמציאותו, רצוני לומר, מציאות האדם, נקמה ממנו ורעה גדולה לו . . .

וסבת זה הטעות כלה היות זה הסכל וחבריו מן ההמון לא יבחנו המציאות רק באיש מבני אדם לא זולת זה, וידמה כל סכל כי המציאות כולו היה בעבורו, וכאלו אין שם מציאות זולתו לבד. וכשיבואהו הענין בחלוף מה שירצה, יגזור מהמציאות כולו רע. ואלו בחן האדם המציאות וציירו וידע מיעוט חלקו ממנו, התבאר לו האמת ונגלה כי זה השגעון הארוך אשר ישתגעו בו בני אדם ברוב רעות העולם, אינם אומרים שהוא בחק המלאכים, ולא בחק הגלגלים והכוכבים, ולא בחק היסודות ומה שהורכב מהן ממוצא או צמח, ולא בחק מיני בעלי חיים גם כן.

People often think that the evils in the world are more numerous than the good things; many sayings and songs of the nations dwell on this idea. They say that a good thing is found only exceptionally, whilst evil things are numerous and lasting. Not only common people make this mistake, but even many who believe that they are wise. Al-Razi wrote a well-known book on theology. Among other mad and foolish things, it contains also the idea that there exists more evil than good. He maintains that if the happiness of man and his pleasure in the times of prosperity be compared with the mishaps that befall him—such as grief, acute pain, defects, paralysis of the limbs, fears, anxieties, and troubles—it would seem as if the existence of man is a punishment and a great evil for him. . . .

This error results from judging the whole universe by what occurs to a single person. Only an ignorant person believes that the whole universe only exists for him, as if nothing else required any consideration. If, therefore, anything happens to him contrary to his expectation, he at once concludes that the whole universe is evil. If, however, he would take into consideration the whole universe, form an idea of it, and comprehend what a small portion he is of it, he will find the truth. For evil is not found among the angels, the spheres, the stars, the elements, and that which is formed of the elements, that is, minerals and plants, or in the various species of living beings.

Text 9b (Optional)

Maimonides, ibid.

יארע לקצת בני אדם מומים גדולים ובטול אברים בכלל היצירה, או מתחדשים משנויים שיארעו ביסודות מאויר הנפסד, או הברקים העצומים הנקרא בלעז לנבי"ש, או שקיעת מקומות . . . שהרעות אשר ימצאו בני האדם בזה המין מעטים מאד מאד ולא יהיו אלא לעתים רחוקים, שאתה תמצא מדינות שיש להם אלפים שנים לא נשקעו ולא נשרפו. וכן יולדו אלפים מבני אדם בתכלית הבריאות, ולא יולד בעל מום רק על דרך פלא ועל צד זרות. ואם יתגבר המתגבר ולא יאמר על צד זרות, הוא מעט מאד ואינו לא חלק ממאה ולא חלק מאלף מן הנולדים בתכלית השלמות.

Some people have great deformities or paralysis of some of the organs. There is also suffering due to changes in the elements that result from, bad air, thunderstorms, or landslides. . . . You will find that these evils are very few and rare. There are countries that have not been flooded or burned for thousands of years. There are thousands of men in perfect health, whereas deformed individuals are an exceptional occurrence. If you object to the term "exceptional," then say "few in number"; they are not one-hundredth, not even one-thousandth of those that are perfectly normal.

Text 9c (Optional)

Maimonides, ibid.

המין הב' מן הרעות הוא מה שיארע לבני אדם מקצתם לקצתם, בהתגבר קצתם על קצתם, ואלו הרעות יותר מרעות המין הראשון . . . אבל מציאותו גם כן מעט, כאיש שיתנכל את איש להרגו או לגנוב ממונו בלילה. ואמנם יכלול זה המין מן הרע אנשים רבים במלחמות הגדולות, וזה גם כן אינו ברוב מה שבישוב.

Another class of evils comprises those that people cause to each other, when some use their strength against others. These evils are more numerous than those of the first kind. . . . It is nevertheless not widespread in any country of the whole world. It is of rare occurrence that a man plans to kill his neighbor or to rob him of his property by night. Many persons are, however, afflicted with this kind of evil in great wars. But these are not frequent, if all of humanity is taken into consideration.

Text 9d (Optional)

Maimonides, ibid.

כל אשר הענין יותר צריך לבעלי חיים הוא נמצא יותר ויותר בחנם, וכל מה שימעט צורך הכרחי, הוא נמצא יותר מעט והוא יקר מאד.

כי הענין ההכרחי לאדם על דרך משל, הוא האויה, והמים, והמזון. אמנם צורך האויר יותר חזק. שאם יפקדהו קצת שעה ימות. אבל המים יעמוד בלעדיו יום או יומים. והאויר יותר נמצא ויותר בזול בלא ספק.

וצורך המים יותר מצורך המזון. כי כשישתה ולא יאכל יעמדו קצת בני אדם ארבעה ימים או חמשה מבלתי מזון. ואתה תמצא המים בכל מדינה ומדינה יותר נמצא ויותר בזול מהמזון.

וכן ימשך הענין במזונות מה שהוא צורך יותר נמצא יותר ויותר בזול במקום ההוא ממה שאינו הכרחי. אמנם המוס"ק והענב"ר והאודם והברקת איני חושב שאחד משלמי הדעת יחשוב שיש לו צורך גדול לאדם אלא לרפואה. והנה יעמדו במקומם ובמקום הדומים להם הרבה מן העשבים ומן העפרים.

זהו פרסום גמילות חסדי השם יתברך למציאותו ואפילו בחק זה החי החלוש.

The more necessary a thing is for living beings, the more easily it is found and the cheaper it is; the less necessary it is, the rarer and dearer it is.

Air, water, and food are indispensable to humanity. Air is most necessary, for if man is without air for a short time he dies, whereas he can be without water a day or two. Indeed, air is more plentiful and cheaper than water.

Water is more necessary than food; some people can survive four or five days without food, provided they have water. Indeed, water exists in every country in larger quantities than food and is also cheaper.

The same proportion can be noticed in the different kinds of foods; that which is more necessary exists in larger quantities and is cheaper than that which is less necessary. No intelligent person, I think, considers musk, amber, rubies, and emerald as very necessary for man except as medicines; and they, as well as other similar substances, can be replaced for this purpose by herbs and minerals.

This shows the kindness of God to His creatures, even to the fragile human being.

Text 10

The Rebbe, *Igrot Kodesh* 20:41

מאשר הנני קבלת מכתבה . . . ולמרות סגנון כתבה ותוכנו . . . לא אבדתי חס ושלום תקותי, אשר סוף סוף לא רק תראה את הטוב בחיים, כולל גם חיי-ה, אלא שבראי' זו תבוא בהרגשה בלב . . .

בעולמנו זה הכל מעורב טוב ורע, ועל האדם לבחור מה להדגיש ובמה להתבונן, ובמה להתענין, כי בחיי כל אחד ואחת שני דרכים ישנם, לראות את הטוב הסובב אותו או וכו' . . .

והרי מאלפנו סיפור חז"ל, אשר אדם הראשון, עוד קודם הגירוש בהיותו בגן עדן, התאונן על ענייניו, וקראוהו כפוי טובה, ובבני ובנות ישראל, שנמצאו במחנות ההסגר של האשכנזים ימח שמם ובתקופה הכי איומה רחמנא ליצלן, ברכו ברכת השחר וכו' הודאה וברכה לבורא עולם ומנהיגו, והרי סוף סוף כל אחד ואחת הוא **בין** הקצוות האמורים.

מובן וגם פשוט, שאין בהנ"ל חס ושלום ענין של הצדקת הדין על מי שהוא, ובפרט וכו', כי אם הדגשת המציאות כמו שהיא. והנקודה - אשר אופן וסוג חיי האדם, אם חיים מלאים שביעת רצון ותוכן, או בקו ההפכי, תלוי במדה חשובה וגדולה - ברצון האדם, המושל בראית עין שכלו להסתכל לצד ימין או לצד שמאל.

I acknowledge receipt of your letter. . . . Despite its tone and content . . . I have not, God forbid, lost hope that eventually you will appreciate the good in life, including the good in *your own* life, and that this appreciation will impact your emotions and frame of mind. . . .

In our world, everything is a mixture of good and bad. Human beings must choose which aspects they will emphasize, contemplate, and pursue. In everyone's life there are two paths—to see the good or [the opposite]. . . .

Igrot Kodesh

A selection of Hebrew and Yiddish letters penned by the Rebbe. As of 2014, 30 volumes have been published in this series. The letters are published in chronological order, starting from 1925 and extending thus far to 1975. Only those letters that are of relevance to the public are published, and all personal information is excised. The letters cover a wide range of issues: communal activism, Chabad philosophy, Talmud, Jewish law, Kabbalah, practical advice, and much more.

How instructive is that which our sages tell us, that Adam was an ingrate. Even before he was banished from the Garden of Eden, [while living in a literal paradise], he complained about his circumstances. On the other hand, there were Jewish men and women who thanked and blessed the Creator and recited the morning blessings while living through most horrifying times in the German concentrations camps. Ultimately, everyone's circumstances will be somewhere between these two extremes. . . .

Needless to say, my intention is not to imply that anyone deserves suffering, God forbid. My point is simply to underscore the reality: The type of lives that we live, whether full of satisfaction and meaning or the opposite, depends, in large measure, on our willpower, which dictates whether we will focus on the positive or on the negative.

Text 11

The Rebbe, *Likutei Sichot* 35:345–346

יש לומר **בדרך אפשר** - לולא ההזמנה דהנפטרת עלי' השלום לחגיגת הספר תורה - הייתה נמצאת **בהתחלת** אַטאק האחרונה שלה - בסביבה שונה לגמרי: ברחוב, או בבית נכרים, על כל פנים - זרים, שלא בנוכחות רופא וידיד ודתי ושברגעים האחרונים שלה שמעה דברי עידוד וראתה פנים דבני ישראל ידידים וכו'. - והאפשר לשַער 1) החילוק בין ב' המצבים? 2) כמה לעבט איבער בן אדם בכל רגע ורגע דרגעיו האחרונים . . . ?!

על פי תורת הבעל שם טוב - אפשר **דאחד** הטעמים **האמתים** שעוררו מן השמים את . . . לנדב ספר תורה וכו', הוא בכדי – שעל ידי זה הנה (סוף סוף) תהי' **עלית** הנשמה דהצעירה מתוך **שלוה פנימית** ובבית יהודי, ובבית שהסימן והשמירה שלו הוא מזוזה, שהתחלתה: שמע ישראל ה' אלקינו ה' אחד.

May I suggest the following:

Were the deceased not invited to the Torah celebration, she would have suffered her fatal attack in a very different setting, perhaps, on the street or in the presence of strangers. She would have been deprived of the comforting presence of a physician, who was also a dear friend of hers and shared her religious values. In her final moments, she would not have heard words of encouragement nor would she have been surrounded by her friends, her coreligionists. The vast difference between these two possible scenarios is self-understood. Moreover, consider how significant are the last moments of life to a dying person. . . .

Based on the teachings of the Ba'al Shem Tov [regarding divine providence], it is possible that one of the true reasons why God inspired so and so to donate the Torah was to allow for the tranquil ascent of this young woman's soul, and that it should occur in a Jewish home, a home that displays and is protected by a *mezuzah* whose firsts words are, "Hear, O Israel, the Lord is our God, the Lord is one."

The Hippies (Optional Section)

QUESTION FOR DISCUSSION

Can you identify the "garden element" in the counterculture movement of the 1960s?

Text 12a

The Rebbe, *Sichot Kodesh* 5730, 1:610–611

אז מ'האט טענות צו די יוגנד פארוואס זיי זיינען מהרס אט די ענינים וואס ס'האט זיך איינגעשטעלט און דאס וואס ווערט אנגערופן בלשון המדינה "עסטאבלישמענט" . . . איז די ערשטע טענה דארף מען האבן צו זייערע מחנכים. וואס בשעת מען האט געוואלט ביי זיי פועל'ן זיי זאלן זיך פירן ווי ס'דארף צו זיין האט מען זיי דאס מסביר געווען אז אזוי ווי א תכלית פון א מענטש'ן איז ער זאל האבן א שיינע דירה און ער זאל האבן א שיינע אקאנט אין באנק, און בשעת מ'וועט איינלאדן אויף א באנקעט זאל מען עם זעצן אויבן אן, און דערצו זאל ער האבן ניט איין מכונה, ניט איין

קאדילאק, נאר צוויי, פאר זיך און פאר דער פרוי . . . בשעת דאס ווערט דער גאנצער יסוד אויף וועלכע מ'בויט דער ארור המן וברוך מרדכי . . . איז פארשטאנדיק פארוואס סוף כל סוף פלאצט די געדולט אויף דעם שקר . . .

וויבאלד אז זיי האלטן אין מיטן וועג דאס מבטל זיין, טאר מען זיי ניט לאזן בלאנדז'שען אין מיטן, און ס'דארף זיין בדרך החינוך "חנוך לנער" דארף דאס זיין "על פי דרכו", בדרכי נועם ובדרכי שלום, אויף צובריינגען זיי צו א טיפערן פארשטאנד אז המן מוז זיין ארור און אז מרדכי דארף זיין ברוך.

The complaints that people have against the younger generation, that they are destroying the system . . . the so-called "establishment," should be addressed to their educators. When parents and teachers taught the younger generation proper behavior, they explained it as the means to be able to afford a nice home, have a large bank account, own two Cadillacs ("his" and "hers"), and to be honorees and seated at the head table at banquets. . . . When this constitutes the reason for choosing between good and evil . . . it is understandable why the youth will ultimately lose all patience for such falsehood. . . .

The youngsters are in the process of a spiritual journey. We cannot allow them to drift and get lost. We must educate them according to their needs, in a pleasant and kind manner, and lead them to a proper understanding of right and wrong.

Text 12b

The Rebbe, *Torat Menachem* 5728, 3:131

דוקא בגלל שהנוער הם חוצפנים ועזי פנים, ואינם מתפעלים משום דבר, לא מהעולם, לא מההורים ובני המשפחה, וגם לא ממה שהם בעצמם הבינו אתמול . . . אלא מכריזים: היום אנחנו בני חורין לעשות מה שאנחנו רוצים (ובפרט כפי שרואים בשבועות האחרונים, שעורכים שביתות וכו') – דוקא בגלל זה נקל יותר להביא אותם לדרך האמיתית של קיום התורה ומצות! . . .

וכאשר יפעלו זאת על הנועה, הנה לא זו בלבד שהם עצמם יהפכו להיות שומרי תורה ומצות, אלא עוד זאת, שמצד טבעם שאינם מתפעלים מאף אחד, יפעלו גם על אחרים, ועד שיהפכו את כל העולם כולו להיות על פי היושר והצדק והמשפט.

Torat Menachem

A Hebrew translation of the transcripts of the Rebbe's talks. This work also comprehensively cross-references and footnotes the material. As of 2014, more than 90 volumes have appeared in this series, covering the years 1950–1968 and 1982–1992. The Rebbe did not edit or review these publications for accuracy.

The youth are brazen, have chutzpah, and are not deterred by anything—not by world opinion not by their parents or families, not even by the opinions they themselves entertained a day earlier. . . . Instead, they proudly proclaim their absolute freedom to do as they wish. (This has become especially evident in the past weeks, as they have held strikes and protests, etc.) Specifically because of their chutzpah, it is easier to draw them to the true path of Torah and *mitzvot*! . . .

When we successfully inspire the youth, they will not suffice with personal Torah observance, but—due to their fierce indomitable spirit—they will also inspire others to do the same. They will be an unstoppable force that will transform the entire world and bring it in alignment with integrity and justice.

Key Points

1. God entrusted us with the task of changing the world for the better. We need to maintain an optimistic outlook and perceive the world in a positive light in order to ensure our motivation and the success of this mission.

2. God refers to this world as His "garden," thus attesting to its inherent beauty and infinite goodness. To perceive this world as a wonderful place is not a matter of subjective choice, but is grounded in reality, in the awareness that God is present and revealed within every detail of Creation.

3. The goodness of the world is not limited to God's perspective, but suffuses Creation in a manner that is perceptible to us too, at least somewhat, although it might require effort to identify the goodness.

4. God desired a "lowest world" whose inhabitants do not intuitively recognize His presence, but reveal that every part of the world is in perfect harmony with its Godly essence.

5. The human "evil inclination" presents us with a wonderful opportunity. Its existence allows us to tame it and channel it for positive purposes, thereby making the world a better place and fulfilling the purpose of our creation.

6. Challenges are not reason to despair, but opportunities for growth. Knowing that God's benevolence pervades everything in our lives allows us to see adversity for what it truly is—an opportunity for unparalleled gain.

7. Pain and suffering challenge our ability to maintain a positive outlook. Nevertheless, we should attempt to identify and focus on the tremendous good that we sometimes take for granted in the world in general and in our lives in particular. We must not allow the negatives to dictate our overall image of ourselves and the world.

Appendix A

Martin E. P. Seligman, *Learned Optimism* [New York: Vintage Books, 2006], p. 5

Martin E. P. Seligman, PhD
1942–

Noted psychologist and bestselling author. Seligman was president of the American Psychological Association in 1998, during which one of his presidential initiatives was the promotion of positive psychology as a field of scientific study. He is a leading authority in the fields of positive psychology, resilience, learned helplessness, depression, optimism, and pessimism. He has written more than 250 scholarly publications and 20 books, including *Flourish*, *Authentic Happiness*, and *Learned Optimism*.

Literally hundreds of studies show that pessimists give up more easily and get depressed more often. These experiments also show that optimists do much better in school and college, at work and on the playing field. They regularly exceed the predictions of aptitude tests. When optimists run for office, they are more apt to be elected than pessimists are. Their health is unusually good. They age well, much freer than most of us from the usual physical ills of middle age. Evidence suggests they may even live longer.

Appendix B

Miriam Adahan, *It's All a Gift* [Jerusalem: Feldheim Publishers, 1992], pp. 2–3

Miriam Adahan

Psychologist and therapist. Adahan is the founder of EMETT ("Emotional Maturity Established Through Torah")—a network of self-help groups dedicated to personal growth. She lives in Jerusalem.

When I moved to Eretz Yisrael, in 1981, we lived for a while in an absorption center. There, I became friendly with a young widow with four children who had come from Iran a year and a half before. Although she lived in a tiny, one-room apartment and worked as a clerk in the local post office, she had a regal dignity which hinted at a refined background. As our eleven-year-old daughters became best friends, the story of her previous life emerged.

In Iran, they had been very wealthy, with servants, fancy cars and expensive vacations abroad. Then came the overthrow of the Shah and the reign of terror against the Jews. One day, a gang of thugs entered her husband's rug store and shot him to death. They defaced the walls with his blood, proclaiming him an agent of the Shah.

Informed of the awful tragedy, the grief-stricken widow knew that she had to leave Iran immediately to save herself and her children. Desperately trying to stay in control, she contacted a man who was known to be helping Jews escape over the treacherous mountains into Turkey. Since unauthorized travel was forbidden and the sale of any household items might arouse suspicion, she had to leave most of her wealth behind. She could not tell anyone of her plans, not even her own children. She could not pack suitcases, as neighbors might see and report her to the police.

Trembling, trying not to let her terror show, she took whatever little cash and jewelry she had on hand and, telling the children that they were going shopping, left her home, never to return. In the darkness of the night, they met their guide at the edge of Teheran. Handing over most of her money, the harrowing nightmare began for this brave widow and her four children, the youngest a girl of three.

For the first few days, they spent eighteen hours at a time on camels. The pain they suffered was so excruciating that they often felt that they would collapse. The mother sustained permanent damage to her back. But each time they complained, their guide yelled that he would shoot them if they said another word. They had no choice but to go on. At one point, the mother was robbed of all her remaining money and jewelry by bandits who preyed on fleeing Iranian Jews.

By day, the sun scorched them. By night, they froze. As the mountains got steeper, they switched to riding donkeys. Often, the precipices were so narrow that one wrong move meant certain death and the donkey and its rider would plunge into the abyss below. Once, in their rush to cross a freezing stream, they all lost their shoes in the mucky water. Then, when they reached the other side, they had to walk barefoot on prickly cactus plants and sharp stones. Wincing in pain, they tried not to cry out as the thorns and pebbles cut into their flesh. Almost stupefied with pain and fatigue, the mother and her oldest son took turns carrying the youngest child.

At another point, they had to make their way across a flimsy bridge made of ropes and wooden slats which stretched between two mountain peaks and spanned a deep ravine. The ropes looked as though they could barely hold their own weight, let alone a group of terrified Jewish refugees. Looking down into the abyss below, the mother froze in utter terror, crying out that she could not possibly go on. Again, their guide took out his gun and threatened her and her children with death if they did not move. Taking her three-year-old by the hand, she forced herself to grab the ropes, fueled by anger toward the Iranian guide who urged them on so gruffly.

After two-and-a-half weeks of this continuous torture, the small group of Jewish refugees arrived at the Turkish border. There, the guide, who had always been so harsh, suddenly embraced each child warmly and said, "Before I leave you, I want to tell you that I, too, am Jewish. I'm sorry I had to be so tough. But if I had been nice to you, you wouldn't have made it. I had to scare you into moving, or you would not have been able to go on." With tears in his eyes he said, "I'm proud of each and every one of you. You are all true *gibborim* [heroes]." With that, he turned and left to go back to the direction of Iran.

Like this heroic family, we, too, are on a journey which is often treacherous and filled with pain. One thing we can know for sure: when we get to the World of Truth, we will see that our Guide always loves us, and that all the difficulties we went through in this world were necessary in order to reveal the greatness and the Godliness in us and in others.

SELECTED CORRESPONDENCE

OF THE REBBE

Self-Assertion—A Religious Advantage*

By the Grace of G-d
In the days of *selichot*, 5728 [September, 1968]
Brooklyn, N.Y.

Greeting and Blessing:

. . . Each era and each country has its particular advantages and difficulties.

In our era there prevails, in certain circles, a strong tendency to self-assertion and independence, not only in material spheres, but also in the ideological: it is the tendency against subordination to the existing order, against accepting things that have not first been scrutinized and fully approved by one's own intellect, and so forth. This, at first glance, would appear to inhibit the acceptance of G-d's kingship.

Moreover, there are certain countries that are relatively young and have been built upon a foundation and by means of personal initiative and energy. This same spirit characterizes the entire individual and social life in these countries, which makes it still more difficult to adjust oneself to accepting G-d's kingship.

The above notwithstanding, we have the undisputed rule that G-d does not demand from human beings anything that is beyond their capacity. Because acceptance of His kingship is the essential point of Rosh Hashanah (and the basis for all our actions throughout the year) and this is valid for all times and places, it is certain that also in our time and in the said countries, it is possible and imperative to attain complete acceptance of G-d's kingship.

Actually, there is a special advantage precisely in our time and in the said countries. People not geared to complete independence, even if they accept G-d unreservedly, are not fundamentally affected, for it is nothing new for them to change their mind and alter their position. However, people who are not accustomed to subordinating themselves, but are consistently independent in their thinking—should these people come to the conviction that they must acknowledge a Supreme Authority, it permeates them deeply and fundamentally, and they find the strength to reorient themselves completely and permanently.

This finds expression not only in their minds and hearts, but also in their thoughts, words, and actions, down to the smallest detail. Indeed, inasmuch as the larger part of the day is filled with actions and verbal expressions, their submission to G-d's kingship expresses itself primarily in speech and deed, in the fulfillment of the *mitzvot*, and in all aspects of daily conduct.

It also brings them to a more earnest and energetic fulfillment of the mitzvah to "Love thy fellow as thyself," particularly in relation to accepting G-d's kingship: to encourage one more person, or many people, to accept G-d's kingship likewise. Here as well, it should not remain in the domain of the intellect and emotion, but should also be actively expressed in thought, speech, and deed of daily life.

May the acceptance of G-d's kingship bring about the immediate fulfillment of our plea, "Accept our prayer with mercy and grace," and may our Father, our King, grant each and every one within the community of Israel a good and sweet year in every respect, "out of His full, open, holy, and ample hand."

* Excerpted and translated from *Likutei Sichot* 9:451–453.

Counting Your Blessings*

By the Grace of G-d
4 Shevat 5716 [Jan. 17, 1956]
Brooklyn

Peace and blessing!

In response to your letter from the month of Kislev, the month of redemption, in which you write about your current situation, that throughout your entire life you have not experienced good, and you request my blessing for yourself, your wife, and your children, may they all be well.

It seems that you do not sense the contradiction in your letter. For a man whom G-d has blessed with a wife and children to say that he has never seen any good is to be startlingly ungrateful.

Certainly, this will not, G-d forbid, negatively affect the blessings that G-d has thus far provided for you. But G-d continuing to provide you, even increasing His blessings, is no reason to continue being an ingrate.

Hundreds, even thousands of people pray every day to be blessed with children and would give everything they have to merit a single son or daughter, but have not as of yet had their prayers answered—may G-d bless them that their hearts' wishes be fulfilled very soon.

But you, the recipient of this blessing—and it seems that it came to you without you having to pray for it especially—apparently don't recognize the fortune and the happiness in the blessings you have. You write twice in your letter that you have never experienced any good and conclude your letter that you don't believe G-d will help you because it has been decreed (G-d forbid!) that you will be destitute all your life!

Understandably, my intention is not that one's livelihood ought to be meager or that one's health ought to be compromised.

I am just pointing out that perhaps this is the reason for the challenges to your health and livelihood—that you don't recognize G-d's blessing in something more essential, namely, the blessing of sons and daughters who are taking the right path in life. When we don't recognize His blessings that are visible and manifest, and in particular when this lack of recognition is so startling as in your letter, then should we be surprised if G-d's blessing does not manifest in other areas of life?

My hope is that these lines, brief in quantity, will suffice to enlighten you to see the situation as it really is.

When you begin to serve G-d with true and inward joy, He will certainly add His blessing for health and sustenance, as can be understood from various texts, including Zohar 2:184b.

Surely, you have a designated routine to study Torah, both the revealed parts and the esoteric. In any case, you should certainly do so from today onward. It would also be proper to inspect your *tefilin* and *mezuzot*, and to give a few coins to charity every day before the morning prayers.

With blessing,

In the name of the Rebbe,

The Secretariat

* Translated from *Igrot Kodesh* 12:270–271.

Backward Step—Forward Leap

By the Grace of G-d
15th of Menachem Av, 5725 [August 13, 1965]
Brooklyn, N.Y.

To All Participants in the Dedication Exercises at Camp Gan Israel Linden, Michigan

Greeting and Blessing:

This is to convey my prayerful wishes to all of you, and particularly to the families of the distinguished friends of the Camp who will be honored on this occasion. The memorial to the late Zeev Hordes, as well as the other distinguished Jews whose memory will be honored, will surely provide visible symbols for their families and friends, to inspire and stimulate them to ever greater accomplishments.

I have chosen the 15th of Av as the date of this letter because of its special significance and also because of its proximity to the day of these dedication exercises.

Our Sages tell us that the 15th day of Av was a very joyous festival in olden days, especially for the younger generation, with particular emphasis on the religious ideals and values of our Jewish way of life.

Coming so soon after Tishah b'Av, the radical transition from a mood of sadness to that of joy is doubly significant. Firstly, it signifies that any sad interlude in Jewish life is only transitory, and is based on the principle of "descent for the purpose of ascent." In other words, any and all sad events in our history which are commemorated on the few sad days on our calendar, are backward steps which are necessary for a greater forward leap.

Secondly, that the very transition from sadness to gladness intensifies the joy, and adds real quality to it, which could not be appreciated otherwise.

The message of these days is best applied in the efforts in behalf of our Jewish youth. All too often we hear about the "lost generation," or our "lost youth." It is therefore most gratifying to see your efforts to provide true guidance, direction and inspiration to the younger generation in your community and environs. Your efforts have, with G-d's help, been fruitful in the past; I hope and pray they will continue in a growing measure, and consequently will enjoy a growing measure of success in the future.

Facing up to the Challenge

By the Grace of G-d
25th of Shevat, 5736 [January 27, 1976]
Brooklyn, N.Y.

Mr. Mordechai Shoel Landow
Miami Beach, Fla.

Greeting and Blessing:

Through our mutual friend, Rabbi Sholom Ber Lipskar, I enquire from time to time as to how things are going with you business-wise, and he reports to me insofar as he knows. I have also seen the newspaper clipping.

I surely do not have to emphasize to you that the true businessman is not the person who can manage his affairs when conditions are favorable and things run smoothly and successfully, but also, and even more so, when he shows that he knows how to cope with an occasional setback. Indeed, facing up to the challenge of adversity makes one a stronger and more effective executive than before, with an added dimension of experience and a keener acumen, to put to good use when things begin to turn upwards. Sometimes, a temporary setback is just what is needed for the resumption of the advance with greater vigor, as in the case of an athlete having to negotiate a hurdle, when stepping back is the means to a higher leap.

In plain words, I trust—on the basis of my acquaintance with you—that you are taking the present difficulty well in your stride, coping with it squarely and making the necessary structural and other improvements, in terms of closer supervision and greater efficiency, as I see also from the clipping, although basically the present difficulty is no doubt a consequence of the general economic situation.

I send you my prayerful wishes that you should very soon have good tidings about a tangible improvement, and that the setback has indeed served as a springboard for the great upturn in the days ahead. All the more so now that we are about to enter the first of the two months of Adar in the current Jewish *Leap Year*—may your *Hatzlocho* [success] be doubled, too, in quantity and quality, i.e. in the resurgence of profits and in their being used in the best possible way, for good, wholesome and happy things, materially and spiritually.

With blessing,

LESSON 2

Realizing Your Potential

Self-exploration is an important endeavor, but it often uncovers unseemly deficiencies. To ignore them is disingenuous; to know about them is disquieting. How can we unconditionally love ourselves yet not fall victim to inertia and complacency that impede us from realizing our potential? Discovering our divine soul—its existence and very practical relevance—will redefine how we view ourselves, our shortcomings, and our latent potential.

Introduction

Know Thyself

LEARNING EXERCISE 1A

Who are you? Describe yourself.

LEARNING EXERCISE 1B

Who are you? Describe yourself. (Again.)

LEARNING EXERCISE 2

What type of things, interactions, or phenomena make you feel important? What makes you feel unimportant?	
What would you like to achieve, but consider too difficult to accomplish?	

A Unique Combination

QUESTION FOR DISCUSSION

Are demanding people usually loving and sensitive? Explain your reasoning.

The Unanimous Court (Optional Section)

Babylonian Talmud

A literary work of monumental proportions that draws upon the legal, spiritual, intellectual, ethical, and historical traditions of Judaism. The 37 tractates of the Babylonian Talmud contain the teachings of the Jewish sages from the period after the destruction of the 2nd Temple through the 5th century CE. It has served as the primary vehicle for the transmission of the Oral Law and the education of Jews over the centuries; it is the entry point for all subsequent legal, ethical, and theological Jewish scholarship.

Text 1

Talmud, Sanhedrin 17a

סנהדרי שראו כולן לחובה פוטרין אותו.

If the Sanhedrin unanimously agrees that a defendant is guilty [in a capital case], he is acquitted.

QUESTION FOR DISCUSSION

What is the logic behind this peculiar law?

The Kabbalah of You

Baring the Soul

Text 2

Rabbi Shne'ur Zalman of Liadi, *Tanya*, ch. 1–2

דלכל איש ישראל אחד צדיק ואחד רשע יש שתי נשמות . . . נפש
אחת מצד הקליפה וסטרא אחרא . . . וממנה באות כל המדות רעות
. . . ונפש השנית בישראל היא חלק אלו-ה ממעל ממש.

Every Jew, irrespective of his or her spiritual standing, possesses two souls. . . . One of these souls, the mundane and unholy one . . . is the source of all undesirable human traits. . . . The second soul of the Jew is a part of God above—literally.

Rabbi Shne'ur Zalman of Liadi (Alter Rebbe)
1745–1812

Chasidic rebbe, halachic authority, and founder of the Chabad movement. The Alter Rebbe was born in Liozna, Belarus, and was among the principal students of the Magid of Mezeritch. His numerous works include the *Tanya*, an early classic containing the fundamentals of Chabad Chasidism, and *Shulchan Aruch HaRav*, an expanded code of Jewish law.

Will the "Real Me" Please Stand Up?

LEARNING EXERCISE 3

Compile a list of activities in which you have engaged over the past twenty-four hours, and in the columns below, divide them into two types: those that stemmed from your self-oriented consciousness, and those that stemmed from your divine-oriented consciousness.

Self-oriented consciousness	Divine-oriented consciousness

Text 3

The Rebbe, *Likutei Sichot* 11:71, and fn. 51

עיקר מציאותו של איש הישראלי היא נפשו האלקית, שהיא חלק אלקה ממעל ממש.

ואף שבבינונים (וכל שכן אלו למטה ממדריגת הבינונים) הנפש הבהמית "היא היא האדם עצמו" (תניא פרק כ"ט), הרי זהו רק בחיצוניות אבל בפנימיות ובאמתית הרי כל איש ישראל אפילו קל שבקלים מוכן למסור נפשו על קידוש השם (שם פרק יח) כי נפשו האלקית היא אמיתית מציאותו.

Our primary identity is that of the divine soul, which is literally a part of God above.

Although *Tanya* (ch. 29) states that the self-oriented consciousness constitutes the core of those who are not *tsadikim,* that is only true superficially. The innermost—and thus truest—part of our identity is our Godly consciousness, as evidenced by the willingness of every Jew, even those on the lowest rungs of spiritual sensitivity, to forfeit their lives rather than renounce their Jewish faith.

Likutei Sichot

Widely considered the Rebbe's magnum opus, the 39 volumes of *Likutei Sichot* feature scholarly essays relating to themes in the weekly Torah portions and the Jewish holidays. The Rebbe initially conveyed these concepts in his public talks and subsequently reworked them for publication. In some volumes, the essays appear in Yiddish, while in others they are in Hebrew. Most volumes also present a collection of the Rebbe's correspondence.

It's No Secret

Text 4

The Rebbe, *Sefer Hasichot* 5750, 1:381

וואלט מען געקענט מיינען, אז דער דמיון צווישן עם ישראל און כביכול דער אויבערשטער (מלך) איז נאר מצד זייער נשמה ובפנימיות (ולולא עבודת האדם קומט עס ניט ארויס בגלוי) . . .

ווי פארשטאנדיק אויך פון דער הוספה אין תניא אויף דעם לשון הכתוב אז א נשמה איז "חלק אלוקה ממעל", און אין תניא איז ער מוסיף ומבאר: "**ממש**". וכידוע, אז נוסף צו דעם פירוש, אז דאס מיינט "ממש" א "חלק אלוקה ממעל" (און ניט א מעין ודוגמא לזה), האט עס אויך דעם פירוש, אז דער "חלק אלוקה ממעל" איז זיך מתלבש אין דעם גוף הגשמי באופן פון "ממש", ביז אז מ'קען דאס אנטאפן מיטן חוש המישוש. ויש לפרש בזה, אז די ממשיות פון א גוף חי פון א איד (וועלכע מ'קען אנטאפן בממשות) און פון אלע זיינע כחות, ווערט באלעבט פון דעם "חלק אלוקה ממעל", און אלע תנועות הגוף שלו (תנועות אצבעות היד וכיוצא בזה), אפילו אין אן ענין של רשות וחול, איז א גילוי החיות פון זיין נפש האלקית.

Sefer Hasichot

A series of 12 volumes of the Rebbe's talks delivered between 1986 and 1992. During these years, the Rebbe would regularly review and edit (parts of) the transcripts of his talks for immediate publication. The language used alternated between Hebrew and Yiddish. These edited talks would appear in two weekly newspapers: the (Yiddish) *Algemeiner Journal* and the (Hebrew) *Kfar Chabad*.

One might mistakenly conclude that our resemblance to the divine is limited to our souls and the innermost recesses of our consciousness (and is not overtly manifest if not for our effort to reveal and act upon it). . . .

[But it is not so.] The *Tanya,* when describing the soul as being a part of God, adds the word *mamash,* which means "literally," implying that the soul is actually a part of God above, and not merely Godlike in some limited sense.

Mamash, however, also translates as "tangibly." This means that our divine core tangibly vivifies and manifests itself within our bodies and in all of its functions and activities. So much so, that every movement of the body (a finger gesture or the like), even when we are involved in a mundane activity, is actually a manifestation of the divine soul.

ממש

MAMASH

מישוש

MISHUSH

FIGURE 2.1

Excerpts from the Rosh Hashanah Liturgy

114 SHACHARIT FOR ROSH HASHANAH THE AMIDAH

countenance You gave us, Lord our God, the Torah of life and loving-kindness, righteousness, blessing, mercy, life and peace. May it be favorable in Your eyes to bless Your people Israel, at all times and at every moment, with Your peace.

ובספר And in the book of life, blessing, peace, and prosperity, deliverance, consolation, and favorable decrees, may we and all Your people the House of Israel be remembered and inscribed before You for a happy life and for peace. Blessed are You, Lord, who blesses His people Israel with peace.

אלהינו Our God and God of our fathers, reign over the entire world in Your glory, be exalted over all the earth in Your splendor, and reveal Yourself in the majesty of Your glorious might over all the inhabitants of Your terrestrial world. May everything that has been made know that You have made it; may everything that has been created understand that You have created it; and may everyone who has the breath [of life] in his nostrils declare that the Lord, God of Israel, is King and His kingship has dominion over all. (Our God and God of our fathers, please find favor in our rest.) Make us holy with Your commandments and grant us our portion in Your Torah; satiate us with Your goodness and gladden our soul with Your salvation. (Lord our God, grant as our heritage, in love

עמידה שחרית לראש השנה 114

תּוֹרַת חַיִּים וְאַהֲבַת חֶסֶד, וּצְדָקָה וּבְרָכָה וְרַחֲמִים וְחַיִּים וְשָׁלוֹם, וְטוֹב בְּעֵינֶיךָ לְבָרֵךְ אֶת עַמְּךָ יִשְׂרָאֵל בְּכָל עֵת וּבְכָל שָׁעָה בִּשְׁלוֹמֶךָ.

וּבְסֵפֶר חַיִּים בְּרָכָה וְשָׁלוֹם וּפַרְנָסָה טוֹבָה, יְשׁוּעָה וְנֶחָמָה וּגְזֵרוֹת טוֹבוֹת, נִזָּכֵר וְנִכָּתֵב לְפָנֶיךָ, אֲנַחְנוּ וְכָל עַמְּךָ בֵּית יִשְׂרָאֵל, לְחַיִּים טוֹבִים וּלְשָׁלוֹם. בָּרוּךְ אַתָּה יְיָ, הַמְבָרֵךְ אֶת עַמּוֹ יִשְׂרָאֵל בַּשָּׁלוֹם:

אֱלֹהֵינוּ וֵאלֹהֵי אֲבוֹתֵינוּ, מְלוֹךְ עַל הָעוֹלָם כֻּלּוֹ בִּכְבוֹדֶךָ, וְהִנָּשֵׂא עַל כָּל הָאָרֶץ בִּיקָרֶךָ, וְהוֹפַע בַּהֲדַר גְּאוֹן עֻזֶּךָ עַל כָּל יוֹשְׁבֵי תֵבֵל אַרְצֶךָ, וְיֵדַע כָּל פָּעוּל כִּי אַתָּה פְעַלְתּוֹ, וְיָבִין כָּל יְצוּר כִּי אַתָּה יְצַרְתּוֹ, וְיֹאמַר כֹּל אֲשֶׁר נְשָׁמָה בְאַפּוֹ: יְיָ אֱלֹהֵי יִשְׂרָאֵל מֶלֶךְ, וּמַלְכוּתוֹ בַּכֹּל מָשָׁלָה: (אֱלֹהֵינוּ וֵאלֹהֵי אֲבוֹתֵינוּ, רְצֵה נָא בִמְנוּחָתֵנוּ) קַדְּשֵׁנוּ בְּמִצְוֹתֶיךָ, וְתֵן חֶלְקֵנוּ בְּתוֹרָתֶךָ, שַׂבְּעֵנוּ מִטּוּבֶךָ וְשַׂמַּח נַפְשֵׁנוּ

QUESTION FOR DISCUSSION

Which of these prayers resonates more with you and is more likely to be recited with greater intensity and emotion? Why?

Text 5

The Rebbe, *Likutei Sichot* 19:296

אידן ווערן נתעורר ביים זאגן "ונתנה תוקף כו' מי ינוח כו" פון טיפעניש פון הארצן נאך מערער ווי די התעוררות ביים זאגן "מלוך על העולם כולו בכבודך" כו' . . .

אף על פי אז דער טעם גלוי אויף דעם איז ווייל זייענדיק א נשמה בגוף, זיינען עניני עולם הזה נעענטער צו אים און דערנעמען אים מער ווי ענינים רוחניים – איז אבער דער טעם פנימי אין דעם, ווייל די כוונה פון עצמותו ית' איז (דוקא) אין דירה **בתחתונים**, ובמילא דערנעמט עס אויך א אידן אין עצמיות הנפש שלו; און דערפאר ווערט ער נתעורר וכו' אין די בקשות דוקא, וואס בפנימיות איז דאס די הזזה עצמית פון עצם הנשמה צו אויספירן די כוונה העליונה צו מאכן די וועלט א דירה לו ית'.

When reciting the *Unetaneh Tokef* prayer [in which we affirm that on this day God decides] who shall find tranquility [and who shall not], etc., we are stirred to the depths of our hearts, more so than when proclaiming, "Reign over the entire word in Your glory."...

The obvious explanation for this is the fact that as souls vested in physical bodies, worldly concerns are closer to our hearts and interest us more than spiritual matters. On a deeper level, however, the explanation for this phenomenon is that our souls sense and mirror God's desire to be present and felt in our physical experience. This is why we are moved to the depths of our souls when we beseech God for material blessing: it is an expression of our deep-seated desire [to be granted the tools and resources that allow us] to implement the divine plan to make this world a home for God.

An Inapplicable Verdict (Optional Section)

Text 6

The Rebbe, *Likutei Sichot* 29:119

עס זיינען דא אזעלכע וואס זייער טוב איז בהעלם לגמרי, אבער א מקצת פונעם טוב הנעלם קומט סוף סוף לידי איזה גילוי – ווארום דער טוב ביי א אידן איז ניט א דבר נוסף אויף זיין מהות ... נאר דאס איז דער עצם און די אמיתיות פון זיין מציאות.

על פי זה איז מובן, אז יעדער איד, יהיה מי שיהיה, אויך בשעת ער איז עובר אן עבירה אויף וועלכן עס קומט מיתת בית דין, מוז זיין א לימוד זכות אויף אים, ווייל זיין אמת'ר רצון, זיין אמיתית **מציאותו** איז דער טוב **שבו**.

בשעת אבער אז סנהדרין "פתחו כולם בדיני נפשות תחלה ואמרו כולן חייב" ... בנוגע צו אזא זאגט מען "הרי זה פטור": וויבאלד אז ביי אים איז דאך זיכער פאראן טוב, נאר **דער בית דין קען עס ניט** "געפינען" דערפאר וואס ער איז בתכלית ההעלם – קען דערפאר ביי אים ניט אויסגעפירט ווערן דער ... פסק פון **דעם בית דין**.

Although the innate goodness in some people is thoroughly hidden, nevertheless, because goodness is not external to our being . . . but constitutes our very essence and is the truth of our existence, therefore, a trace of the person's concealed goodness inevitably must find some expression.

Accordingly, there must be a favorable way to view any individual, even one who has committed a capital crime, inasmuch as his true desire and his truest identity is the goodness that is at his core.

This is why a defendant is acquitted . . . if the Sanhedrin immediately and unanimously agrees upon his guilt. The defendant, without a doubt, possesses goodness, but due to its concealment, it has not been identified by the members of the Sanhedrin. The verdict of this court, therefore, cannot be applied . . . to this defendant.

The Practical Implications of Divinity

QUESTION FOR DISCUSSION

What are the practical implications of this understanding of our core identity?

Why Do We Matter?

Text 7

Rabbi Abraham J. Twerski, *Seek Sobriety Find Serenity* [New York: Pharos Books, 1993], p. 327

If we know we are great, we do not have to prove it.

Little children climb onto a chair or table and announce, "See how big I am! I can almost touch the ceiling." . . .

All that changes when we grow up is that we do not stand on chairs to demonstrate our height. The underlying pattern is unchanged, however. In whatever way we feel small, we try to show that we are big.

We see people who are name-droppers, or who otherwise try to impress people with their importance. We think,

Rabbi Abraham J. Twerski, MD
1930–

Psychiatrist and noted author. Rabbi Twerski is a scion of the Chernobyl Chasidic dynasty and a well-known expert in the field of substance abuse. He has authored more than 50 books on self-help and Judaism, and has served as a pioneer in heightening awareness of the dangers of addiction, spousal abuse, and low self-esteem. He served as medical director of the Gateway Rehabilitation Center in Pittsburgh and as associate professor of psychiatry at the University of Pittsburgh School of Medicine.

"What a huge, inflated ego that person has." Actually, the person feels terribly depleted and acts in desperation to convince others of his or her importance. This person wants to have a feeling of self-worth, hoping to hear the equivalent of "Look how big Johnny is" when the child stands on the chair.

Text 8

Rabbi Tzvi Freeman, *Bringing Heaven Down to Earth* II [Vancouver, B.C.: Class One Press, 2007], p. 195

Rabbi Tzvi Freeman
1955–

Rabbi, computer scientist, and writer. A published expert, consultant, and lecturer in the field of educational technology, Rabbi Freeman held posts at the University of British Columbia and the Digipen School of Computer Gaming. Rabbi Freeman is the author of *Bringing Heaven Down to Earth* and *Men, Women & Kabbalah*. He is a senior editor at Chabad.org.

You cannot reach deeper within another than you reach in your own self.

If you love yourself for your achievements, your current assets, the way you do things and handle the world—and despise yourself for failure in the same—it follows that your relationship with another will also be transient and superficial.

To achieve deep and lasting love of another person, you need to first experience the depth within yourself—an inner core that doesn't change with time or events. If it is the true essence, it is an essence shared by the other person as well, and deep love becomes unavoidable.

The Girl Who Cried Wolf

LEARNING EXERCISE 4

The Pew Research Center's 2013 survey of U.S. Jews asked:

Can a person be Jewish if he/she . . .

. . . works on the Sabbath?	**Yes / No**
. . . is strongly critical of Israel?	**Yes / No**
. . . claims not to believe in God?	**Yes / No**
. . . professes belief in the Christian messiah?	**Yes / No**

Text 9

Talmud, Sukah 56b

מעשה במרים בת בילגה שהמירה דתה, והלכה ונשאת לסרדיוט
אחד ממלכי יוונים. כשנכנסו יוונים להיכל היתה מבעטת בסנדלה
על גבי המזבח ואמרה: לוקוס לוקוס! עד מתי אתה מכלה
ממונן של ישראל ואי אתה עומד עליהם בשעת הדחק.

Miriam the daughter of Bilgah apostatized and married a Syrian-Greek military officer. When the Syrian-Greeks invaded the Sanctuary, she [joined them,] kicked the altar with her sandal and cried out, "Wolf! Wolf! How long will you consume Israel's money but not come to their assistance in their time of distress?!"

QUESTIONS FOR DISCUSSION

1. **How would you describe Miriam's relationship to her Jewish heritage?**
2. **Is there a way to put a positive spin on her disrespectful behavior?**

Text 10a

The Rebbe, *Sichot Kodesh* 5735, 1:45

Sichot Kodesh

Transcripts (mostly in Yiddish) of most of the Rebbe's public addresses (*farbrengens*) between 1950 and 1981, published in 50 volumes. For the talks that the Rebbe delivered on Shabbat and holidays, when audio recordings and taking notes are proscribed, a team of trained memorizers (*chozrim*) would reconstruct and transcribe the Rebbe's talk from memory. The Rebbe did not edit or review these transcripts for accuracy.

אפילו המירה דתה, און אפילו נישאת לסרדיוט, און זי איז געגאנגען מיט די וואס האבן איינגענומען דעם בית המקדש, אריינגעטראגן אהינצו דער ענין פון א ד"א וואס מהאט דארט מקריב געווען, איז אף על פי כן, מאנט מען פון איר אט דאס וואס זי האט געקלאפט מיט א סנדל אויפ'ן מזבח . . .

זאגט מען ניין! וואו אפגעשניטן! וואס אפגעשניטן! דאס איז מערניט בחיצוניות . . . א אידישע מיידל וואס המירה דתה רחמנא ליצלן, ונישאת לסרדיוט, איז דעם אויבערשטן נוגע ווי אזוי זי וועט זיך פירן אז זי וועט דערזען דעם מזבח . . .

אט דא באוויזט מען די גרויסקייט פון א אידישע נשמה, אז וואס ס'איז ניט געווען בחיצוניות, און וואס ס'האט זיך מיט איר ניט געטאן, ביז א דבר הכי שפל, בלייבט ער "בשעת החטא היתה באמנה אתו", מיט עצמות ומהות אליין.

Miriam apostatized, wedded an enemy of the Jewish people, and was part of the entourage that invaded the Temple and offered a swine on the altar. Despite all this, the sages make an issue of the fact that she disrespectfully struck the altar with her sandal. . . .

[Why did the sages focus on this act? Isn't this offense far eclipsed by the fact that she severed her ties with her Jewish heritage?]

Absolutely not!

What severed? Where severed?! Such a notion is an utter impossibility!

Her failings were only external to her identity. . . . Although a Jewish girl rejects her faith, God forbid, and marries an enemy of our people, nevertheless, [because she is still intimately connected with God], He still cares how she behaves when she approaches the altar. . . .

This demonstrates the greatness of the soul. No matter our external spiritual state, and no matter the depraved depths to which we may sink, our souls remain faithful to God, even at the moment of our failing.

Text 10b

The Rebbe, ibid., p. 46

אפילו אין אזא מין מעמד ומצב פון "המירה דתה ונישאת לסרדיוט", און געגיינגען מיט די גויים וואס זיינען געגיינגען אין בית המקדש . . . וואס האט איר אבער געארט? פארוואס איז דער מזבח ניט מגין אויף א אידן?

וואס דא זעט מען וואס א אידיש קינד איז: נישאת לסרדיוט, דער סרדיוט וואס האט מלחמה געהאלטן מיט אידן, און האט איינגענומען ירושלים, האט איינגענומען דעם בית המקדש, איינגענומען דעם מזבח, און זי גייט מיט עם מיט אלס אזא מין וואס איז שייכות צו אים, בשעת דערנאך אבער זי דערזעט וואס טוט זיך מיט א צווייטן אידן, שרייט זי "לוקוס לוקוס" פארוואס העלפסטו ניט קיין אידן.

Miriam rejected her faith, married the enemy, and joined the invasion of the Temple.... Nevertheless, what bothered her was why the altar was not protecting the Jews.

We see here the essence of a Jewish daughter. Miriam married an officer who waged war against the Jewish people, conquered Jerusalem, and invaded the Temple and desecrated its altar. And she went along with him, associating herself with the enemy's cause. Still, when she observed the tragedy that was befalling her fellow Jews, she screamed, "Wolf! Wolf! Why do you not come to the Jews' assistance?!"

FIGURE 2.2

No Jew Is Lost

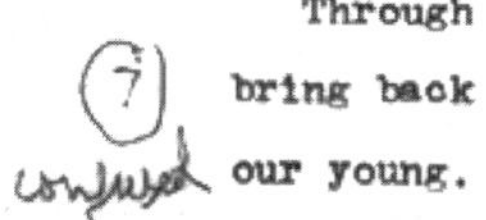

Through these encounters we hope to strengthen Yiddishkeit bring back our ~~lost~~ youth and prevent further drifting of our young.

Doesn't your community have a need for a Speakers' Bureau? How about starting one?

This notification about a speaker bureau said, ". . . to strengthen Yiddishkeit, bring back our lost youth, and prevent further drifting . . ." The Rebbe deleted the word "lost," and wrote on the side "confused?" as a possible replacement.

Modern Conversos

Text 11

The Rebbe, *Igrot Kodesh* 10:100

אינני יודע אם הבא לקמן היה גם כוונת כבודו כשנתן לי תשורתו הקובץ ברכות ותפלות "מאה ברכות", אבל בטח יש גם בזה השגחה פרטית, כי זהו מעין סידור הנדפס בשביל האנוסים, או אפשר גם על ידם, לאחר שבאו למקום מנוחה בו יכלו להתנהג כפי רצונם האמיתי בחיים היום-יומיים ובגלוי . . . ומזמן לזמן כשהנני מסתכל בקובץ זה . . . הנה בדרך ממילא עולה בכל פעם הרעיון אשר באמת הרי כל אחד ואחד במדה ידועה, ואולי גם במדה חשובה, אנוס הוא, ועושה כמה ענינים מפני כפית הסביבה אם במישרין או בעקיפין, או על כל פנים כלשון המורה הגדול (רמב"ם הל' גירושין ספ"ב) "אנוס מיצרו הרע ובאמת הוא רוצה להיות מישראל ורוצה לעשות כל המצוות ולהתרחק מהעבירות".

Igrot Kodesh

A selection of Hebrew and Yiddish letters penned by the Rebbe. As of 2014, 30 volumes have been published in this series. The letters are published in chronological order, starting from 1925 and extending thus far to 1975. Only those letters that are of relevance to the public are published, and all personal information is excised. The letters cover a wide range of issues: communal activism, Chabad philosophy, Talmud, Jewish law, Kabbalah, practical advice, and much more.

I do not know if the following was also your intention when you gave me the gift, the booklet of blessings and prayers titled *Me'ah Berachot* (*One Hundred Blessings*). Either way, it was certainly by divine providence.

This is a prayer booklet that was printed for converso Jews, perhaps even by conversos themselves, who immigrated to countries where they found respite, locales that allowed them the opportunity to openly behave in their everyday lives in accordance with their true wishes. . . .

Every so often when I look at this booklet . . . I can't help but think that truthfully, we are all conversos to a degree, perhaps even to a great degree, inasmuch as we act in many ways upon direct or indirect societal pressures. At the very least, [we are conversos due to internal coercion], as the great teacher, Maimonides wrote, "[We are] induced by the evil inclination [to act in manners inconsistent with our true will]. For in truth we want to be part of the Jewish nation, fulfill all of God's commandments, and distance ourselves from wrongdoing" (*Mishneh Torah,* Laws of Divorce 2:20).

Text 12

The Rebbe, *Torat Menachem* (5723), 36:224–225

לאמיתתו של דבר, שם זה (לשוב אל המקורות) אינו מתאים, כי, כאשר אומרים "מקור" סתם, אזי מדמיינים שזהו ענין שנמצא באיזה מקום רחוק, וצריך לילך מהלך רב וגדול עד שמגיעים אליו. ואילו אליבא דאמת, כיון ש"לכל ישראל אחד צדיק ואחד רשע . . נפש . . (ש)היא חלק אלקה ממעל ממש (כמ"ש בהתחלת ספר התניא), הרי אינו צריך לילך מרחק רב עד שיגיע למקור; זהו ענין שנמצא במוחו ולבו, וצריך רק להסיר את המכסה, ההעלם וההסתר שהוטל על זה.

In truth, the term "returning to the source" [used to describe people who embrace the path of the Torah] is inappropriate. The word "source" implies a faraway entity, one that one must travel great distances to reach. The reality, however, is that because (as stated in the beginning of *Tanya*) we all have a divine soul, we do not need to traverse great distances to arrive at our source. It is there already in our hearts and minds; we need only to remove the cover that conceals it.

Torat Menachem

A Hebrew translation of the transcripts of the Rebbe's talks. This work also comprehensively cross-references and footnotes the material. As of 2014, more than 90 volumes have appeared in this series, covering the years 1950–1968 and 1982–1992. The Rebbe did not edit or review these publications for accuracy.

Text 13

The Rebbe, English Letters

English Letters

The Rebbe's correspondence includes many thousands of letters in English. Dr. Nissan Mindel, a member of the Rebbe's secretariat, was responsible for these letters. The Rebbe would dictate his responses to Dr. Mindel, who would draft letters for the Rebbe's review and editing. It is not always clear whether the letters we possess are Mindel's initial drafts, or the final version authorized by the Rebbe to be sent to the recipient.

The nature of a Jew is that he always desires to act in accordance with the Torah and *mitzvot*. However, sometimes there may be some circumstance which overshadows this desire, or immobilizes it. . . . Once the external constraint is removed, the true (innate) will is free to reassert itself and to act in accordance with the innate nature.

In light of the above, it should be clear that there can be no question of hypocrisy when a Jew learns Torah and conducts his life in accordance with the Torah and *mitzvot,* even if some of his other actions, even feelings, do not always harmonize with his Torah study and observance; because the incongruity lies not in acting according to the Torah and *mitzvot,* rather it lies in acting *contrary* to the Torah and *mitzvot*.

FIGURE 2.3

The Ten Mitzvah Campaigns

Campaign	Details
Tefilin	Jewish men (age 13 and over) should don *tefilin* every day, except for Shabbat and festivals. (Est. 1967)
Torah Study	Every Jew should study Torah daily. (1974)
Mezuzah	A Jewish home should have kosher *mezuzot* on its doorposts. (1974)
Tsedakah	Everyone should give charity daily. (1974)
A Home Filled with Holy Books	Jewish sacred books should be present in Jewish homes. (1974)
Shabbat and Holiday Candles	Jewish women and girls should light candles every Friday afternoon before sunset and in honor of festivals. (1974)
Kosher	Jews should eat kosher food. (1975)
Family Purity	Jewish married couples should observe Torah marital laws. (1975)
Jewish Education	Jewish children should be taught about their heritage and be provided with a quality Jewish education. (1976)
Love Your Fellow	Jews should reach out to one another with love, concern, and a sense of unity. (1976)

When Impossible Is Impossible

Text 14

Midrash, *Tana Devei Eliyahu Rabah* 25

Tana Devei Eliyahu (*Seder Eliyahu*)

A Midrashic work. Midrash is the designation of a particular genre of rabbinic literature. The term "Midrash" is derived from the root *d-r-sh,* which means "to search," "to examine," and "to investigate." This particular Midrash deals with the divine precepts, their reasons, and the importance of Torah, prayer, and repentance. The work is divided into two sections: *Seder Eliyahu Rabah* and *Seder Eliyahu Zuta*

שכל אחד ואחד מישראל חייב לומר: מתי יגיעו מעשי למעשה אבותי אברהם יצחק ויעקב.

Every Jew must ask, "When will my actions be on par with those of Abraham, Isaac, and Jacob?"

Text 15

Talmud, Megilah 6b

אם יאמר לך אדם:

"יגעתי ולא מצאתי", אל תאמין.

"לא יגעתי ומצאתי" אל תאמין.

"יגעתי ומצאת" תאמין.

If someone tells you:

"I have toiled, but I have not succeeded"—do not believe it.

"I have not toiled, yet I have succeeded"—do not believe it.

"I have toiled and succeeded"—believe it.

Text 16

The Rebbe, *Igrot Kodesh* 29:203

טרם יקראו ואני אענה – מכבר עשיתי כעצתו ונשלח לשם הר"ר משה יצחק שי' העכט – וכנראה **ממכתבו זה ומהקודמו** עדיין אינו מכירו ואת הכוחות שניתנו להנ"ל ועל כל פנים ישתדל להכירו **עתה**, **ותיכף ומיד** ישתנה הכל: המצב רוח, הבטחון בהשם, השמחה היום יומית וכו' וכו'.

I preempted you and responded even before you made your request. I already did precisely as you advised. Rabbi Moshe Yitzchak Hecht was sent to your city. It appears from your letter (and from the previous one) that you are unfamiliar with Rabbi Hecht or the abilities and powers he has been granted. In any event, endeavor now to acquaint yourself with him, and immediately everything will change—your disposition, your trust in God, your everyday joy, etc.

QUESTION FOR DISCUSSION

Can you deduce from the Rebbe's answer what question he was answering? How would you formulate the question?

FIGURE 2.4

Not Small After All

B"H

May Flower n.v.

2

I am going to write to Mendy but please check if he received the letter because his adress he gave me 2 or 3 years ago and I don't know if it is still the same . If he did not receive anything from me please drop me a note with Mendy Katzman's address, thank you.
Give also my regards to Levy Krinsky and his nice father.
I would like you to extend the Rebbe my most sincere appreciation and other good feelings but for lack of good English I do not know what words to use. Just tell the Rebbe that a small Jew from Curacao felt that the Rebbe Shelita touched my soul; thank you for doing it.
I would like to write to the Rebbe myself but I do not know how to write the words in Hebrew adressing to the Rebbe.
Please help me with that either you write to me in Hebrew I'll copy it and the rest of the letter I'll write in as good English as possible.

Once again thank you, as we say here Masha Masha Danki pa tur Kos.

A gezinte meniche Kol Tov,
have a Koshere Pesach,

Shalom,
Haime Groisman.

Haime Groisman wrote this letter to Rabbi Moshe Kotlarsky. Toward the end, he wrote, "Just tell the Rebbe that a small Jew from Curacao felt . . ." The Rebbe responded with the letter on the right.

For the background of this correspondence, see chabad.org/133497

RABBI MENACHEM M. SCHNEERSON
Lubavitch
770 Eastern Parkway
Brooklyn, N. Y. 11213
Hyacinth 3-9250

מנחם מענדל שניאורסאהן
ליובאוויטש
770 איסטערן פארקוויי
ברוקלין, נ. י.

By the Grace of G-d
3rd of Nissan, 5744
Brooklyn, N. Y.

Mr. Chaim Yosef Groisman
P. O. B 2073
Breederstraat 74 (o)
Curacao, N. A.

Greeting and Blessing:

I was pleased to receive your regards through our esteemed mutual friends.

I must, however, take exception to your referring to yourself as "a small Jew from Curacao." There is surely no need to emphasize to you at length that every Jew, man or woman, has a Nefesh Elokis, which is a "part of G-dliness Above," as explained in the Tanya, beginning of chapter two. Thus, there is no such thing as "a small Jew," and a Jew must never underestimate his or her tremendous potential.

With the approach of the Yom Tov Pesach, I take this opportunity of extending to you my prayerful wishes that the Festival of Our Freedom bring you and yours true freedom, freedom from anxiety material and spiritual, from anything which might distract from serving G-d wholeheartedly and with joy, and to carry over this freedom and joy into the whole year.

Wishing you and yours a Kosher and happy Pesach.

With blessing, M. Schneerson

Key Points

1. Our truest self is a Godly soul. A spiritual experience is a moment of unrestricted contact with our deepest essence.

2. Our corporeal lives and physical activities are themselves vehicles of the soul's expression.

3. Our longing for material blessing is an expression of our deep-seated desire to be granted the resources that allow us to implement the divine plan to make this world a home for God.

4. Because goodness is not secondary to our core identity, even a negative act must yield some expression of goodness.

5. Faults, failures, and bad habits do not define who we are. When we tap into our inherent value and immutable perfection, we can truly love ourselves and others.

6. Our essence is an indistinguishable spark of God. No matter how we behave, our Jewishness can never be extinguished.

7. Our souls desire whatever God desires. Thus, the deepest and truest desire of each Jew, when stripped of all superficiality, is to perform all of God's instructions (*mitzvot*).

8. *Teshuvah* means to return to our true selves and harmonize our lives with our innermost essence, our Godly consciousness.

9. There can be no question of hypocrisy when we choose to do a mitzvah, even if other areas of our lives are not harmonious with Judaism. The incongruity lies not in the choice to do a mitzvah, but in the choice to delay living from our essential core completely and proudly.

10. Our divine souls are infinite. We are thus empowered to accomplish far beyond our perceived abilities.

SELECTED CORRESPONDENCE

OF THE REBBE

An Un-American Welcome

By the Grace of G-d
22nd of Adar II, 5733 [March 26, 1973]
Brooklyn, N.Y.

Mr. Mordechai Shoel Landow

Greeting and Blessing:

Your letter of March 1st reached me with some delay. I regret that my acknowledgment has been unavoidably delayed by the intervening days of Purim. Please accept my apology.

First of all, I want to express my gratification at your response to the suggestions which I proposed to you during your visit here. It was, of course, a pleasure to make your personal acquaintance.

Frankly, I had wondered what your reactions might be to my "un-American" manner of welcoming you. For, the accepted American way, if I am not mistaken, is to greet one with a shower of compliments and praise, even if not always fully merited. In your case, of course, it would have been very well deserved credit, for I was fully aware of your accomplishments and generosity in behalf of the Lubavitch work in your community, given in the best tradition of inspiration and dedication, even to the extent of getting your friends involved in it. Yet, instead of verbalizing my appreciation at length, I glossed over it briefly, and immediately challenged you with new and formidable projects.

However, the fact is that I felt impelled to use the precious time at our disposal to discuss with you those matters which, in my estimation, are of vital importance, namely the expansion of our program in Miami and also the project in our Holy Land, knowing that however much we could extend the late hour, the time would still be too short to discuss the vital need of these matters in all their ramifications.

My guiding principle in this case, as when meeting with people in general, is the *bon mot* I heard from my father-in-law of Saintly memory: "When two Jews meet, they should not be content with the benefit that the meeting brings to each of them, but they should immediately be concerned with the prospect of bringing a benefit to a third Jew, a fourth, and to as many Jews as possible." Moreover, I was hopeful that you would accept my suggestions in the right spirit, precisely because you have already made a magnificent start. And as I wrote to you in my previous letter, quoting our Sages of blessed memory, "He who has 100 desires 200," etc., or, in other words, since achievement is the greatest incentive to further and more ambitions achievement, I had reason to believe that your achievement in the past will widen your horizons and intensify your desire for even greater things. Hence, without losing time, I embarked upon the practical aspects of our meeting for the benefit of so many of our fellow Jews. This, I felt, would ensure also our share of the benefit, yours and mine, and yours even more than mine, since the actual implementation of these projects is something which Divine Providence has entrusted in your hands.

As for the projects themselves, I can hardly overemphasize their importance. The development of the educational facilities in Miami on all levels up to and including the highest, goes beyond the thing itself, for, as the point was mentioned, Miami is a showcase for American Jewry from all parts of the U.S.A., so that every accomplishment there, in the area of Torah education and revival of Yiddishkeit, has the significance of a "pilot" project for others to emulate. Similarly, giving new direction to the networks and other media would trigger off beneficial repercussions on a global scale.

Thus, even a small accomplishment in these areas could be multiplied on an unforeseen scale; how much more so a substantial accomplishment.

As Miami is the showcase for American Jewry, so Eretz Yisroel is the showcase for world Jewry, due to the considerable and growing tourism. Add to this the fact that it is the "Holy Land" also for other faiths, and attracts non-Jewish tourists, too, in growing numbers. Eretz Yisroel must therefore serve as a model for all. The project has still greater merit because it is directly connected with the influx of the new immigrants.

In the light of all that has been said above, you can well understand that your letter has greatly relieved my mind, for you have indeed shown yourself big enough to overlook the scanty praise and to give your serious and favorable attention to the tasks at hand. I feel certain that the Zechus [merit] of your good deeds already accomplished has stood you in good stead.

I am very gratified to note that the activities in Miami are proceeding at an accelerated pace. No doubt these include the summer camp and day camp which came up in our conversation, as well as making your influence increasingly felt in the networks and news media, after the promising start you made.

As for the third project, namely, the one for Eretz Yisroel, may I say, with all due respect, that I do not agree with your contention that you are not equipped to develop it. I am certain that you are. However, it would in any case have to wait until the Miami program is well advanced, so as not to detract attention from the latter. Actually, I regret to say, there is also a different factor, which makes the present moment not very opportune for the immediate implementation of the Eretz Yisroel project. For, such a project must, of course, have the utmost cooperation of various departments of the Israeli government. But, unfortunately, for various reasons, the present moment is not very auspicious to embark upon the project, so that it must be postponed for the time being.

Finally, with reference to the conclusion of your letter, on the subject of ritual observance, I need not emphasize to you, a successful businessman, that although knowledge and motivation etc. are very desirable things, the essential thing, after all, is the actual deed. As for the "disappointment" at the lack of greater progress, I would like to cite a basic Chasidic principle, actually deriving from the Alter Rebbe, in his classical work, the *Tanya*. It is to the effect that inasmuch as a Jew must utilize to the full all his capacities towards increasing the good and the holy within himself and the environment, "disappointment" (which usually is a negative factor, being closely linked with discouragement) can also be converted into a positive force, to redouble one's efforts in the right direction. Indeed, it can be made into a springboard for an even greater accomplishment, as in the case of a person who has to make a wide leap, which he can do only by going back (in his feelings of sophistication—*not*, G-d forbid, in doing Mitzvos) a few steps in order to gain momentum for that extra leap. May G-d grant that your hope for complete observance will be realized even sooner than you expect, and the Zechus Horabim (the benefit for many) will help you, since your way of life and conduct will surely be an inspiration to many.

With esteem and with blessings for good tidings,

P.S. I was pleased to receive personal regards from you through Prof. Yirmyahu Branover, who informed me that he gained the distinct impression that the Eretz Yisroel project has become much closer to your heart, not just theoretically, but also from the practical viewpoint. And while, as mentioned above, the time now is not opportune, the situation might change at any moment, though the Miami program must have top priority, as above; and, hopefully, the other project will have its turn at the proper time.

A Soul Seeking Expression

By the Grace of G-d
16th of Tammuz, 5720 [July 11, 1960]
Brooklyn, N.Y.

After the very long interval, I was pleased to receive your letter of June 17th, in which you write about your wedding in a happy and auspicious hour. I was also especially interested to read about your having settled down to a family life based on the foundations of our Torah, which is called the Law of Life.

Judging from the description of your experiences with a sense of humor, I trust that both you and your wife are sincerely determined to live up to the Jewish way of life, which will ensure a happy and harmonious life, both materially and spiritually. The important thing is to start with a firm determination, and then, as our Sages said, "One Mitzvah brings another in its train," and these are the channels and vessels to receive and enjoy G-d's blessings.

You write about meeting a Jew in the course of your travels who comes to the synagogue to help make up a minyan, yet at the same time reads the newspaper. Everyone, of course, reacts to an experience in a way that is closest to him. Thus, for my part, I make the following two extreme observations:

First, I see in it the extreme Jewish attachment which one finds in every Jew. For here is a person who has wandered off to a remote part of the world, and has become so far removed, not only geographically, but also mentally and intellectually, as to have no concept of what prayer is or what a house of G-d is, etc.; yet one finds in him that Jewish spark, or as the Old Rebbe, the founder of Chabad, expressed it in his Tanya: "The Divine soul which is truly a part of G-d." This Divine soul, which is the inheritance of every Jew, seeks expression as best it can, and in the case of this particular Jew, it seeks expression in at least enabling other Jews to pray congregationally, and he therefore goes out of his way to help them and at the same time to be counted with them.

My other observation, following from the above, is as follows: If, where the odds are so great against Jewish observance, yet a Jew can remain active and conscious of his Jewishness, it can easily be seen what great things could have been accomplished with this particular Jew if, at the proper time, he should have received the right education in his early life, or at least the proper spiritual guidance in his adult life. This consideration surely emphasizes the mutual responsibility which rests upon all Jews, and particularly on those who can help others.

I will not deny that the above is said not in a spirit of philosophizing, but with a view to stimulate your thinking as to your own possibilities in your particular environment, and what the proper attitude should be.

We must never despair of any Jew, and at the same time we must do all we can to take the fullest advantage of our capacities and abilities to strengthen the Jewish consciousness among all Jews with whom we come in contact. For one can never tell how far-reaching such influence can be.

To conclude this letter on the happy note of the beginning of your letter relating to your marriage, may I again reiterate my prayerful wishes that you establish and conduct your home on everlasting foundations of the Torah and Mitzvos, and thus enjoy a totally happy and productive life, both materially and spiritually, which go hand in hand together.

I trust both you and your wife will find the enclosed copies of my recent message interesting and useful.

Hoping to hear good news from you always.

The Harmonious Life

By the Grace of G-d
26th of Teves, 5725 [December 31, 1964]
Brooklyn, N.Y.

Greeting and Blessing:

This is to acknowledge receipt of your letter with the enclosure, in which you write about your problem of acute anxiety, and ask my advice.

The best and most effective thing to do, in a situation such as yours, is to study thoroughly those sections and chapters in our sacred books where the matter of Divine Providence and Bitochon [trust in G-d] are discussed, such as Chovos Halvovos, Shaar Habitochon, and similar. It is well to keep in mind those chapters and verses in the Tehillim [Psalms] which speak of these subjects, as well as the Midrashim and interpretations of our Sages on them. These things should be studied with such depth that they should become a part of one's thinking. In this way there will be no room left for any kind of anxiety or worry, and as King David said in the Tehillim, "G-d is with me, I shall not fear. What can man do unto me!"

As you well know, the matter of Hashgocho Protis is the basis of true monotheism, a concept which to us means not only that G-d is one, but that there is oneness in the whole of Nature. In other words, the whole universe has one Supreme Being, Who not only is the Creator of everything, but also is the Master, continually supervising every detail of his handiwork. The corollary of this is that there cannot be a single point in the whole order of the world which is separated from the Supreme Being, or in any way not subject to His control. At the same time it is obvious that the Supreme Being is also the Essence of Perfection and Goodness. And although many things in the world seem imperfect, and require completion or perfection, there can be no doubt that there is a perfect order in the world, and even the lowest in the scale of Creation, namely the inanimate things, display wonderful perfection and symmetry, as can be seen from the atoms and molecules of inorganic matter. Hence, the conclusion must be that even those things which require completion are also part of the perfect order, and necessary for the fulfillment of the good, as all this is explained at length in the teachings of Chassidus. It is explained there that in order for a man to attain perfection, it is necessary that he should also have the feeling that he is not only on the receiving end, but also a contributor, and according to the expression of our Sages of blessed memory, "A partner in the Creation." This is why many things have been left in the world for him to improve and perfect.

I also want to make the further observation, and this is also essential, that there is really no basis for anxiety at any time, and as you yourself mentioned in your letter, that you find no reason for it. Even in such cases where you think you know the reason for your anxiety, the reason is undoubtedly imaginary, or at any rate, not the real cause. For the real cause is that one's daily life is not in complete harmony with the true essence of a Jew. In such a case it is impossible not to have an awkward feeling that things do not seem to fit somehow, and it is this disharmony which is at the bottom of the anxiety, and it is in proportion to the discrepancy between his way of life and his true natural self.

Everybody recognizes that anxiety has to do with the psyche. But in the case of a Jew, the so-called psyche is really the Neshama [soul]. Some Jews have a particularly sensitive soul, in which case the above-mentioned disharmony would create a greater anxiety. In such a case even subtle and "minor" infractions of Dikdukei Mitzvoth [details of *mitzvot*] would create anxiety. But even in the case of an ordinary soul of the average Jew, there must inevitably be created some anxiety if there is a failure to observe the fundamental Mitzvoth. It is very possible that the above may have a bearing on your situation. If this is so, then all that is necessary is to rectify matters, and bring the daily life and conduct into complete harmony with the essence of the soul, through strict adherence to the Torah and Mitzvoth. Then the symptoms will disappear of themselves.

It is necessary to mention also that in your case, where your position gives you a great deal of influence on your environment, your influence is an integral part of your harmonious life, and it is therefore essential that your influence, too, should be in harmony with the Torah and Mitzvoth in the fullest measure.

I suggest that you should also have the Mezuzoth of your home checked, as also your Tefillin, and before putting on your Tefillin every weekday morning, to put aside a small coin for Tzedoko [charity].

Hoping to hear good news from you in regard to all the matters discussed above.

With blessing,

P.S. As for the question of seeing me personally in connection with this year's occurrence, the calendar of appointments is filled to capacity and for a long time in advance. But the important thing is that it is not at all necessary for you to take the trouble and time to see me personally, inasmuch as all I could tell you is what I wrote to you above.

You Never "Lose" Your Judaism

5735 [1975]

Mrs.
Johannesburg, South Africa

Blessing and Greeting:

I am in receipt of your letter. As requested, I will remember you in prayer for the fulfillment of your heart's desires for good in the matters about which you write.

It is well to remember that since the teachings and obligations of the Torah, which a Jew is duty-bound to observe, come from G-d, the Creator of man, it is certain that G-d provides the necessary ability to carry out His directives. It would, of course, be illogical to presume that G-d would request a Jew to do something beyond his capacity. It is true that some things are harder to carry out than others, but we have the assurance that nothing stands in the way of the will[1] and, given the proper effort, it is possible to overcome all difficulties.

I must take exception to what you call at the conclusion of your letter "*my lost Judaism.*" The expression "lost" does not really fit here, for no person can lose something that is his or her true essence and inwardness. What is possible is that this true essence of a person is sometimes in a state of "suspended animation," or covered with various layers of foreign substances, even such that are at variance with this essence. But this essence cannot be "lost"; it can only be dormant, as it were, instead of being active and on the surface, as it should be.

Needless to say, the purpose of the above remark is not to discuss the semantics, but to emphasize that your Judaism is actually intact deep inside of you, and it is entirely up to you to make it an integral and active ingredient of your daily life. You don't have to look for it elsewhere; all you have to do is to brush off those external layers that, for one reason or another, have covered your inner essence.

May G-d grant that you will have good news to report.

With blessing,

1 Zohar, Part II, 162:b.

It Most Certainly Will Assert Itself

5730 [1970]

Mr.
Manchester, England

Greeting and Blessing:

After the long interval, I was pleased to receive your recent letter.

Thank you very much for the good news in regard to the progress of the *mikvah*. . . .

I read with particular interest your reference to your efforts in behalf of your uncle. You write that you think that you have not succeeded even in stirring his conscience. However, while you may not have noticed any visible signs of it, there can be no doubt that you have in some way touched his innermost consciousness. According to the Rambam, a Jew, regardless of his professed attitudes, or even his conduct, always retains an innermost desire to submit to the will of G-d. The Rambam, who was a great physician, of the spirit as well as of the body, can be relied upon in such matters. He explains this phenomenon by pointing to the fact that in some Jews the innermost consciousness and essence may sometimes be covered up and hidden, so that the individual himself may not be aware of what his true essence is. However, sooner or later this innermost aspect and essence of the Jew must assert itself and come to the fore. When it does, the individual will be grateful to any and all who have helped bring it about, and who have done so a year, a month, or even a day sooner than he could have done so by his own unaided efforts.

Thus, this is clearly the responsibility of every Jew towards every other Jew, since all Jews are like the parts of one body. Certainly it is the responsibility of one who is a relative. And wherever the responsibility is the greater, it is also certain the additional capacities have been given to carry it out.

In light of the above, you will understand my feelings that you should maintain contact with your uncle from time to time, and be confident that eventually your sincere approach, and words coming from the heart, will find the proper response.

With blessing,

LESSON 3
Eliminating the Divide

The secret of Jewish survival is the Torah, which century after century has been studied and taught with commitment and love. But what does the Torah mean to us? Of what value is it in our everyday lives? Valuing the Torah for what it really is can enhance our lives in intriguing and dramatic ways and allow us to reconcile conflicts between our spiritual aspirations and our quest for happiness.

Unforgettable Words

Text 1a

Flavius Josephus, *The Jewish War*, VII [London: Penguin, 2003], pp. 385–386

Josephus
ca. 37–100

Jewish historian. Born Yosef ben Matityahu Hakohen, he changed his name to Titus Flavius Josephus upon becoming a Roman citizen. His two principal works, *The Jewish War* and *Antiquities of the Jews,* are considered primary sources in documenting Jewish history during the Second Temple period. Despite surrendering his garrison to the Romans during the great revolt and later accepting Roman patronage, Josephus viewed himself as a faithful Jew.

Most of the spoils that were carried were heaped up indiscriminately, but more prominent than all the rest were those captured in the Temple at Jerusalem—a golden table weighing several hundred weight, and a lampstand similarly made of gold but differently constructed from those we normally use. The central shaft was fixed to a base, and from it extended slender branches placed like the prongs of a trident, and with the end of each one forged into a lamp: these numbered seven, signifying the honour paid to that number by the Jews. After these was carried the Jewish Law, the last of the spoils. Next came a large group carrying images of Victory, all fashioned of ivory and gold. Behind them drove Vespasian first with Titus behind him. . . . All day long the city of Rome celebrated the triumphant issue of the campaign against her enemies, the end of civil strife, and the beginning of hope for a joyful future.

Text 1b

Simon Schama, "The Beginning," *The Story of the Jews*, Part I
[Oxford Film and Television Production, 2013]

Given the hammer blows of the Roman legions, and coming as they did after century upon century of blows from Egyptians, Syrians, and Babylonians, there would have been scant reason to suppose that the Jews would survive as a people—and yet, two thousand years later the Jews are still here. How?

Well, one answer could be found back at the Arch of Titus—not something that's here, but something that's not. When Josephus describes the procession of loot and prisoners paraded through the streets of Rome, he says, "And last of all of the spoils was carried the Laws of the Jews." But, where are the laws? Where are the Torah scrolls? Conspicuously, tellingly, they are absent.

What were scrolls of law anyway, just many words on parchment, not really worth the time of a sculptor or the cost of the marble. But words copied, memorized, internalized, made unforgettable, will beat swords anytime. You can't hold words captive.

The Roman Empire has come and gone, but go into a synagogue any Saturday and you'll still hear those words.

In September 1913, Dr. Sigmund Freud, the "godless" Jew, was in Rome, and he sent a post card of the arch of Titus to a friend. On it he wrote, *Der Jude übersteht's*, the Jew survives it.

Simon Michael Schama
1945–

British historian. Schama was born in London, the son of Jewish parents with roots in Lithuania, Romania, and Turkey. He is professor of history and art history at Columbia University. He is perhaps best known for writing and hosting the 15-part BBC documentary series *A History of Britain*. His book, *Two Rothschilds and the Land of Israel* is a study of the Zionist aims of Edmond James de Rothschild and James Armand de Rothschild.

LEARNING EXERCISE 1

It is important that I study Torah because . . .

1. ____________________

____

2. ____________________

____

3. ____________________

____

The Torah and the World

Aphorisms from Talmudic Times

Text 2a

Talmud, Bava Kama 92a

מנא הא מילתא דאמרי אינשי "בתר עניא אזלא עניותא"?

What is the Torah source for the popular saying, "Poverty follows the poor"?

Babylonian Talmud

A literary work of monumental proportions that draws upon the legal, spiritual, intellectual, ethical, and historical traditions of Judaism. The 37 tractates of the Babylonian Talmud contain the teachings of the Jewish sages from the period after the destruction of the 2nd Temple through the 5th century CE. It has served as the primary vehicle for the transmission of the Oral Law and the education of Jews over the centuries; it is the entry point for all subsequent legal, ethical, and theological Jewish scholarship.

Text 2b

Ibid., 93a

מנא הא מילתא דאמרי אינשי "בתר מרי ניכסי ציבי משך"?

What is the Torah source for the popular saying, "Following a person of means will leave you chunks of fat"?

QUESTIONS FOR DISCUSSION

1. **What is the Talmud's underlying assumption in asking these questions? What is the basis of this assumption?**
2. **Why does the Talmud engage in this seemingly pointless exercise? What is the significance in finding Torah sources for popular adages?**

Dualistic Model vs. Blueprint Model

Text 3

Zohar 2:161a

וכד בעא קודשא בריך הוא למברי עלמא, הוה מסתכל בה באורייתא, בכל מלה ומלה, ועבד לקבלה אומנותא דעלמא. בגין דכל מלין ועובדין דכל עלמין באורייתא אינון. ועל דא קודשא בריך הוא הוה מסתכל בה וברא עלמא.

When God resolved to create the world, He looked into the Torah, into its every word, and fashioned the world accordingly. For the Torah contains every phenomenon and every entity of every world. God, therefore, consulted the Torah and created the world.

Zohar

The most seminal work of Kabbalah, Jewish mysticism. The Zohar is a mystical commentary on the Torah, written in Aramaic and Hebrew. According to Arizal, the Zohar contains teachings of Rabbi Shimon bar Yocha'i who lived in the Land of Israel during the 2nd century. The Zohar has become one of the indispensable texts of traditional Judaism, alongside and nearly equal in stature to the Mishnah and Talmud.

Optional Section

Text 4a

Rabbi Shne'ur Zalman of Liadi, *Tanya*, ch. 4

שכתוב בזהר דאורייתא וקודשא בריך הוא כולא חד. פירוש: דאורייתא היא חכמתו ורצונו של הקדוש ברוך הוא.

The Zohar states that the Torah is one with God. This means to say that the Torah is God's wisdom and will.

Rabbi Shne'ur Zalman of Liadi
(Alter Rebbe)
1745–1812

Chasidic rebbe, halachic authority, and founder of the Chabad movement. The Alter Rebbe was born in Liozna, Belarus, and was among the principal students of the Magid of Mezeritch. His numerous works include the *Tanya*, an early classic containing the fundamentals of Chabad Chasidism, and *Shulchan Aruch HaRav*, an expanded code of Jewish law.

Text 4b

Rabbi Shne'ur Zalman of Liadi, ibid.

נמשלה התורה למים: מה מים יורדים ממקום גבוה למקום נמוך, כך התורה ירדה ממקום כבודה, שהיא רצונו וחכמתו יתברך, ואורייתא וקודשא בריך הוא כולא חד, ולית מחשבה תפיסא ביה כלל, ומשם נסעה וירדה בסתר המדרגות ממדרגה למדרגה בהשתלשלות העולמות, עד שנתלבשה בדברים גשמיים ועניני עולם הזה.

The Torah is allegorically compared to water because the nature of water is to descend from a higher place to a lower place. Similarly, the Torah is God's will and wisdom and is absolutely one with God, Whom no mind can grasp. Yet, the Torah descended from its position of glory, through various spiritual levels, level after level, until it clothed itself in corporeal substances and worldly concepts.

End of Optional Section

A Non-Relationship

QUESTION FOR DISCUSSION

Is there a practical difference whether we view the Torah as the blueprint of Creation or not?

FIGURE 3.1

The Dualistic Model

1. The Torah and nature, including human nature, pull us in opposite directions.
2. At times, the Torah might not be practical.
3. We need to make painful sacrifices and relinquish a normal and healthy life in order to enjoy a thriving spiritual life.
4. If we disregard the Torah's instructions, we only undermine our spiritual aspirations.

No Contradiction

Text 5

The Rebbe, *Igrot Kodesh* 15:314

יהי רצון שהתחלת הדיון על דבר בעית האניות תביא הזזה **ממשית** לפתרון הענין מתאים להוראות תורתנו . . .

וכיון שאמרו חז"ל אסתכל באורייתא וברא עלמא, הרי אי אפשר ונגד השכל הוא אשר ענינים שבעולם יפריעו וימנעו קיום האמור בתורה, שהרי אי אפשר, שמובן גם על פי שכל הפשוט, שהמסובב יהיה חזק יותר מהסבה.

May God help that the start of deliberations regarding the problem of the ships [in terms of the violation of Shabbat] should result in a meaningful breakthrough that leads to a solution that is consistent with the teachings of our Torah. . . .

Our sages say that "God looked into the Torah and created the world." Accordingly, it is logically impossible that anything in the world should impede the fulfillment of the Torah's directives. It is self-understood that the effect cannot prevail over its cause.

Igrot Kodesh

A selection of Hebrew and Yiddish letters penned by the Rebbe. As of 2014, 30 volumes have been published in this series. The letters are published in chronological order, starting from 1925 and extending thus far to 1975. Only those letters that are of relevance to the public are published, and all personal information is excised. The letters cover a wide range of issues: communal activism, Chabad philosophy, Talmud, Jewish law, Kabbalah, practical advice, and much more.

Text 6

The Rebbe, *Likutei Sichot* 1:1–2

בעת עס . . . דוכט זיך אז צוליב דער וועלטלעכער נאטירלעכער ארדענונג איז דאס אים שווער, אדער גאר אוממעגלעך - איז בשעת ער דערמאנט זיך אז . . . "קודשא בריך הוא אסתכל באורייתא וברא עלמא" - דער אויבערשטער האט אריינגעקוקט אין תורה (אין די עשרה מאמרות) און דערמיט באשאפן די וועלט, איז מצד דעם אפלייג אז די גאנצע עקזיסטענץ און "פאראן" פון וועלט איז נאר פון די עשרה מאמרות **שבתורה**, ווייסט ער במילא, אז די מציאות פון וועלט קען ניט זיין קיין שטער צו מצוות, ווארום אין **דער זעלבער תורה** שטייט דאך "אנכי ה' אלקיך" מיט אלע תרי"ג מצוות.

Likutei Sichot

Widely considered the Rebbe's magnum opus, the 39 volumes of *Likutei Sichot* feature scholarly essays relating to themes in the weekly Torah portions and the Jewish holidays. The Rebbe initially conveyed these concepts in his public talks and subsequently reworked them for publication. In some volumes, the essays appear in Yiddish, while in others they are in Hebrew. Most volumes also present a collection of the Rebbe's correspondence.

When it . . . appears that natural circumstances make it difficult, or perhaps even impossible, to follow the teachings of the Torah, one should recall that . . . "God looked into the Torah and created the world." This premise, that all of existence comes from the Torah, leads us to the conclusion that nothing that exists can hamper our performance of any of the 613 *mitzvot* that are contained in the very same Torah.

Text 7

Midrash, *Bamidbar Rabah* 12:3

אמר לו הקדוש ברוך הוא: איני מבקש לפי כחי אלא לפי כחן.

Bamidbar Rabah

A Midrashic work. Midrash is the designation of a particular genre of rabbinic literature. The term "Midrash" is derived from the root *d-r-sh,* which means "to search," "to examine," and "to investigate." The first part of *Bamidbar Rabah* is notable for its inclusion of esoteric material; the second half is essentially identical to *Midrash Tanchuma* on the book of Numbers. It was first published in Constantinople in 1512, together with four other Midrashic works on the other four books of the Pentateuch.

God said to Moses, "I don't issue commandments consistent with My capabilities, but consistent with the Jews' capabilities."

The Ultimate Guide to Life

Text 8

The Rebbe, *Sefer Hasichot* 5748, 2:590 fn. 10

התורה מגלה אמיתית המציאות ותכלית של כל דבר . . .

היינו שהשימוש בהדבר צריך להיות מתאים **לאמיתת** מציאותו וטבעו של הדבר שבעולם, כשמשתמשים בו על פי הוראת התורה, ובאם לא כן חס ושלום הרי זה לא רק היפך התורה והיפך רצון ה', אלא גם היפך **המציאות והטבע** של הדבר ההוא.

The Torah reveals the true nature and function of everything. . . .

Practically, this means that when we use an object as per the Torah's directives, our usage is consistent with the true nature of that object. If, God forbid, we do not do so, we are not only contravening the Torah's instructions and God's will; we are also in conflict with the object itself by using it in a manner that is contrary to its own nature and existence.

Sefer Hasichot

A series of 12 volumes of the Rebbe's talks delivered between 1986 and 1992. During these years, the Rebbe would regularly review and edit (parts of) the transcripts of his talks for immediate publication. The language used alternated between Hebrew and Yiddish. These edited talks would appear in two weekly newspapers: the (Yiddish) *Algemeiner Journal* and the (Hebrew) *Kfar Chabad*.

Reframing Reward

Text 9

The Rebbe, *Igrot Kodesh* 3:376

התורה היא המקור והצינור לכל הבריאה וההשפעות שבעולם, וכמאמר, "אסתכל באורייתא וברא עלמא", וכך הוא בכל יום וכמו שכתוב, "המחדש בטובו בכל יום תמיד מעשה בראשית", ולכן אם כל עניני התורה ומצוות הם כדבעי אז גם כל הענינים הגשמיים בבריאה כדבעי.

ויעויין הקדמת השל"ה בית אחרון דמסיק דשכר המצוות הוא טבעי.

The Torah is the source of all of Creation and the conduit through which God's effluence flows to the world. As it is said, "God looked into the Torah and created the world"; and this reoccurs every day, as it is said, "In His goodness, God renews each day, continuously, the work of Creation." Therefore, when matters of Torah and *mitzvot* are as they should be, matters of this physical world are also as they should be.

Indeed, in the introduction to *Shenei Luchot Haberit*, Rabbi Yeshayahu Horowitz concludes that the reward we receive for mitzvah observance is a natural consequence of our actions.

FIGURE 3.2

A Comparison of the Two Paradigms

Dualistic Model	Blueprint Model
The Torah and nature, including human nature, pull us in opposite directions.	The Torah and nature, including human nature, pull us in the same direction.
At times, the Torah might not be practical.	The Torah is always practical.
We need to make painful sacrifices and relinquish a normal and healthy life in order to enjoy a thriving spiritual life.	We do not need to relinquish a normal and healthy life in order to enjoy a thriving spiritual life.
If we disregard the Torah's instructions, we only undermine our spiritual aspirations.	If we disregard the Torah's instructions, we undermine not only our spiritual aspirations, but also our general well-being.

Text 10

Rabbi Yoel Kahn, *Kfar Chabad* [Kislev 5752], 500:7–8

Rabbi Yoel Kahan
1930-

Lead expert on Chabad philosophy. Rabbi Kahan served as the senior member and leader of the team that would memorize and transcribe the Rebbe's talks and discourses that were delivered on Shabbat and holidays when audio recordings and taking notes is proscribed. The leading authority on Chabad philosophy and the Rebbe's teachings, he is in the midst of publishing a comprehensive encyclopedia on Chabad Chasidism of which 10 volumes have already appeared. He also serves as the senior educator of Chasidic teachings at the central Lubavitcher yeshivah.

אחד הדברים שהחדיר כ"ק אדמו"ר לרבבות יהודים, זו הגישה הזאת. לא רק שהתורה היא אמת מוחלטת בלי שום ערעור, אלא שהתורה היא אמיתת מציאותו של העולם. כשרוצים לברר את "פשיטות" המציאות של דבר כלשהו בעולם, מביטים בתורה, כי לא ייתכן אחרת, שהרי העולם נברא על פי התורה . . .

כ"ק אדמו"ר החדיר שבראש ובראשונה צריך לבדוק התפילין, המזוזות, כשרות המאכלים, ההקפדה על לימוד התורה וכו'. בראש ובראשונה צריך יהודי לפשפש במעשיו ולנסות למצוא מהו הפגם הרוחני שהיה יכול להביא את התופעות הבלתי רצוית. גישה זו נובעת מכך, שאצל כ"ק אדמו"ר נתפס ב"פשיטות", שהתורה והמצוות הן המקור של כל עניין בעולם.

Among the ideas that the Rebbe imbued in tens of thousands of Jews is a particular approach to Torah. In this view, not only is the Torah true, it is also the truth of the world. Thus, when we want to determine the nature of any created entity, we look to the Torah. There exists no other option, inasmuch as the world was created through Torah. . . .

The Rebbe imbued within us the instinct to [respond to any sort of negative situation by] having our *tefilin* and *mezuzot* inspected, recommitting to be particular about eating kosher food, being meticulous to study Torah on a regular basis, and so forth. In such situations, we need to examine our behavior and strive to identify the spiritual flaw that might lie at the root of the unwanted occurrence. This approach is based on the premise that Torah and *mitzvot* are the source for everything in this world.

Not Outsiders

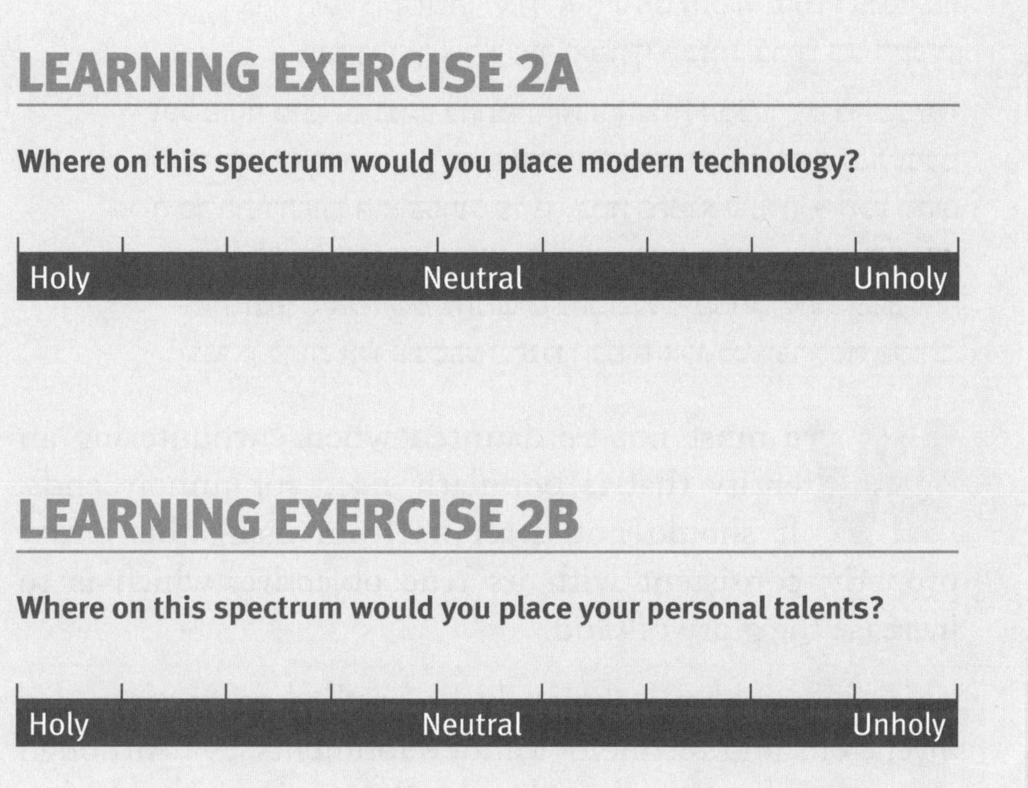

Text 11

The Rebbe, *Sefer Hasichot* 5748, 2:593

אפילו ווען מ'טרעפט אן א זאך וואס אנדערע ("אינשי") נוצן עס אויף היפך הקדושה, דארף א איד ניט נתפעל ווערן דערפון און נוצן די זאך צוליב איר (אמת'ן) **תכלית**, כבודו של הקב"ה.

ועל פי זה מובן גם בנוגע להתפתחות והתגלות המכשירים כו' שנתגלו בדורות האחרונים . . . שאף שיש אפשרות להשתמש בהם לענינים היפך התורה (וכן הוא בפועל על ידי כמה רחמנא ליצלן) – מכל מקום צריך להשתמש בהם לעניני קדושה, הפצת התורה והיהדות וכיוצא בזה, ובפרט אלה שמשתמשים בהם בעניני מסחר, שהרי בשביל זה נבראו כחות אלו שבטבע ונתגלו חכמות אלו, כמדובר כמה פעמים.

We must not be daunted when encountering an entity that is popularly used for unholy ends. It should not deter us from using this entity properly, consistent with its true objective, which is to increase the glory of God.

This approach can obviously be applied to modern-day inventions and technological developments. . . . Although it is possible to exploit these technologies in ways that are inconsistent with Torah values—and unfortunately, many people actually do so—we ought to use them for holy ends, such as disseminating Torah and Judaism. (This is particularly pertinent for those who already make use of these technologies for commercial matters.) In fact, God embedded within nature the capabilities for such technologies and orchestrated their discovery specifically for these holy purposes, as we have frequently discussed.

Text 12 (Optional)

Michel Schwartz, "The Rebbe and the Artist," www.chabad.org

The Rebbe wanted to introduce a new feature in *Talks and Tales*, an illustrated page with five or six items, little known facts about Jewish customs, lore and legend, which would add a new dimension to the publication. The Rebbe wanted this feature to be something that the children would look forward to reading from issue to issue. It was to be titled, "Curiosity Corner." . . .

When describing the feature, the Rebbe said, "It should look like Ripley (*Es zol oyszehn vee Ripley*)." I was taken by surprise.

For many years, in many newspapers throughout the country, a square measuring approximately 5" × 5" contained the work of Robert Ripley, titled "Believe It Or Not." Here was this venerable rabbi aware of a column, which appeared daily in the *New York Mirror*, now a defunct Hearst publication, asking me to make our feature in Ripley's style.

On another occasion, the Rebbe asked me to create a true to life character about whom adventure stories could be written. This time he suggested that the format and look should be "like Dick Tracy."

Michel Schwartz
1926–2011

Artist and calligrapher. At the age of 13, Schwartz enrolled in the New York School of Art and Design alongside his studies at the Lubavitch school in Brooklyn. After graduating from art school, Schwartz became a well-known graphic designer. His artistic works adorned the walls and tables of Israeli presidents and prime ministers. In a 1970 feature, *Fortune* magazine called him, "a visionary of unobstructed and unparalleled foresight."

Text 13

The Rebbe, *Likutei Sichot* 16:456

בשעת דער אויבערשטער האט געגעבן א אידן א חוש וכשרון מיוחד, דארף ער וויסן אז דאס איז ניט צוליב אים אליין, נאר ער דארף עס אויסנוצן אין זיין עבודה צו מאכן פון וועלט א משכן, א דירה לו יתברך –

פונקט ווי עס איז געווען ביי די נשים אין זמן פון בנין המשכן, אז האבנדיק א כשרון מיוחד, וואס אנדערע האבן עס ניט געהאט, האבן זיי פארשטאנען, אז אט דער כשרון וואס דער אויבערשטער האט זיי געגעבן דארף פון זיי אויסגענוצט ווערן אויף בויען א משכן וואס דארט וועט זיין השראת השכינה . . .

על דרך זה איז עס אין אנדערע ענינים וואס דער אויבערשטער גיט א אידן – ווי לדוגמא, בשעת דער אויבערשטער גיט אים א פארדינסט וואס איז מער ווי געוועגלעך, זאל ער וויסן, אז ער דארף מוסיף זיין אין נתינת הצדקה.

When God gifts us a special talent, we need to understand that it is not for our personal benefit; rather, we need to utilize the talent for our divine service of making this world into a home for God.

When our ancestors constructed the Tabernacle, the Torah tells us that a group of talented women weaved various materials for its sake. Seeing that they were blessed with a specific uncommon talent, they understood that this God-given gift should be dedicated to building a Tabernacle that would be graced by God's presence. . . .

The same principle applies to all that God gives us. For example, when God blesses us with profits that exceed the norm, we ought to understand that it is in order for us to increase our charitable giving.

Text 14

The Rebbe, *Igrot Kodesh* 4:223

די הויפּט קונסט פון א מאלער אין חכמת הציור איז, אז ער זאל זיך קאנען אפּטראגן פון דער חיצוניותדיקייט פון דער זאך, און ניט קוקנדיק אויף דער אויסערליכער פארם, זאל ער קאנען אריינבליקן אין דער זאך "אינעווייניק" און דערזען דארט די פּנימיות ועצמות הדבר, און קענען דאס דערנאך איבערגעבן בציור, אזוי אז דער וואס זעט דעם ציור פון דעם מאלער זאל פאר עם אנטפּלעקט ווערן אין דער זאך דאס וואס ער האט פריער ניט באמערקט, ווייל דער תוך איז געווען פארשטעלט פון ענינים טפלים. אזוי ארום אנטפּלעקט דער מאלער דעם עצמות און מהות פון דער זאך וואס ער צייכנט, און דער וואס זעט עס, דערזעט עס אין אן אנדער אמת'ער ליכט און כאפּט זיך, אז ער איז פריער געווען אין א טעות.

ככל הדברים האלה וככל החזיון הזה, איז איינער פון די עקרים בעבודת האדם לקונו. ווי מיר ווייסן פון דער תורה בכלל און פון חסידות בפרט, איז כל הבריאה כולה נעמט זיך פון דבר ה', און דער דבר ה' איז דאס מהווה ומקיים בכל עת ובכל רגע. נאר מצד דעם ג-טליכן כח הצמצום והגבורה, שטייט דער דבר ה' בהעלם והסתר און עס זעט זיך בלויז די חיצוניות.

איז דער ענין פון עבודה, וואס שטיצט זיך אויף דער אמונה פשוטה אז אין עוד מלבדו, אז מען זאל מיט דעם שטאנדפּונקט צוגיין צו יעדן ענין אין לעבן, און מען זאל זען ארויסברייינגען כל אחד כפי יכולתו, וואס מער דעם אלקות שבכל דבר, און קלענער מאכן, אויף וויפל עס לאזט זיך, דעם העלם והסתר פון דער חצוניות אויף אלקות שבתוכו.

The essential skill of the artist is the ability to look past superficial appearances and penetrate the essence of the object he or she is striving to artistically convey, and to then translate and depict that impression. The resulting art reveals to the viewers what they could not recognize on their own when observing the original object: the essence that was obscured by superficial layers. The artist enables observers to see things from a different perspective and thus realize the limitations of their previous awareness.

This point is precisely analogous to one of the key areas of our divine service. The Torah, and specifically Jewish mysticism, teaches us that all of Creation emanates from, and is constantly sustained by, the word of God, which constitutes the essence of every being. However, because of the process of divine concealment, God's word is hidden, and only the external layer of Creation—the material substance—is visible.

Our task is to approach all areas of life fortified by an unshakeable belief in God's omnipresence. Then, using our unique abilities, we ought to bring to the fore the Godly essence of everything and minimize the concealment posed by physical externalities.

Text 15

Pirkei Avot 6:11

כל מה שברא הקדוש ברוך הוא בעולמו, לא בראו אלא לכבודו.

Everything that God created in His world, He created only for [the role it plays in increasing] His glory.

Pirkei Avot
(Ethics of the Fathers)

A 6-chapter work on Jewish ethics that is studied widely by Jewish communities, especially during the summer. The first 5 chapters are from the Mishnah, tractate Avot. Avot differs from the rest of the Mishnah in that it does not focus on legal subjects; instead, it is a collection of the sages' wisdom on topics related to character development, ethics, healthy living, piety, and the study of Torah.

LEARNING EXERCISE 3

An area of my life—i.e., a talent or opportunity—that I have yet to utilize in my service of God:	
How I might be able to use this talent or opportunity for its true purpose:	

Constructing Our Micro-Universe

Text 16

The Rebbe, *Sichot Kodesh* 5733, 1:74

ערשט איז געווען דער "אסתכל באורייתא" און נאך דעם איז געווען דער "וברא עלמא". על דרך זה מאנט מען פון יעדער איד אז ערשט דארף זיין "מבית הכנסת לבית המדרש", "ומבית המדרש" ארויס "לדרך ארץ". דאס הייסט, אז איידער ער גייט ארויס אין וועלט דארף ערשט זיין א הכנה אין תורה, און פון תורה גייט ער ארויס אין וועלט.

God first looked into the Torah and then created the world. The same is asked of every one of us. Every morning, we pray and then study some Torah, and only then do we proceed to our jobs. Before entering the mundane world, we need to prepare ourselves with Torah.

Sichot Kodesh

Transcripts (mostly in Yiddish) of most of the Rebbe's public addresses (*farbrengens*) between 1950 and 1981, published in 50 volumes. For the talks that the Rebbe delivered on Shabbat and holidays, when audio recordings and taking notes are proscribed, a team of trained memorizers (*chozrim*) would reconstruct and transcribe the Rebbe's talk from memory. The Rebbe did not edit or review these transcripts for accuracy.

Text 17

The Rebbe, *Sichot Kodesh* 5733, 1:128

נוסף לזה וואס עס דארף זיין "אסתכל באורייתא" (בכללות) בנוגע לעניני העולם, אז בשעת מ'וויל ארוסקריגען דעם תוכן פנימי פון יעדער זאך אין וועלט — דארף מען קוקן אין תורה, הנה נוסף לזה דארף זיין א התבוננות מיוחדת בפרשת השבוע אויף ארויסנעמען הוראות בנוגע לעניני השבוע, וואס דאס איז דער "אסתכל באורייתא וברא עלמא" בשייכות צו די הנהגה פון א אידן אין דער וואך בפרט.

In general, it is important to "look into the Torah" in order to know how to navigate life and to understand the inner meaning of everything in this world. In addition, every week has its distinctive "looking into the Torah": we need to contemplate specifically the weekly Torah portion to derive lessons uniquely relevant for each particular week.

Key Points

1. The Torah is the blueprint for all of Creation. Accordingly, the Torah and the world are inherently interrelated, and every worldly entity and phenomenon reflects preexisting Torah realities.

2. At times, it appears that circumstances make it difficult to follow the Torah's instructions. However, the fact that "God looked into the Torah and created the world" leads us to the logical conclusion that nothing can hamper our performance of a mitzvah.

3. When we use an object as per the Torah's directives, our usage is consistent with the true nature of that object. If, however, we do not do so, we are not only contravening God's will; we are also doing a disservice to the object, by using it in a manner that is contrary to its own nature and purpose of existence.

4. Because the Torah is the source of all of Creation and the conduit through which God's effluence flows, when matters of Torah and *mitzvot* are as they should be, matters of this physical world are also as they should be.

5. Because the Torah is the source of all of Creation, everything that exists has a divine purpose that is its raison d'être. This includes modern technologies and personal talents.

6. Before we "create" our personal world, we ought to emulate God and "look into the (blueprint, the) Torah." It is therefore important to designate time for Torah study every morning before work.

SELECTED CORRESPONDENCE

OF THE REBBE

Chasidism Is Not Asceticism

5724 [1964]

Mr.
Toronto, Ontario, Canada

Greetings and Blessing:

This is to acknowledge receipt of your letter.

It is surprising to me to note in your letter that it is your impression of Chassidim that they do not participate in the life of the outside world, etc. As a matter of fact, the reverse is true, for there is hardly any human activity that Chassidim exclude from their sphere of interest. This attitude is the direct result of the emphasis in Chassidut on the authentic concept of monotheism. The Chassidic concept of the oneness of G-d goes much further that the generally accepted view that there is one Deity and no other, since it places the stress on the fact that *there is only One G-d and nothing else.*[1] For inasmuch as G-d's word (wherewith He brought the world into existence) constantly and without interruption creates and vitalizes the whole universe and every particular of it, and because without this creative force, which is the true essence of every existing thing, nothing could exist, it follows that there is no reality other than G-d, and there is actually nothing but G-dliness. Chassidut emphasizes that it is one of the central aspects of man's purpose in life to establish this truth and to spread it to the utmost extent of his influence. This is not merely an idea, but a way of life that finds expression in the everyday reality and which completely permeates the inner being of the Chassid.

A corollary of this viewpoint is another fundamental principle found in the teachings of Chasidut, namely, that Divine Providence extends to each and every particular in the Creation, not only to each individual of the human race, but to each particular in the realm of the animal, the vegetable and even the mineral worlds, as is well known to everyone who studies Chasidut.[2]

Thus it is fundamental for the Chassidic philosophy and way of life not to exclude any part of the world from its sphere of interest.

As for your point that you have not come across the names of any Chassidim who participate in certain movements, such as civil rights, etc., this is also surprising, inasmuch as many have taken an active part in this and other constructive movements. However, many more among those who participate in such constructive movements do so while avoiding publicity and unwanted exposure in the press.

With blessing,

Torah: Source of Contentment

By the Grace of G-d
12th of Kislev 5725 [November 17, 1964]
Brooklyn, NY

Mrs.
Springfield, N.J.

Blessing and Greeting:

I received your letter, in which you write about your state of health and frame of mind, etc.

As I see from your letter, it is unnecessary for me to emphasize to you that there are many things in your

[1] *Tanya, Shaar Hayichud v'Haemuna,* ch. 1.

[2] *Hayom Yom*, 28 Cheshvan (p. 108), 29 Sivan (p. 66).

life for which you can be truly grateful to G-d. Of course, this does not mean that your present state of anxiety, which you describe, is not altogether unjustified. Nevertheless, one must see things in their totality and not only the negative aspects.

For a person of your background and faith, it should not be difficult to contemplate on G-d's benevolent Providence, which extends to each and everyone individually, and that G-d is the Essence of Goodness, and it is in the nature of the good to do good. Reflecting on these thoughts one must come to the same conclusion as did King David, author of Psalms, who declared, "G-d is with me, I shall not fear." On the contrary, there is every reason to be in a state of joy and gladness of heart, especially as such a happy frame of mind would reflect beneficially upon every one of the family. The important thing is, as already mentioned earlier, that you have indeed many things for which to be grateful and happy.

It very often happens that a person in a frame of mind similar to yours looks for an explanation and for the cause in the wrong direction, for it seems to him that that is where the cause of his problem lies, although in reality the cause may be quite different. This is particularly true in the case of a Jew, or a Jewess, whose true happiness lies in leading a full Jewish life, in the daily life. That is, a life which is in complete harmony with the way of the Torah and *mitzvot*, which were given to us at Mt. Sinai, and which made us into a holy nation. The details of the Jewish way of life have been clearly spelled out in the *Shulchan Aruch*, the code of Jewish law and daily conduct. If, for one reason or another, the daily life does not fully harmonize with the Jewish way of life as commanded by G-d, it is impossible for the Jew to be completely happy and contented, inasmuch as something very essential is lacking in his daily life. He may not be aware of this, and consequently is looking for the cause of his disquietude in another direction.

On the other hand, when a Jew is determined to live in full accord with the Jewish way of life, this is within the reach of each and every Jew, although it may be easier for one than for another. But everyone can attain this, inasmuch as G-d, the Creator of man and Master of the world, Who commanded this, also provided the capacity for the fulfillment of His commands.

Needless to say I am aware of the question, how is it that many people who apparently have deviated from the way of the Torah and *mitzvot,* yet they appear to be quite happy, etc. The answer is simple. No one truly knows what is going on in the heart and mind of another person, and besides, it may be possible for an individual to conceal his inner anxiety and unhappiness, although sooner or later it is bound to come forth.

It would be well that your husband should have his *tefillin* checked, and before putting them on every weekday morning, he should put aside a small coin for *tzedoko* [charity]. It would also be advisable to have the *mezuzot* of your home checked to make sure they are *kosher*, and before lighting the candles, you should also put aside a small coin for *tzedoko.*

Hoping to hear good news from you,

With blessing,

To Be Fruitful and Multiply

By the Grace of G-d
16th of Adar, 5736 [February 17, 1976]
Brooklyn, NY

Mr.
Omaha, Neb.

Greeting and Blessing:

Your letter reached me with considerable delay. May G-d grant the fulfillment of your heart's desires for good. The way to ensure it, as you surely realize, is living up to G-d's Will through adherence to his Torah and *mitzvot* in the daily life, though these have to be observed, of course, for their own sake. And inasmuch as the Torah and *mitzvot* are infinite, being derived from, and rooted in, the Infinite, there is always room for advancement in this area.

With regard to the subject of overpopulation which you mention in your letter, and you wonder what the Torah attitude is in this respect—you surely know that the first Divine commandment in the Torah is "Be fruitful and multiply." And since the Torah is Torat Emet and Torat Chayim, and is eternal, it is certain that all its directives are factual and practical and eternally valid, and in the best interests of all who follow them

Herein is the answer to all arguments about overpopulation. As a matter of fact, this question is not likely to present a real problem for a very long time, if at all. If there are pockets of malnutrition in the world, it is not because the world lacks in resources to feed its population, but rather a problem of distribution, and the failure to utilize fully known resources. Hence, if the world's natural resources will be adequately utilized and distributed, and the world's human inhabitants will behave with justice and compassion, in accordance with G-d's Will, thus deserving of G-d's blessings and bounty, there will be no need to worry about overpopulation.

Furthermore, in view of your interest in the general field of world health, etc., as you mention in your letter, it is surprising that you are apparently not well informed about the latest scientific research and findings which have to do with the immense natural resources on land and in the sea, not to mention the almost unlimited possibilities of the fledgling atomic and other, as yet untapped, sources of energy. Thus even from the purely secular, scientific view there is no cause for alarm for centuries to come.

So much for the subject matter of your letter.

Now, inasmuch as everything is by Divine Providence, and you have written to me on a matter which, viewed without misconception or prejudice, is of no immediate concern to you and me, it occurs to me that perhaps the real reason behind your writing to me is to give me an opportunity to call your attention to something more practical and immediate, namely the need to strengthen daily life and conduct in accordance with the Torah and *mitzvot*—in which there is always room for improvement in one's personal life and in one's surroundings.

I trust you know that it is the total commitment to Torah and *mitzvot* as a way of life that has been the lifeline of the Jewish people, ever since, its destiny as an independent and unique nation has been tied up with our receiving the Torah at Sinai and out Covenant with G-d. This adherence to the Torah and *mitzvot* has sustained and preserved our people in the face of overwhelming odds for thousands of years and has give us the strength to survive all our enemies. There were, of course, dissident and rebellious groups from the earliest times, beginning with worshippers of the Golden Calf, and right through ancient, medieval, and modern times, to this very day. But our history has clearly shown that the outcome of deviation from the Torah way has always been the same: either the deviationists realized their mistake and returned to the fold, or they were completely and forever lost to the Jewish people.

Therefore, no matter what field or pursuit a Jew chooses—certainly a field which is concerned with the survival of mankind—his primary concern must be with the survival and wellbeing of our Jewish people. Every Jew can and must be active in this direction, by personal example and precept, to strengthen and disseminate the Torah and *mitzvot* in the daily life, to the fullest extent of his ability and opportunities.

With blessing,

LESSON 4

Synching with the Divine

"The world was wrong. When they thought that the most important fact about the Rebbe was that here was a man with thousands of followers, they missed the most important fact: That a good leader creates followers, but a great leader creates leaders."

—Lord Rabbi Jonathan Sacks

Chasidic Mystery

Afterlife

Text 1

Michael A. Hiltzik and Mathis Chazanov,
"Life After the Rebbe a Puzzle," *Los Angeles Times*, June 14, 1994

"Can Chabad Outlive the Rebbe?" asked the headline in a recent edition of a leading Jewish journal, as the 92-year-old leader of one of Judaism's most aggressive and charismatic sects lay comatose in a New York hospital.

After the death Sunday of Menachem Mendel Schneerson, the seventh leader, or rebbe, of the Chabad Lubavitch movement, that question is at hand. At stake is the future of an organization that Schneerson personally transformed in his 44 years of leadership from a provincial sect into what Allen Nadler, an expert on the group's activities, describes as the "most famous and powerful movement in contemporary Orthodox Judaism." . . .

In an interview Monday, [Director of Chabad activities on the West Coast, Rabbi Shlomo] Cunin himself gave no indication that his faith has been rocked by Schneerson's death. . . .

But other observers say that even if it survives in some form, Chabad cannot help but be seriously shaken by the passing of its charismatic leader.

QUESTION FOR DISCUSSION

What assumption was this prediction based upon?

Text 2

Carolyn Drake, "A Faith Grows in Brooklyn," *National Geographic*, February 2006

Now headquartered in Crown Heights, Brooklyn, the group was relatively small and little known when Schneerson became rebbe in 1951. During his 43-year tenure he pioneered a system of *shluchim*, or emissaries, charged with going out into the world to open Chabad centers, spreading knowledge of the Torah and Judaism. Some feared that the Lubavitch movement would dwindle after the rebbe's death in 1994. But today there are more than 3,000 centers in 70 countries—nearly half of them founded after Schneerson's death.

International Conference of *Shluchot* – 2012

QUESTIONS FOR DISCUSSION

1. Why was the observers' prediction about Chabad's survival incorrect?
2. In your estimation, what is the secret of Chabad's success and endurance?

Lubavitch World Headquarters - 770

Of Leaders & Followers

Text 3a

Rabbi Herbert Weiner, *9½ Mystics* [New York: Collier Books, 1992], pp. 190–191

I remembered that this was my last chance and resolved to ask even the most embarrassing questions in an effort to solve the enigma of Lubavitch. I explained to the Rebbe that more than a year had passed since I began trying to understand the movement, and that I had come to him now with a confession: I did not understand. Would he mind if I started this interview by asking him about the character of a Hasid?

Rabbi Menachem Mendel smiled and told me to go ahead; as before I could speak English but he would answer in Yiddish.

"Isn't the fact that Hasidim turn to the Rebbe for almost every decision in their lives—isn't this a sign of weakness, a repudiation of the very thing that makes a man human, his *b'chirah*, freedom of will?"

Rabbi Herbert Weiner
1919–2013

Born in Boston, Weiner graduated from the University of Massachusetts at Amherst in 1942. During World War II, he served as a radio officer in the Merchant Marine. In 1948, Weiner became the founding rabbi of Temple Israel of South Orange, N.J., a Reform congregation, and served there until his retirement in 1982. Weiner was the author of two books: 9½ *Mystics*, and *The Wild Goats of Ein Gedi*, both of which were recipients of the National Jewish Book Award.

QUESTION FOR DISCUSSION

Based on your knowledge, how would you answer this question?

Text 3b

Rabbi Herbert Weiner, ibid.

The Rebbe's answer came without hesitation, as if he had dealt with the question before. "A weak person is usually overcome by the environment in which he finds himself. But our Hasidim can be sent into any environment, no matter how strange or hostile, and they maintain themselves within it. So how can we say that it is weakness which characterizes a Hasid?"

QUESTION FOR DISCUSSION

Did the Rebbe's answer address Rabbi Weiner's question? If yes, how so? If no, why not?

QUESTIONS FOR DISCUSSION

1. **Is Rabbi Sacks's assertion, in your estimation, accurate—considering how devoted the Rebbe's followers are to him?**
2. **What do you think is the appropriate balance between being a follower of a rebbe (or any leader) and being independent-minded?**

"Do as You Understand!"

Dual Coronation

LEARNING EXERCISE 1

Based on your knowledge and experience, which person described below would you consider the ideal religious person?

1. One who follows God's instructions without question or need to understand why
2. One who has questions, but obeys nonetheless
3. One whose obedience of God's will is accompanied by an understanding of and appreciation for the reasons for the *mitzvot*.

Text 4a

Exodus 24:3–7

וַיָּבֹא מֹשֶׁה וַיְסַפֵּר לָעָם אֵת כָּל דִּבְרֵי ה' . . . וַיֹּאמְרוּ,
"כֹּל אֲשֶׁר דִּבֶּר ה' נַעֲשֶׂה וְנִשְׁמָע".

Moses came [from atop Mount Sinai] and told the nation all of God's words. . . . The people responded, "All [the commands] that God spoke we will do and we will understand."

Text 4b

Babylonian Talmud

A literary work of monumental proportions that draws upon the legal, spiritual, intellectual, ethical, and historical traditions of Judaism. The 37 tractates of the Babylonian Talmud contain the teachings of the Jewish sages from the period after the destruction of the 2nd Temple through the 5th century CE. It has served as the primary vehicle for the transmission of the Oral Law and the education of Jews over the centuries; it is the entry point for all subsequent legal, ethical, and theological Jewish scholarship.

Talmud, Shabbat 88a

בשעה שהקדימו ישראל נעשה לנשמע, באו ששים ריבוא של מלאכי השרת לכל אחד ואחד מישראל קשרו לו שני כתרים: אחד כנגד נעשה ואחד כנגד נשמע.

When the Jews preceded "we will do" to "we will understand," sixty myriads of ministering angels came and placed two crowns upon each and every Jew: one corresponded to "we will do" and the other corresponded to "we will understand."

QUESTION FOR DISCUSSION

Does this Talmudic statement provide an answer to the question in Learning Exercise 1?

A Groundbreaking Mission

Text 5a

Deuteronomy 1:22

וַתִּקְרְבוּן אֵלַי כֻּלְּכֶם וַתֹּאמְרוּ, "נִשְׁלְחָה אֲנָשִׁים לְפָנֵינוּ
וְיַחְפְּרוּ לָנוּ אֶת הָאָרֶץ, וְיָשִׁבוּ אֹתָנוּ דָּבָר".

You all approached me and said, "Let us send men ahead of us to explore the land on our behalf and bring us back a report."

Text 5b

Numbers 13:1–2

וַיְדַבֵּר ה' אֶל מֹשֶׁה לֵּאמֹר: "שְׁלַח לְךָ אֲנָשִׁים וְיָתֻרוּ אֶת
אֶרֶץ כְּנַעַן אֲשֶׁר אֲנִי נֹתֵן לִבְנֵי יִשְׂרָאֵל".

God spoke to Moses saying: "Send for yourself men to scout the Land of Canaan, which I am giving to the children of Israel."

Text 5c

Rashi, ad loc.

Rabbi Shlomo Yitschaki
(Rashi)
1040–1105

Most noted biblical and Talmudic commentator. Born in Troyes, France, Rashi studied in the famed *yeshivot* of Mainz and Worms. His commentaries on the Pentateuch and the Talmud, which focus on the simple understanding of the text, have appeared in virtually every edition of the Talmud and Bible.

שלח לך—לדעתך. אני איני מצוה לך, אם תרצה שלח.

"Send for yourself"—that is, do as per your understanding. I am not commanding you; if you wish, you may send.

Text 6

Mishnah, Avot 2:4

Pirkei Avot
(Ethics of the Fathers)

A 6-chapter work on Jewish ethics that is studied widely by Jewish communities, especially during the summer. The first 5 chapters are from the Mishnah, tractate Avot. Avot differs from the rest of the Mishnah in that it does not focus on legal subjects; instead, it is a collection of the sages' wisdom on topics related to character development, ethics, healthy living, piety, and the study of Torah.

עשה רצונו כרצונך . . .

בטל רצונך מפני רצונו.

Make His will into your will. . . .

Nullify your will before His will.

QUESTION FOR DISCUSSION

What is the difference between "Make His will into your will" and "Nullify your will before His will"?

Text 7

The Rebbe, *Sefer Hasichot* 5749, 2:538

כשהקדוש ברוך הוא אמר למשה "שלח לך, לדעתך, אני איני מצוה לך, אם תרצה שלח" – הרי לא זו בלבד שמשה **לא חשש** שיש כאן ענין בלתי-רצוי, אלא **אדרבה** – הי' **שמח** על החידוש שבדיבור זה ("וידבר גו' שלח לך"), שעבודת המטה תוכל להיות באופן של בחירה חפשית לגמרי – ללא ה"הכרח" דציווי הקדוש ברוך הוא, כי אם **מדעתו ומרצונו של האדם** ("לדעתך .. אם תרצה"), שיהיו מתאימים **מעצמם** לרצונו של הקדוש ברוך הוא.

Moses was not at all anxious when God told him, "'Send for yourself,' as per your understanding. I am not commanding you; if you wish, you may send." To the contrary, *he rejoiced,* for he perceived that this directive introduced a new phase. This new and loftier level of divine service is wholly a product of our free will and even lacks the subtle "coercion" implicit in a directive from God. Rather, the service is completely consistent with our own understanding and wishes ("as per your understanding . . . if you wish"), which are completely in synch with the will of God.

Sefer Hasichot

A series of 12 volumes of the Rebbe's talks delivered between 1986 and 1992. During these years, the Rebbe would regularly review and edit (parts of) the transcripts of his talks for immediate publication. The language used alternated between Hebrew and Yiddish. These edited talks would appear in two weekly newspapers: the (Yiddish) *Algemeiner Journal* and the (Hebrew) *Kfar Chabad*.

Text 8

The Rebbe, *Hayom Yom*, Menachem Av 29

Hayom Yom

In 1942, Rabbi Yosef Y. Schneersohn, the sixth rebbe of Chabad, gave his son-in-law, the future Rebbe, the task of compiling an anthology of Chasidic aphorisms and customs arranged according to the days of the year. In describing the completed product, Rabbi Yosef Yitschak wrote that it is "a book that is small in format but bursting with pearls and diamonds of the choicest quality."

עס דארף זיין עבודה בכח עצמו. העכער איז אז מ'נעהמט פאר'ן האנט און מ'פירט. טייערער איז אז עס איז בכח עצמו.

Our service must be a product of our own efforts. Although superior heights are attained when we are taken by the hand and led, it is far more precious when we go by our own strength.

QUESTION FOR DISCUSSION

What are the benefits of the *avodah beko'ach atsmo* model?

Self-Subsistent Flames

Text 9

Mishnah, Avot 4:12

יהי כבוד תלמידך חביב עליך כשלך,

וכבוד חברך כמורא רבך,

ומורא רבך כמורא שמים.

The honor of your student should be as precious to you as your own.

Your honor of your colleague should be as great as your reverence for your teacher.

Your reverence for your teacher should be on par with your reverence for God.

Text 10a

Numbers 8:1–2

וַיְדַבֵּר ה' אֶל מֹשֶׁה לֵּאמֹר: "דַּבֵּר אֶל אַהֲרֹן וְאָמַרְתָּ אֵלָיו: בְּהַעֲלֹתְךָ אֶת הַנֵּרֹת, אֶל מוּל פְּנֵי הַמְּנוֹרָה יָאִירוּ שִׁבְעַת הַנֵּרוֹת".

God spoke to Moses, saying: "Speak to Aaron and say to him: 'When you cause the [flames of the Tabernacle] lamps to ascend, the seven lamps shall cast their light toward the face of the menorah.'"

Text 10b

Rashi, ad loc.

על שם שהלהב עולה, כתוב בהדלקתן לשון עליה, שצריך להדליק עד שתהא שלהבת עולה מאליה.

Because the flame rises, the Torah describes their kindling in terms of ascending: the one lighting the menorah is required to kindle the lamp until the flame rises by itself.

Text 10c

The Rebbe, *Sefer Hasichot* 5751, 2:600–601

כאטש אז דער אויבערשטער גיט כחות א אידן צו טאן זיין עבודה ("הקדוש ברוך הוא עוזרו") אין "נר מצוה ותורה ואור" . . . און אזוי אויך באקומט א איד כחות פון אהרן הכהן (רועה ישראל) וועלכער צינדט אן דעם "נר ה'" למטה, און אויך כחות פון זיינע עלטערן און מחנכים, און פון אנדערע מענטשן ארום . . .

פונדעסטוועגן, באשטייט שלימות ואמיתית העבודה אין דעם, אז (לאחרי וואס ער ווערט "אנגעצונדן" דורך אנדערע) ווערט ער א "שלהבת עולה **מאלי'**", ד.ה. אז די "נר מצוה ותורה אור" נעמט אים אויף אזויפיל דורך, אז דאס לייכט פון אים – פון זיין מציאות (אלס נשמה **בגוף**) – אליין ("מאלי'"), אזוי אז ער דארף ניט אנקומען צו פעולת המשפיע (דעם "מדליק הנר"), זייענדיק א "שלהבת עולה **מאלי'**".

God grants us the powers to perform our service of igniting and illuminating [ourselves and the world] with the light of Torah and *mitzvot*. . . . In addition, we receive powers from Aaron the High Priest (the Shepherd of Israel), who ignites the "candle of God" here in this world. We also receive guidance and inspiration from our parents, educators, and the people with whom we interact. . . .

Nevertheless, [we cannot suffice with the powers and guidance we receive from God and others, because] the ultimate and truest service necessitates us to be "flames that rise on our own" (after we are "ignited" by others). The light of Torah and *mitzvot* must permeate us to the extent that we ourselves become independent sources of illumination and no longer require the efforts of a mentor (the one who ignited the flame)—because we have become self-subsistent flames.

QUESTION FOR DISCUSSION

How does a leader cultivate in his or her followers the ethic of self-initiated and self-motivated work?

Text 11

The Rebbe, *Likutei Sichot* 2:500–501

איצטער הערט זיך איין אידן! בכלל ביי חב"ד האט מען געמאנט אז מען דארן אליין טאן, ניט פארלאזן זיך אויף די רביים . . . איז דארפן מיר אלע אליין טאן, מיט די רמ"ח אברים ושס"ה גידים פון גוף, און די רמ"ח אברים ושס"ה גידים פון נשמה, עס שטייט דאך "הכל בידי שמים חוץ מיראת שמים". איך זאג זיך ניט אפ חס ושלום פון העלפן. העלפן וויפל מען וועט קענען. אבער הכל בידי שמים חוץ מיראת שמים.

במילא אויב מען טוט ניט אליין – איז וואס וועט העלפן וואס מ'גיט כתבים, מ'זינגט ניגונים, מ'זאגט לחיים.

דער רבי פלעגט אמאל זאגן לייגט זיך ניט קיין פויגעלעך אין בוזעם. מען דארף אליין מהפך זיין דעם שטות דלעומת זה און דעם קאך פון נפש הבהמית אויף קדושה.

Likutei Sichot

Widely considered the Rebbe's magnum opus, the 39 volumes of *Likutei Sichot* feature scholarly essays relating to themes in the weekly Torah portions and the Jewish holidays. The Rebbe initially conveyed these concepts in his public talks and subsequently reworked them for publication. In some volumes, the essays appear in Yiddish, while in others they are in Hebrew. Most volumes also present a collection of the Rebbe's correspondence.

Listen up, fellow Jews! The rebbes of Chabad demanded that their Chasidim take personal action, and not rely on the rebbe. . . . After all, even God Himself does not impress piety or proper conduct upon anyone. We must all work, therefore, with the entirety of our bodies and souls. I will not withhold my assistance, God forbid, I will help to the best of my abilities, but I cannot do the work on your behalf.

Of what good will it be for me to publish Chasidic discourses, sing Chasidic songs, and say *lechayim* (at Chasidic gatherings)—if you all don't do your part?

The Rebbe [my father-in-law] would say: "Don't be delusional." Each one of us must personally transform our foolish tendencies and material passion into holiness [because no one else can do it on our behalf].

Text 12

The Rebbe, *Torat Menachem* 5748, 2:215–216

מענה כללי להשלוחים שי׳: כאשר מתעוררים ספקות ושאלות בקשר לאופני פעולת השליחות בהפצת היהדות והמעיינות חוצה . . .

הרי, המענה הכללי שצריכים לסמוך על שיקול דעתם, "אין לו לדיין אלא מה שעיניו רואות", בכל מקום לפי ענינו.

The following is my general response to *shluchim* [emissaries] who have doubts or questions as to which methods are appropriate or advisable in the course of implementing their *shlichut* of disseminating Judaism and the wellsprings of Chasidic teachings:

My answer is that they should act upon their own understanding of the situation. "A judge must rule based on the evidence before him" (Talmud, Sanhedrin 6b), in every location according to its unique needs and circumstances.

Torat Menachem

A Hebrew translation of the transcripts of the Rebbe's talks. This work also comprehensively cross-references and footnotes the material. As of 2014, more than 90 volumes have appeared in this series, covering the years 1950–1968 and 1982–1992. The Rebbe did not edit or review these publications for accuracy.

International Conference of *Shluchim* – 2010

Application Time

Text 13

Rabbi Yeshayahu Halevi Horowitz, *Shenei Luchot Haberit, Asarah Ma'amarot* 1

נוסף על מה שהוקבע אמונה האלקות בלבבך מצד אביך, דהיינו
הקבלה איש מפי איש, דע אתה בעצמך מצד ההשגה.

וזהו רמז הפסוק, "זה א-לי ואנוהו, אלקי אבי וארממנהו" (שמות טו,ב).

רצה לומה, כש"זה א-לי", שהוא א-לי מצד השגתי וידיעתי, אז "ואנוהו", מלשון
"אני והו", רצה לומה, אני והוא דבוקים ביחד כביכול, כי הידיעה נתפסת בלב.

אמנם כשאין לי הידיעה מצד ההשגה, רק מצד הקבלה שהוא "אלקי אבי",
אז "וארממנהו", כי הוא רם ונשגב ממני, ואני מרוחק מאתו במצפון הלב.

Rabbi Yeshayah Halevi Horowitz (*Shelah*)
1565–1630

Kabbalist and author. Rabbi Horowitz was born in Prague and served as rabbi in several prominent Jewish communities, including Frankfurt am Main and his native Prague. After the passing of his wife in 1620, he moved to Israel. In Tiberias, he completed his *Shenei Luchot Haberit*, an encyclopedic compilation of Kabbalistic ideas. He is buried in Tiberias, next to Maimonides.

In addition to the belief in God implanted in our hearts by our parents who transmitted to us the age-old Jewish tradition, we must strive to intellectually understand God.

This is alluded to in the verse: "This is my God, *ve'anvehu* [lit.: and I will glorify Him], the God of my father, and I will exalt Him" (Exodus 15:2).

When "this is *my* God," when my relationship with Him is a product of my own comprehension and knowledge, then *ve'anvehu,* a contraction of the Hebrew words *ani vahu,* "I and He." I and He are then united [in a meaningful relationship], for my understanding of Him permeates the emotions of the heart.

If, however, I do not comprehend the divine and I depend on the faith of my family tradition (the "God of my father"), then "I exalt Him." God remains exalted and beyond me, and I remain emotionally distant from Him.

LEARNING EXERCISE 2

What are some areas of Jewish practice or belief that I could better "own" by transitioning from follower to understander?

1. ______________________________

____

____

2. ______________________________

____

____

3. ______________________________

____

____

Total Transformation

Text 14

Mishnah, Avot 1:17

ולא המדרש עיקר, אלא המעשה.

The essential thing is not study, but the deed.

Text 15 (Optional)

The Rebbe, *Hayom Yom*, Kislev 17

חסידות חב"ד פותחת שערי היכלי חכמה ובינה, לידע ולהכיר את מי שאמר והי' העולם בהשגה שכלית, מעוררת רגשי הלב להתפעל באותה מדה שבלב המחוייבת מהשכלה זו, ומורה דרך אשר כל אחד ואחד לפום שיעורא דילי' יכול לגשת אל הקדש לעבוד את הוי' במוחו ולבו.

Chabad Chasidism:

opens the chambers of wisdom and understanding, and enables us to intellectually comprehend and recognize God;

stirs the heart and arouses within us the appropriate emotion [for example, comprehension of God's infinite kindness leads us to love God];

guides each individual, commensurate with his or her abilities, to approach God and serve Him with both mind and heart.

The Ultimate Divine Dwelling

Text 16

The Rebbe, *Likutei Sichot* 29:100

די שלימות החביבות והתענוג דלמעלה איז ווען ביי אידן איז
פאראן אויך די הבנה והשגה אין עניני תורה ומצוות.

ווארום נתאוה הקדוש ברוך הוא להיות לו דירה בתחתונים, אז **אלע** "תחתונים" זאלן ווערן א "דירה" וכלי צו ג-טלעכקייט. בשעת ביי א אידן טוט זיך אויף בלויז דער "נעשה" – עשי', קבלת עול – איז אף על פי אז אין דעם דריקט זיך אויס זיין ביטול צום רצון העליון, איז דאס אבער ניט אן ענין וואס דרינגט דורך זיין מציאות בכל פרטי', אויך די כחות פנימיים; כדי עס זאל זיך דורכפירן די כוונה פון "דירה בתחתונים" איז ניט גענוג וואס א איד איז זיך מבטל צום רצון העליון, נאר ער כולו ובכל פרטיו מוז ווערן א "כלי" ("דירה") צו קדושה, וואס דאס איז דוקא ווען עס איז (אויך) דא (כוחותיו הפנימיים) "נשמע", הבנה והשגה.

We cause God the greatest pleasure imaginable when we intellectually grasp the Torah and *mitzvot*; this is the type of service He treasures most.

God's desire for a "dwelling place in the lower worlds" requires *all* elements of the lower realms to be an "abode" for and in concert with God. When we negate our own understanding and feelings and choose to do as God commands, though such behavior expresses tremendous subservience to God, it also demonstrates that God's will has not fully permeated us, for our intellectual and emotional faculties have yet to become an abode for God. To fully realize God's desire, our entirety must become an abode for holiness, and this occurs only when our minds comprehend God's plan.

Key Points

1. There are two levels of divine service: (a) Rejecting and ignoring one's own will and understanding, choosing instead to conform to God's will. (b) Using one's intellectual capacity to *transform* one's will and desires to the point that they mirror and are fully in synch with the divine plan.

2. The second level of service, known as *avodah beko'ach atsmo*, is far greater than the first. Its benefits include: increased passion, intensified personal investment, and greater endurance. In addition, it allows one to intuit the proper choices in those areas that God does not issue specific instructions.

3. The independence and autonomy offered by *avodah beko'ach atsmo* must be preceded by and anchored in unequivocal commitment to God's instructions.

4. *Avodah beko'ach atsmo* is also the ideal in leader-follower relationships, such as rebbe and Chasid. The Chasid not only follows the rebbe's instructions, but also strives to be in synch, in both mind and heart, with the principles and ideas of the rebbe.

5. The ideal leader fosters and cultivates *avodah beko'ach atsmo* in his or her followers. This endeavor was a cornerstone of the Rebbe's leadership style.

6. *Avodah beko'ach atsmo* is not peripheral to Chabad Chasidism, but is the foundation of its philosophy and is the reason why it demands rigorous study and comprehension of the divine.

7. Self-motivated divine service constitutes the ultimate purpose of Creation, inasmuch as it facilitates the transformation of this world into one that is in synch with its Creator.

Appendix A

Adapted from the Rebbe, *Likutei Sichot* 20:284

There was once a mighty king who had an only son. The prince was regal, kind, wise, and multitalented. With pride the king watched as the son capably assumed more and more responsibilities in the royal palace. Whatever venture the prince embarked upon was wildly successful.

One day, the ministers and servants at the royal palace received the most stunning news imaginable. For no apparent reason whatsoever, the king had banished his beloved son from the palace. He dispatched him without a penny, and even commanded that he remove his royal garb before his hasty departure. The king exiled his son to a faraway province, a place where the residents were barely aware of the existence of the royal family, a place where his lineage would hardly impress anyone or gain him any sort of advantage.

Years went by, and the prince was all but forgotten by the members of the royal palace. One day, a large caravan was seen approaching the palace. At its head, in a royally bedecked chariot, sat the prince, clad in glorious regal clothing. Accompanying the prince were many servants and attendants and multiple wagons laden with the riches that the prince had amassed. It seems that the prince had done quite well in his place of exile; from scratch he had made for himself a fortune, and had even been elected as governor of that remote province.

At the grand reception that the king held in honor of his dear son's homecoming, the years' old question was finally answered, as the king explained to all the assembled the reason behind the banishment.

"For years," the king began, "I watched in awe as my son, the apple of my eye, succeeded in all his endeavors; but I was always troubled by one thought. All of his successes can be attributed to the fact that he dwells in the royal palace, avails himself of the royal coffers, and has access to the greatest minds and finest artists. Deep in my heart I always knew that my son is great in his own right and intrinsically royal, and, in fact, needs none of these advantages in order to succeed. It was to prove this point that I sent him off to a land where he would have to earn everything on his own merit. And never for a moment did I doubt that this day would arrive, the day when my son would return and reclaim his position in the palace—a position that he himself has now rightfully earned."

SELECTED CORRESPONDENCE

OF THE REBBE

Inquire and Probe; But Don't Lose Sight

By the Grace of G-d
26th of Tammuz, 5733
[July 26, 1973]
Brooklyn, N.Y.

Greeting and Blessing:

I was pleased to receive your letter of the 18th of Tammuz, following our conversation when you visited here. May G-d grant that just as your letter included good news, so you should be able to continue reporting good news in the same vein and in a growing measure.

You mention that you had some questions and doubts, etc. Of course, one must not feel any shame in asking clarification, and certainly should not keep any doubts within oneself, but seek answers. However, there is only one condition: Whatever the questions and doubts may be, this must not affect one's simple faith in G-d and in His Torah and *Mitzvos*, even if the answers have temporarily eluded one. This condition goes back to the day when the Torah was received at Sinai on the principle of *Naaseh* before *V'Nishma,* the guiding principle for all posterity. But after *Naaseh* follows *V'Nishma*, for G-d, the Essence of Goodness, desires us to follow the path of Truth on the basis of faith, but then to follow it up with knowledge and understanding, for then the totality of the person is involved in serving G-d to the fullest capacity.

However, one must always bear in mind the limitations of the human intellect in general, and particularly in relation to the area of G-dliness, which is essentially beyond human comprehension. By way of analogy, even within the realm of human intellectual achievement, a small child cannot possibly comprehend an advanced mathematical or scientific formula conceived of by a great professor, though the latter was a small child at one time, and the former could one day surpass even the mind of the professor. It is quite different in the relation between the human mind and the Divine Mind, where the difference is not in degree but in kind; between a created being and the Creator. Therefore, the Torah and *Mitzvos*, G-d's Wisdom and Will, can at best be comprehended only in a limited way. To the extent of a person's capacity, he is welcome to inquire and probe, but, as above, without losing sight of the basic condition.

What has been said above is especially pertinent in the present Three Weeks, commemorating the destruction of the Beth Hamikdosh [Holy Temple] and our Exile. For, as we say in prayer: "Because of our sins we have been exiled from our land," etc. Hence, every one of us must do our utmost to rectify and reverse the cause, by studying more Torah and doing more *Mitzvos*, and spreading them throughout the environment, and thus hasten the reversal of the effect and the fulfillment of the Divine prophecy that these days shall be converted into days of joy and gladness, with our true and complete *Geulo* through Moshiach Tzidkeinu.

Enclosed is a copy of a general message which I trust will interest both of you. For, as mentioned during our conversation, Mrs. —— has also an important part to play in spreading the fountains of Torah and *Mitzvos* among her friends and in her circles. In addition to the essential thing, this is also the way to widen the channels to receive G-d's blessings in all needs, materially and spiritually. May you both have *Hatzlocho* [success] in this and enjoy it in good health and with gladness of heart.

With blessing,

LESSON 5

Redefining Failure

We all make mistakes. Such is life. But why was it intended to be this way? This lesson explores how failure is not an anomaly in the design of creation, but the tool through which the highest form of success is carved.

The Anatomy of Failure

A Glitch in the Plan?

LEARNING EXERCISE 1

Rate, on a scale from 1–5 (1=poor; 5=magnificent), the perfection and excellence of the following entities:

Earth's ecosystem	1	2	3	4	5
Human nature	1	2	3	4	5
Our nation's legislature	1	2	3	4	5
The constitution of the human body	1	2	3	4	5
The solar system	1	2	3	4	5

QUESTION FOR DISCUSSION

Are we, as human beings endowed with free choice, the exception to God's perfect universe? Do we at times subvert and undermine God's plan?

A Cosmic Set-Up

LEARNING EXERCISE 2A

What is one of your greatest regrets in terms of interpersonal relationships?

____

____

____

What is one of your greatest regrets in terms of your relationship with God?

____

____

____

What is one of your greatest regrets in terms of character, integrity, or missed opportunities?

____

____

____

LEARNING EXERCISE 2B

List three events or circumstances that factored into your failure in your interpersonal relationship:

a) ______________________________

b) ______________________________

c) ______________________________

List three events or circumstances that factored into your failure in your relationship with God:

a) ______________________________

b) ______________________________

c) ______________________________

List three events or circumstances that factored into your failure in character, integrity, or missed opportunities:

a) ______________________________

b) ______________________________

c) ______________________________

Text 1a

Genesis 1:26

וַיֹּאמֶר אֱלֹקִים נַעֲשֶׂה אָדָם בְּצַלְמֵנוּ כִּדְמוּתֵנוּ.

God said, "Let us make man in our image and likeness."

Text 1b

Midrash, *Bereishit Rabah* 8:8

בשעה שהיה משה כותב את התורה, היה כותב מעשה כל יום ויום. כיון
שהגיע לפסוק הזה שנאמר, "ויאמר אלקים, 'נעשה אדם בצלמנו כדמותנו'",
אמר לפניו: "רבון העולם! מה אתה נותן פתחון פה למינים? אתמהא!"

אמר לו, "כתוב! והרוצה לטעות יטעה".

When Moses transcribed the Torah, he chronicled God's doings on each of the [six] days [of Creation]. When Moses reached this verse: "And God said, 'Let us make man in our image and likeness,'" he was dumbfounded. "Master of the Universe!" Moses exclaimed. "Why are You wording the verse in a manner that will provide fodder for heretics?"

God responded: "Write [as I have dictated]! And those who wish to err are free to do so."

Bereishit Rabah

An early rabbinic commentary on the Book of Genesis. It bears the name of Rabbi Oshiya Rabah (Rabbi Oshiya "the Great") whose teaching opens this work. This Midrash provides textual exegeses and stories, expounds upon the biblical narrative, and develops and illustrates moral principles. Produced by the sages of the Talmud in the Land of Israel, its use of Aramaic closely resembles that of the Jerusalem Talmud. It was first published in Constantinople in 1512 together with four other Midrashic works on the other four books of the Pentateuch.

Text 1c

The Rebbe, *Sichot Kodesh* 5737, 1:134

משה רבינו שרייט, "ווי קען מען שרייבן נעשה לשון רבים?!" און דער אויבערשטער ענטפערט אים, "כתוב!" כדי ס'זאל זיין די אפשריות לטעות.

איז דאך לכאורה ניט פארשטאנדיק: דער אויבערשטער איז דאך עצם הטוב, און טבע הטוב להטיב, איז ווי קען ער זאגן, "כתוב, והרוצה לטעות יטעה"?

Sichot Kodesh

Transcripts (mostly in Yiddish) of most of the Rebbe's public addresses (*farbrengens*) between 1950 and 1981, published in 50 volumes. For the talks that the Rebbe delivered on Shabbat and holidays, when audio recordings and taking notes are proscribed, a team of trained memorizers (*chozrim*) would reconstruct and transcribe the Rebbe's talk from memory. The Rebbe did not edit or review these transcripts for accuracy.

Moses vociferously protests: "How can You write 'Let *us* make' in the plural form?" To which God responds: "Write [as I have dictated]," in order that there be the possibility for error.

This seemingly defies understanding. God is the quintessence of goodness, and it is the nature of the good to bestow goodness—how then can God say, "Write! And those who wish to err are free to do so"?

Text 2a

The Rebbe, *Likutei Sichot* 5:66–67

אויך די ירידות אין וועלט און אין מענטשן וואס ווערן געשאפן דורך **זיינע** מעשים און לויט זיין בחירה חפשית – וויבאלד אז אויך זיי זיינען "על פי ההשגחה העליונה" ובמילא פירן זיי דאך צו א געוויסן תכלית – זיינען אויך זיי, די ירידות, א חלק פון דעם תכלית.

און הגם אז מעשה החטא גופא איז דאך זיכער **היפך** רצון העליון – איז אבער דער מצב פון ירידה אין וועלט און אין מענטשן, וואס ווערט געשאפן דורכן חטא, ניט קיין זאך פון היפך רצון העליון, דאס הייסט, ס'איז ניט קיין ירידה אמיתית, נאר א חלק פון דער עלי' וואס קומט דורך איר.

Likutei Sichot

Widely considered the Rebbe's magnum opus, the 39 volumes of *Likutei Sichot* feature scholarly essays relating to themes in the weekly Torah portions and the Jewish holidays. The Rebbe initially conveyed these concepts in his public talks and subsequently reworked them for publication. In some volumes, the essays appear in Yiddish, while in others they are in Hebrew. Most volumes also present a collection of the Rebbe's correspondence.

The deteriorations that the world and an individual suffer as a result of human actions and free choice are also in accordance with God's plan, and therefore must also lead to a [productive] goal. As such, these deteriorations, too, are part of God's intended goal.

Although the sinful act is certainly contrary to God's will, the decline in the state of the world or the individual that results from the sin is not contrary to His will. It follows, then, that the decline is not a true descent, but a necessary component of the ascent to which it leads.

Text 2b

The Rebbe, *Sefer Hama'amarim* 5735, p. 290

ומאחר שזה בא מעצם הטוב, וטבע הטוב להטיב, הרי זה סימן שזוהי
עלי' כזאת שאין דרך אחרת לבוא אלי', דאם הי' דרך קלה יותר וטובה
יותר ובלי היסורים ובלא ענין הירידה, אם כן למה עשה הוי' ככה?

Because [the deterioration] was enabled by God, the quintessence of goodness, and it is the nature of the good to bestow goodness, it must be that there is no other way to arrive at an ascent of this magnitude. For if there was an easier and straighter path to the destination, one that does not involve hardship and painful plunges, why would God allow for the more difficult path?

Sefer Hama'amarim

Transcripts of the Rebbe's *ma'amarim*, in-depth explorations and analyses of mysticism and Chabad philosophy delivered by Chabad rebbes. For the discourses delivered on Shabbat and holidays, when audio recordings and taking notes are proscribed, a team of trained memorizers (*chozrim*) would reconstruct and transcribe the discourses from memory. The Rebbe did not edit or review these transcripts for accuracy. Thus far, more than 20 volumes have been published.

The Upside of the Downside

Beyond "Forgive and Forget"

QUESTION FOR DISCUSSION

What is the gain that results from failure?

Text 3

Rabbi Yitschak Abohav, *Menorat Hama'or*, *Ner* 5, *Kelal* 3 2:10

גדולה תשובה שהיא מכפרת דבר קל ודבר חמור, ליחיד ולרבים,
כשהיא נעשית כהלכתה ולא ישוב עוד למשובתו.

וזהו חסד גדול שעושה הקדוש ברוך הוא עם החוטאים,
שְׁמוחה עונם ולא יזכרו ולא יפקדו לעולם.

Rabbi Yitschak Abohav
14th century

Preacher and author. Born in Spain, Rabbi Abohav, a businessman, was distressed over the lack of Jewish scholarship in his time. Toward the end of his life, therefore, he dedicated much time to preaching and writing. Abohav wrote *Menorat Hama'or,* a work on ethics based on the sections of the Talmud. The work became a popular household book in medieval Jewish homes.

Great is *teshuvah*! It secures atonement for sins both large and small, those committed by an individual as well as those committed by a community—provided that the *teshuvah* is proper and [is accompanied by the sincere intent] never again to lapse.

Teshuvah is an extraordinary kindness that God extends to those who go astray. He erases their sin, and never again does He recall their offenses.

Text 4

Talmud, Berachot 34b

מקום שבעלי תשובה עומדין צדיקים גמורים אינם עומדין, שנאמר (ישעיהו נז,יט): "שלום שלום לרחוק ולקרוב" – לרחוק ברישא והדר לקרוב.

In the place where penitents stand, even the perfectly righteous cannot stand. This is alluded to in the verse, "Peace, peace to those distant and those near" (Isaiah 57:19): First [God extends His greetings of peace] to those who were distant [and have since repented], and then to those [who were always] near.

Babylonian Talmud

A literary work of monumental proportions that draws upon the legal, spiritual, intellectual, ethical, and historical traditions of Judaism. The 37 tractates of the Babylonian Talmud contain the teachings of the Jewish sages from the period after the destruction of the 2nd Temple through the 5th century CE. It has served as the primary vehicle for the transmission of the Oral Law and the education of Jews over the centuries; it is the entry point for all subsequent legal, ethical, and theological Jewish scholarship.

QUESTION FOR DISCUSSION

How is it that the penitent is on a higher level than one who never failed in the first place?

Text 5

Talmud, Yoma 86b

גדולה תשובה שזדונות נעשות לו כזכיות, שנאמר (יחזקאל לג,יט)
"ובשוב רשע מרשעתו ועשה משפט וצדקה, עליהם הוא יחיה".

Great is *teshuvah*! It causes willful transgressions to be transformed into merits. As it says: "If the wicked man turns away from his wickedness and behaves with justice and righteousness, he shall live on account of them" (Ezekiel 33:19).

Text 6

Rabbi Shne'ur Zalman of Liadi, *Tanya*, ch. 7

Rabbi Shne'ur Zalman of Liadi
(Alter Rebbe)
1745–1812

Chasidic rebbe, halachic authority, and founder of the Chabad movement. The Alter Rebbe was born in Liozna, Belarus, and was among the principal students of the Magid of Mezeritch. His numerous works include the *Tanya*, an early classic containing the fundamentals of Chabad Chasidism, and *Shulchan Aruch HaRav*, an expanded code of Jewish law.

. . . תשובה גדולה כל כך שזדונות נעשו לו כזכיות ממש, שהיא תשובה מאהבה
מעומקא דלבא באהבה רבה וחשיקה ונפש שוקקה לדבקה בו ית', וצמאה
נפשו לה' כארץ עיפה וציה. להיות כי עד הנה היתה נפשו בארץ ציה וצלמות,
היא הסטרא אחרא, ורחוקה מאור פני ה' בתכלית, ולזאת צמאה נפשו ביתר עז
מצמאון נפשות הצדיקים, כמאמרם ז"ל, "במקום שבעלי תשובה עומדים כו'".

ועל תשובה מאהבה רבה זו אמרו שזדונות נעשו לו
כזכיות, הואיל ועל ידי זה בא לאהבה רבה זו.

Teshuvah that is motivated by a great love for God emanates from the depths of the heart; it springs from a soul that passionately desires to cleave to God and thirsts for Him like parched desert soil [yearns for water]. Inasmuch as this person's soul had been in a [spiritual] barren wilderness and in the shadow of death and infinitely removed from the light of God's countenance, his soul now thirsts [for God] even more than the souls of the righteous. Hence our sages say: "In the place where penitents stand, not even the perfectly righteous can stand."

Teshuvah from love, our sages have said, cause "willful transgressions to become transmuted into merits." For [in retrospect,] it is those willful transgressions that [led to the spiritual thirst that] caused this great love for God.

Text 7 (Optional)

II Samuel 22:29

כִּי אַתָּה נֵירִי ה', וה' יַגִּיהַּ חָשְׁכִּי.

For You, O God, are my candle; and God causes my darkness to illuminate.

Text 8

The Rebbe, *Sichot Kodesh* 5737, 1:135

דער גאנצער ענין פון אפשריות לחטא . . . [איז] נאר כדי ס'זאל צוקומען די מעלה פון בעל תשובה . . . ווארום דער גאנצער ענין איז געמאכט געווארן כדי ס'זאל זיין א מציאות פון א "נדח", און די כוונה בזה איז – ס'זאל זיין "לבלתי ידח ממנו נדח" (שמואל ב, יד,יד).

וואס דערמיט איז מובן ווי אזוי מ'קען מתקן זיין על ידי התשובה, ווארום דער ענין החטא איז דאך מלכתחלה בשביל המעלה דתשובה.

God allows for the possibility of sin . . . only to enable us to arrive at the level of the *ba'al teshuvah*. . . . The purpose of sin is to facilitate the possibility of a "banished" person, and the objective of the banishment is so that the "banished person *does not* remain banished." [As it says (II Samuel 14:14): "God devises ways so that a banished person does not remain banished from Him."]

Based on this premise, we can understand how it is possible to correct past failings through *teshuvah*. For the notion of sin in the first place is only to allow for the advantage to be gained through *teshuvah*.

QUESTION FOR DISCUSSION

Can you think of a foolish choice that you made that ultimately led you to a better place and/or to be a better person?

From the Depths of Life to the Depths of Identity

Text 9a

The Rebbe, *Sefer Hasichot* 5752, 2:428–429

(א) די לוחות הראשונות, וואס אויף זיי זיינען חקוק די עשרת הדברות הראשונות וועלכע זיינען געזאגט געווארן בא מתן תורה (אנהויבנדיק פון דעם אל"ף פון "אנכי"), איז דער אל"ף (די התחלה ויסוד) פון אלע ענינים, כולל גאנץ בריאת העולם . . .

(ב) די ירידה פון דעם חטא העגל וואס האט געבראכט צו שבירת הלוחות – איז מרמז דעם ענין הבי"ת, די כללות'דיקע ירידה אין עולם ("בראשית ברא גו'"), וואס לאזט אן ארט אויף דעם ענין החטא והשבירה כו' . . . און די כוונה אין דעם איז, אז דורך דער עבודה למטה, ביז אפילו אין מצב של ירידה, זאל מען אויספירן די כוונת הבריאה, "בשביל התורה" (כדלקמן).

(ג) די לוחות האחרונות באדייטן דעם ענין הגימ"ל – די עלי' וואס קומט דורך דער ירידה ושבירת הלוחות.

Sefer Hasichot

A series of 12 volumes of the Rebbe's talks delivered between 1986 and 1992. During these years, the Rebbe would regularly review and edit (parts of) the transcripts of his talks for immediate publication. The language used alternated between Hebrew and Yiddish. These edited talks would appear in two weekly newspapers: the (Yiddish) *Algemeiner Journal* and the (Hebrew) *Kfar Chabad*.

The first tablets—upon which were engraved the Ten Commandments (which start with an *alef*), as spoken by God by the Giving of the Torah—constitute the beginning and foundation of everything, including all of creation. . . .

The spiritual decline that we suffered after the sin of the Golden Calf—which resulted in the shattering of the tablets—alludes to the *beit*. The *beit* symbolizes the spiritual decline associated with the creation of this world that permits the possibility of sin and the shattering [of the tablets].

The second tablets express the *gimel*—the spiritual ascent that resulted from the spiritual deterioration and the shattering of the first tablets.

Text 9b

The Rebbe, ibid., p. 430

היות אז דער אל"ף מצד עצמו (הגילוי מלמעלה) איז ניט בערך
און נעמט ניט דורך די תחתונים (דער בי"ת פון "בראשית"),
איז אין דעם שייך דער ענין השבירה כו' . . .

מה שאין כן דורך די לוחות האחרונות, וועלכע קומען דורך
עבודת האדם (תשובה), און די לוחות עצמן זיינען מעשה ידי
משה – ווערט אויסגעפירט תכלית וכוונת הבריאה.

The *alef*, because it is a revelation from above, is beyond us and fails to permeate our reality (the *beit*). Thus, there is the possibility for [the *alef*] to be shattered....

The second tablets, on the other hand—which were the product of human effort (*teshuvah*) and which were fashioned by Moses [as opposed to the first tablets, which were fashioned by God]—are the vehicle for the realization of God's ultimate plan.

Text 10

The Rebbe, freely adapted from *Likutei Sichot* 9:63–66

Ultimate refinement does not result from a revelation from above or any external source of inspiration. Rather, it results from tapping into one's own core, at which place the person is a Godly being and at oneness with the Creator. Such refinement is not imposed from without, but springs forth from the depths within.

The penitent, due to his prior failings and transgressions, is very distant from spiritual consciousness or inspiration. His sins have caused the severing of his "spiritual antennae" that sense and respond to the divine. His *teshuvah*, therefore, is the purest expression of his own desire to connect with God.

QUESTION FOR DISCUSSION

Can you think of a time when a foolish choice that you made led you to identify more strongly with your core values?

The Proper Perspective

The Time to Celebrate

QUESTIONS FOR DISCUSSION

1. **Does what we have learned imply that we should celebrate our failures and mistakes?**
2. **Does it lessen the gravity of our mistakes and preclude feelings of guilt and remorse?**

Text 11

The Rebbe, *Likutei Sichot* 9:241

דאס איז דער טעם פארוואס "יישר כחך ששברת" שטייט ערשט ביי דעם ציווי אויף די לוחות שניות . . . ווייל דאן דוקא ווערט נתגלה דער עילוי צו וועלכן אידן זיינען צוגעקומען דורך שבירת הלוחות.

God's congratulating Moses for breaking the first tablets is [alluded to] in the Torah in His instruction to Moses to fashion the second tablets. . . . For only at that point the advantage that the Jews gained through the shattering of the first tablets became apparent.

Text 12

Mishnah, Yoma 8:9

האומה, "אחטא ואשוב, אחטא ואשוב", אין מספיקין בידו לעשות תשובה.

If one says, "I will sin and then repent; I will sin again and repent yet again," he is not given the opportunity to do *teshuvah*.

Mishnah

The first authoritative work of Jewish law that was codified in writing. The Mishnah contains the oral traditions that were passed down from teacher to student; it supplements, clarifies, and systematizes the commandments of the Torah. Due to the continual persecution of the Jewish people, it became increasingly difficult to guarantee that these traditions would not be forgotten. Rabbi Yehudah Hanasi therefore redacted the Mishnah at the end of the 2nd century.

Breaking the Cycle of Failure

Text 13

Talmud, Kidushin 20a

אמר רב הונא: כיון שעבר אדם עבירה ושנה בה הותרה לו.

"הותרה לו" סלקא דעתך?

אלא, נעשית לו כהיתר.

Rav Huna said: "When a person transgresses and repeats it a second time, it becomes permitted for him."

[The Talmud asks:] Can one really think that [a repeat offender] is permitted [to transgress]?

Rather, [Rav Huna is saying that] the deed becomes permissible in the eyes of the offender.

QUESTION FOR DISCUSSION

Why is it more difficult to make the correct choice in an area in which one has repeatedly failed in the past?

Text 14

The Rebbe, *Likutei Sichot* 5:66–67

אין וועלכן מצב א איד זאל זיך ניט געפינען, אפילו אין א מצב ירוד ופחות ביותר, און אפילו ווען ער אליין האט דערפירט צו זיין דאזיקן ניט-גוטן מצב, דורך דעם וואס ער האט בוחר געווען אין רע, און וויבאלד אז "הוא הפסיד את עצמו" איז "ראוי לו לבכות ולקונן על חטאיו ועל מה שעשה לנפשו וגמלה רעה" –

איז אבער אל יתייאש אדם וחס ושלום צו טראכטן אז אבדה תקותו – ווארום וויבאלד אז אויך דער געשאפענער צושטאנד זיינער קומט דאך, מלבד זיין בחירה, מצד השגחה העליונה, פירט עס אים דעריבער (דורך תשובה כו') צו אן עילוי נעלה ביותר.

A person must never despair, God forbid, regardless of one's personal state. This holds true even if one's spiritual state is abjectly low and wretched, even if the person made irresponsible choices and is therefore to blame for bringing this miserable state of affairs upon himself.

Although this person "ought to wail and bemoan his transgressions and the evil that he has wrought his soul" (Maimonides, *Mishneh Torah*, Laws of *Teshuvah* 5:2), he must never lose hope for a brighter future. He must realize that his state, though caused by his free choice, is part of the divine plan. It must be then that it will lead, through *teshuvah*, to even greater heights [than what would have been otherwise possible].

Application Time

LEARNING EXERCISE 3

Step 1: Review the answers you provided to Learning Exercise 2a.

Step 2: Take a moment to meditate on God's greatness and goodness, and the immensity of His love for you.

Step 3: Contemplate the fact that God would never allow you to fail or fall unless there was the possibility for you to grow and benefit from the experience.

Step 4: a) In which way can your failure in the area of interpersonal relationships make you a better person?

____

____

____

____

In which way can you use it to benefit others?

____

____

____

____

b) **In which way can your failure in your relationship with God make you a better person?**

____

____

____

In which way can you use it to benefit others?

____

____

____

c) **In which way can your character failure or missed opportunity make you a better person?**

____

____

____

In which way can you use it to benefit others?

____

____

____

Part of the Ultimate Plan

Text 15

The Rebbe, *Sefer Hama'amarim Melukat* 1:371

על ידי . . . הפיכת הזדונות לזכיות (על ידי התשובה), מבררים
ומזככים גם ענינים הכי תחתונים ונעשים דירה לו יתברך.

When we transform willful transgressions into merits through *teshuvah,* we refine and elevate the lowest elements of Creation—and they, too, become part of and are included in "God's dwelling" [in the lowest realm].

Sefer Hama'amarim Melukat

Of the many *ma'amarim* (in-depth explorations and analyses of mysticism and Chabad philosophy) delivered by the Rebbe, close to 200 were reworked, edited, and released for publication by the Rebbe. Most of the discourses were edited by the Rebbe between 1986–1992. The Rebbe himself distributed a select few of these discourses to the thousands who queued up to receive them.

Key Points

1. The possibility for human error and failure was deliberately incorporated by God into the fabric of Creation. The events and experiences that enable us to make unwise choices are "programmed" by God.

2. Even after we fail, we are never outside the pale of God's benevolent master plan.

3. God allows us to make mistakes and suffer their consequences only because of their potential to lead us to greater heights than would have been possible otherwise. This then is the ultimate raison d'être of our failures.

4. Failure cannot be celebrated as long as it has not been transformed through *teshuvah*. Until that point, failure is bad, and a reason for remorse and grief, not celebration.

5. On the other hand, our knowledge that the failure was allowed by God, for the purpose of leading us to a better place, precludes feelings of despair and empowers us to break the cycle of failure and do *teshuvah*.

6. The advantage that can result from sin and failure is *teshuvah* (repentance).

7. By doing *teshuvah* we not only secure God's forgiveness, but actually redefine past negative events and transform them into positive ones.

8. Moreover, *teshuvah* is an expression of our truest selves. Through *teshuvah* we reveal our most essential bond with God and recognize how we are completely in synch with Him.

9. The advantages to be gained from failure and *teshuvah* are necessary in order to arrive at the ultimate and most profound levels of *dirah betachtonim*.

Appendix A

Rabbi Yanki Tauber, "The Best Kept Secret in the World," www.Chabad.org

Rabbi Yanki Tauber
1965–

Chasidic scholar and author. A native of Brooklyn, NY, Rabbi Tauber is an internationally renowned author who specializes in adapting the teachings of the Lubavitcher Rebbe. He is the executive editor of Chabad.org, the largest Jewish content website, and has written numerous articles and books, including *Once Upon a Chassid* and *Beyond the Letter of the Law.*

Life, as we all know, is a series of blunders. We never, never ever, get it right the first time.

Is it supposed to be this way? Obviously not. Why not? Well, if something is a blunder, then, by definition, it's something that should *not* have happened. But never mind semantics—let's talk gut feeling. I trust my intuition more than any syllogism. Well, every time I begin to see another of my life's blunders developing, every filament in my gut screams: "Noooo! This should *not* be happening. . .!"

And yet, strip life of all its false starts, of all its wrong turns, missed opportunities, naive presumptions, fumbling first attempts and learned-it-the-hard-way experiences, and what's left? Nothing worth writing home about, never mind going through all that trouble to live a life for.

Okay, then, let's say we put intuition and gut feeling aside and say that blunders *are* supposed to happen, as part of G-d's grand plan to make life worthwhile. But if that's the case, we're back in the bland and meaningless space of a pre-programmed life that's not worth going through all that trouble for. Besides, how could my blunders be things that G-d wanted all along to happen, if many, most, (all?) of them result from actions which G-d specifically told me He doesn't want to happen?

That's the crazy thing about blunders. Without them, there's nothing. Yet if there's one thing we can about them say with absolute conviction, it's that they're not supposed happen. How can something not supposed to be and supposed to be at the same time?

G-d knows, but He's not telling.

SELECTED CORRESPONDENCE

OF THE REBBE

To Go Back in Time*

By the Grace of G-d
The eve of Shabbat Teshuvah
6 Tishrei, 5739 [October 7, 1978]
Brooklyn, N.Y.

To the sons and daughters of
our people Israel, everywhere,

Greeting and Blessing:

In a previous letter, we have noted the unique quality and preeminence of repentance—that in a mere moment and with one turn, one is able to rectify all that should have been achieved in the past. (Parenthetically, it is plain and obvious that the above must not, G-d forbid, serve as an excuse for wrongdoing, for our sages have said, "Whoever says, 'I will sin and repent later,' is not given an opportunity to repent.")

Now, we will amplify the said point in order to underscore how much this affects the conduct of a Jew and the conduct of every person.

By way of introduction:

Upon reflection, a person would conclude that the world contains much more materiality than spirituality. Moreover, the more an entity is corporeal and gross, the greater it is in quantity. For example, inanimate matter is much greater in volume than the vegetative kingdom, and the latter is quantitatively greater than the animal kingdom, which, in turn, by far surpasses in quantity the highest of the four kingdoms—humankind.

We find a similar pattern within the human body. The legs are larger than the rest of the body. And the body itself is much greater in size than the head wherein the entities that vivify and direct the activities of the human being are located—the faculty of speech; the senses of smell, hearing, and sight; and the intellect.

People might therefore become disheartened, G-d forbid, wondering how they can properly fulfill their real purpose in life on this earth—which is, to quote our sages, "I was created to serve my Creator"—seeing that most of their time is necessarily taken up with materialistic things, such as eating, drinking, sleeping, earning a livelihood, etc. Add to this the fact that the earliest years of a human being, before reaching maturity, are spent in an entirely material mode of living.

The answer:

We are told, "Let all your doings be for the sake of Heaven" (Mishnah, Avot 2:12) and "Know G-d in all your ways" (Proverbs 3:6). The meaning of these directives is that we need to understand that the material preoccupations of our daily lives (which take up most of our time) do not constitute an end in themselves; instead, they are and need to serve as a medium to attain a higher, spiritual realm of life, namely, G-dliness.

In this way, we imbue spiritual content into all of the material things that we utilize for spiritual purposes. Thus, all of these mundane matters are elevated and attain completion.

In addition to the above, there is also the concept of prompt repentance, which has the power to transform all of the mundane experiences of the past into spiritual ones.

* * *

There are very significant differences between different hours and moments of time in terms of their con-

* Translated from *Torat Menachem, Igrot Melech* 1:192–196.

tent and value. Thus, one cannot compare an hour of prayer and outpouring of the soul before G-d with an hour of sleep. To use an analogy of coins: there may be coins of identical size and shape, yet differing in their intrinsic value, depending upon whether they are made of copper, silver, or gold.

Yet, the "G-d who does wonders" provided repentance with an extraordinary quality, that it can transcends all limitations, including the limitations of time, so that in one moment it can transform the all of the past to become absolutely perfect.

* * *

G-d ordained the beginning and end of each year as especially favorable times for repentance. G-d also provided the assurance that anyone who resolves to do teshuvah can do so in a mere moment. In this short amount of time, a person can transform the quantity of the material past into a meritorious quality of spirituality and holiness. This short time suffices as well to prepare the future, the coming year and thereafter, so that it will be proper, by following the Torah and fulfilling the mitzvot in everyday life. Thereby one elevates oneself and the environment at large to the highest possible level of spirituality and holiness, thus making this material world a fitting home for G-d.

* * *

May G-d grant that everyone actively strive for the above, in accordance with the prayer of the Prophetess Hannah, which we read on the first day of the New Year: "My heart rejoices in G-d, my strength is uplifted through G-d . . . I rejoice in His help . . . and He will exalt the reign of His Mashiach."

With blessing for success in all the above, and to be definitively sealed in the Book of Life for a good year, both materially and spiritually,

A *Teshuvah* Primer

By the Grace of G-d
Erev Shevuoth [May 15, 1956]
Brooklyn, New York

Sholom U'Brocho [Greeting and Blessing]:

In reply to your (undated) letter, you should bear in mind the following points:

(a) There can be no question but that Teshuvo [repentance] is effective in every case, and whatever the transgression, for Teshuvo is one of G-d's commandments, and G-d does not require of us the impossible.

(b) It is likewise certain that any kind of depression, despondency or sadness, is a trick of the Yetzer Hora [evil inclination] to discourage one from serving G-d, as is explained at length in the books of Mussar, and in the books of Chassidus [Chasidism]; and you would do well to refer to Tanya, Ch. 26 and further.

(c) Even where one has relapsed in committing the same transgression for which one has done Teshuvo, and, moreover, even while doing Teshuvo one is not certain whether he could resist the temptation should it recur, this must in no way prevent him from studying the Torah and observing its Mitzvoth, included among which also the Mitzvah of Teshuvo, for every action of man has its repercussions both down here below and Above, and you surely know the saying of our Sages "No transgression extinguishes a Mitzvah" (even though it extinguishes the reward of a Mitzvah). I refer you again to Iggereth Hatshuvo (part III of the Tanya), Ch. 11.

I advise you from now on to stop weighing and dwelling on things which are of no practical value, and especially the kind of thought that only leads to despondency, but concentrate ever growing efforts on Torah and Mitzvoth.

I wish you to celebrate the Festival of Our Receiving the Torah with inner and lasting joy.

With blessing,

Regarding the Past

By the Grace of G d
8th of Adar II, 5727 [March 20, 1967]
Brooklyn, N. Y.

Blessing and Greeting:

Your cable reached me with some delay. I also received your recent correspondence.

Upon receipt of your cable, the following reply was cabled back to you, "Replying to your cable, wishing you successful treatment, good news, with blessing."

May G-d grant that you should have good news to report, especially as we are now in the auspicious month of Adar. The auspiciousness of this month is, of course, connected with the miraculous Purim festival, in which Jewish women have a particularly important part, for Esther, together with Mordecai, brought about the turn of events. And although Mordecai was as much the essential figure as Esther, and as we say in the Purim prayer, "In the days of Mordecai and Esther," yet the Megilah containing the story of Purim, and which is one of the sacred books of the Tanach, is not called after Mordecai, nor after Mordecai and Esther jointly, but solely after Esther—Megilas Esther—the "Book of Esther."

With reference to your letter, I read with considerable interest your outline of your curriculum vitae. I am gratified to note that you are conducting your home in the way of our sacred Torah, called Toras Chaim [the Torah of Life] because it is both the source of true life as well as the true guide in the daily life, despite the difficulties which you had in the past, and are still experiencing to some extent.

To be sure, that period of time in the past when the daily life should have been different requires rectification, especially by means of a determined effort to improve the present and future, so as to make up for the past. On the other hand, human nature is such that things that come easily are taken for granted, and are not so appreciated and cherished as things for which one had to fight and struggle. Thus, the level of Yiddishkeit [Judaism] which you and your husband have attained through real efforts has permeated you more deeply and thoroughly, and may G-d grant that you should both continue in this direction together with your children, without allowing yourself to be hindered or influenced in any way by the difficulties which you describe in your letter. On the contrary, the difficulties themselves can serve as a challenge and stimulus to greater spiritual advancement, as is also explained in Chassidic literature. . . .

I send you my prayerful wishes for the fulfillment of your heart's desires for good, especially for a Refuo [recovery] and good health, and the fulfillment of the Mitzvos with joy and gladness of heart, and hope to hear good news from you.

With blessing,

LESSON 6

Opening Our Eyes

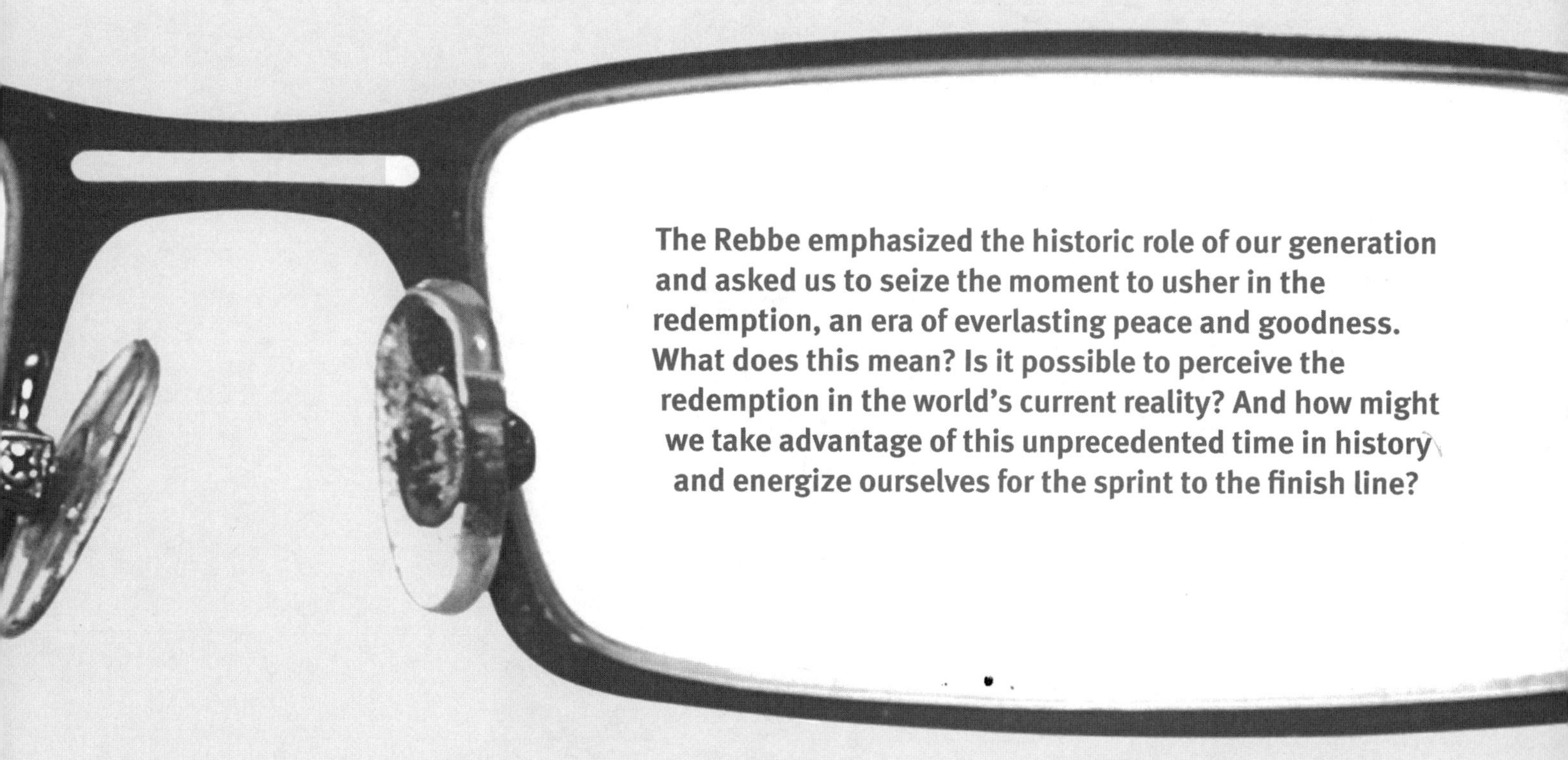

The Rebbe emphasized the historic role of our generation and asked us to seize the moment to usher in the redemption, an era of everlasting peace and goodness. What does this mean? Is it possible to perceive the redemption in the world's current reality? And how might we take advantage of this unprecedented time in history and energize ourselves for the sprint to the finish line?

Focus on Redemption

LEARNING EXERCISE 1

Why does Jewish law mandate the ritual washing of the hands before eating bread?

A. For hygienic reasons

B. Because water is a metaphor for the Torah, of which we should always be mindful

C. To symbolize the need for pure intentions when partaking of the world's pleasures

D. Because we anticipate the Messianic redemption at any moment

E. A and C

Text 1

The Rebbe, *Igrot Kodesh* 12:414

מיום הלכי ל"חדר" ועוד קודם לזה התחיל להתרקם בדמיוני ציור
גאולה העתידה – גאולת עם ישראל מגלותו האחרון, גאולה כזו
ובאופן כזה שעל ידה יהיו מובנים יסורי הגלות הגזירות והשמדות.

From the time that I was a child attending *cheder* [primary school], and even earlier than that, the picture of the future redemption began to take form in my imagination: the redemption of the Jewish people from their final exile, a redemption that will finally allow us to understand the purpose of the suffering, harsh decrees, and annihilations of exile.

Igrot Kodesh

A selection of Hebrew and Yiddish letters penned by the Rebbe. As of 2014, 30 volumes have been published in this series. The letters are published in chronological order, starting from 1925 and extending thus far to 1975. Only those letters that are of relevance to the public are published, and all personal information is excised. The letters cover a wide range of issues: communal activism, Chabad philosophy, Talmud, Jewish law, Kabbalah, practical advice, and much more.

Text 2

The Rebbe, *Sefer Hama'amarim Melukat* 1:5

והנה זה תובעים מכל אחד ואחת מאתנו . . . נמצאים אנחנו בעיקבתא
דמשיחא, בסיומא דעקבתא, והעבודה – לגמור המשכת השכינה,
ולא רק שכינה כי אם עיקר שכינה, ובתחתונים דוקא.

We are now at the conclusion of the final period of exile. The task that is now demanded of each and every one of us . . . is to complete the process of drawing the essence of the Divine Presence into the lowest realm.

Sefer Hama'amarim Melukat

Of the many *ma'amarim* (in-depth explorations and analyses of mysticism and Chabad philosophy) delivered by the Rebbe, close to 200 were reworked, edited, and released for publication by the Rebbe. Most of the discourses were edited by the Rebbe between 1986–1992. The Rebbe himself distributed a select few of these discourses to the thousands who queued up to receive them.

QUESTION FOR DISCUSSION

In your estimation, why are some people bothered by the Rebbe's and Chabad's strong emphasis on Mashiach and the redemption?

Text 3

Maimonides, *Mishneh Torah*, Laws of Kings 11:1

המלך המשיח עתיד לעמוד ולהחזיר מלכות דוד ליושנה
לממשלה הראשונה ובונה המקדש ומקבץ נדחי ישראל
וחוזרין כל המשפטים בימיו כשהיו מקודם . . .

וכל מי שאינו מאמין בו או מי שאינו מחכה לביאתו לא בשאר
נביאים בלבד הוא כופר אלא בתורה ובמשה רבינו.

Rabbi Moshe ben Maimon (Maimonides/Rambam)
1135–1204

Halachist, philosopher, author, and physician. Maimonides was born in Cordoba, Spain. After the conquest of Cordoba by the Almohads, he fled Spain and eventually settled in Cairo, Egypt. There, he became the leader of the Jewish community and served as court physician to the vizier of Egypt. He is most noted for authoring the *Mishneh Torah*, an encyclopedic arrangement of Jewish law, and for his philosophical work, *Guide for the Perplexed*. His rulings on Jewish law are integral to the formation of halachic consensus.

The Mashiach will appear one day and renew the Davidic dynasty and restore its sovereignty. He will build the Temple and gather the dispersed of Israel. At that time, we will observe all the *mitzvot* [related to the Temple and the Holy Land] as we did in days of yore. . . .

One who does not believe in this redemption or does not await its coming denies not only the statements of the prophets [who spoke of the redemption], but also the words of the Torah and our teacher Moses.

Revealing the Alef

A Dreamy Reality

FIGURE 6.1

גולה	גאולה
Exile	Redemption

Text 4

The Rebbe, *Sefer Hasichot* 5751, 2:505–506

גאולה איז ניט דער טייטש, אז דורך ארויסגיין פון גלות פארלאזט מען דעם לעבן, די פעולות און דער וועלט וואס איז געווען (פריער) אין גלות. אדרבה: גאולה הייסט, אז די מציאות וואס איז פריער געווען פארשקלאפט אין גלות ווערט (ניט בטל חס ושלום, נאר) **אויסגעלייזט** . . . אלע (חיוב'דיקע) זאכן אין גלות פארבלייבן אויף ווייטער, נאר עס ווערט בטל זייער גלות-צושטאנד: עס ווערט בטל דער העלם והסתר וואס פארדעקט אויף זייער אמת'ע און פנימיות'דיקע מציאות . . .

על פי זה איז פארשטאנדיק פארוואס דער ווארט "גאולה" איז **כולל** דעם ווארט "גולה", אבער – מיט א תוספת אל"ף: די גאולה איז ניט מבטל (די עבודה אין) גלות, אדרבה: די גאולה באשטייט פון אויפהויבן (דעם לעבן אין) "גולה" (דורך אויסלייזן אלע ענינים פון גלות) און דערפון גופא מאכן "גאולה" – דורך דעם וואס מ'איז מגלה אין אלע ענינים פון "גולה" דעם אל"ף פון אלופו של עולם – מ'נעמט אראפ דעם העלם והסתר אין די עניני גלות וועלכע פארדעקט אויף איר אמת'ע מציאות און תכלית, מ'איז מגלה דעם אלופו של עולם שבזה – די תכלית פון אלע עניני גלות צוליב וועלכער דער אויבערשטער האט זיי באשאפן – אזוי אז פון "גולה" ווערט "גאולה".

Sefer Hasichot

A series of 12 volumes of the Rebbe's talks delivered between 1986 and 1992. During these years, the Rebbe would regularly review and edit (parts of) the transcripts of his talks for immediate publication. The language used alternated between Hebrew and Yiddish. These edited talks would appear in two weekly newspapers: the (Yiddish) *Algemeiner Journal* and the (Hebrew) *Kfar Chabad*.

Redemption does not imply a departure from our current state—from our lives, routines, and world. To the contrary, the definition of redemption is that the very entity that was previously in a state of exile is—not nullified, God forbid, but—redeemed. . . . All the positive elements that are part of our current reality will remain intact; only their exilic condition will be eliminated. The concealment of each entity's true nature will be removed. . . .

This explains why the word *ge'ulah* (redemption) includes within itself the word *golah* (exile), with the added letter *alef*. Redemption will not do away with exile and our efforts therein. To the contrary, redemption's characteristic is that it lifts up and redeems the entire state of exile and transforms exile itself into redemption. This is done by removing all of exile's concealments, everything that obscures each thing's true nature and purpose, and revealing within everything the *alef*, which alludes to the Master (*aluf*) of the World. When we reveal the Master of the World in each thing—that is, the purpose for which God created it—then from exile itself, redemption emerges.

Text 5a

Psalms 126:1

שִׁיר הַמַּעֲלוֹת, בְּשׁוּב ה' אֶת שִׁיבַת צִיּוֹן הָיִינוּ כְּחֹלְמִים.

A song of ascents: When God returns the exiles to Zion, we [will realize that we] had been like dreamers.

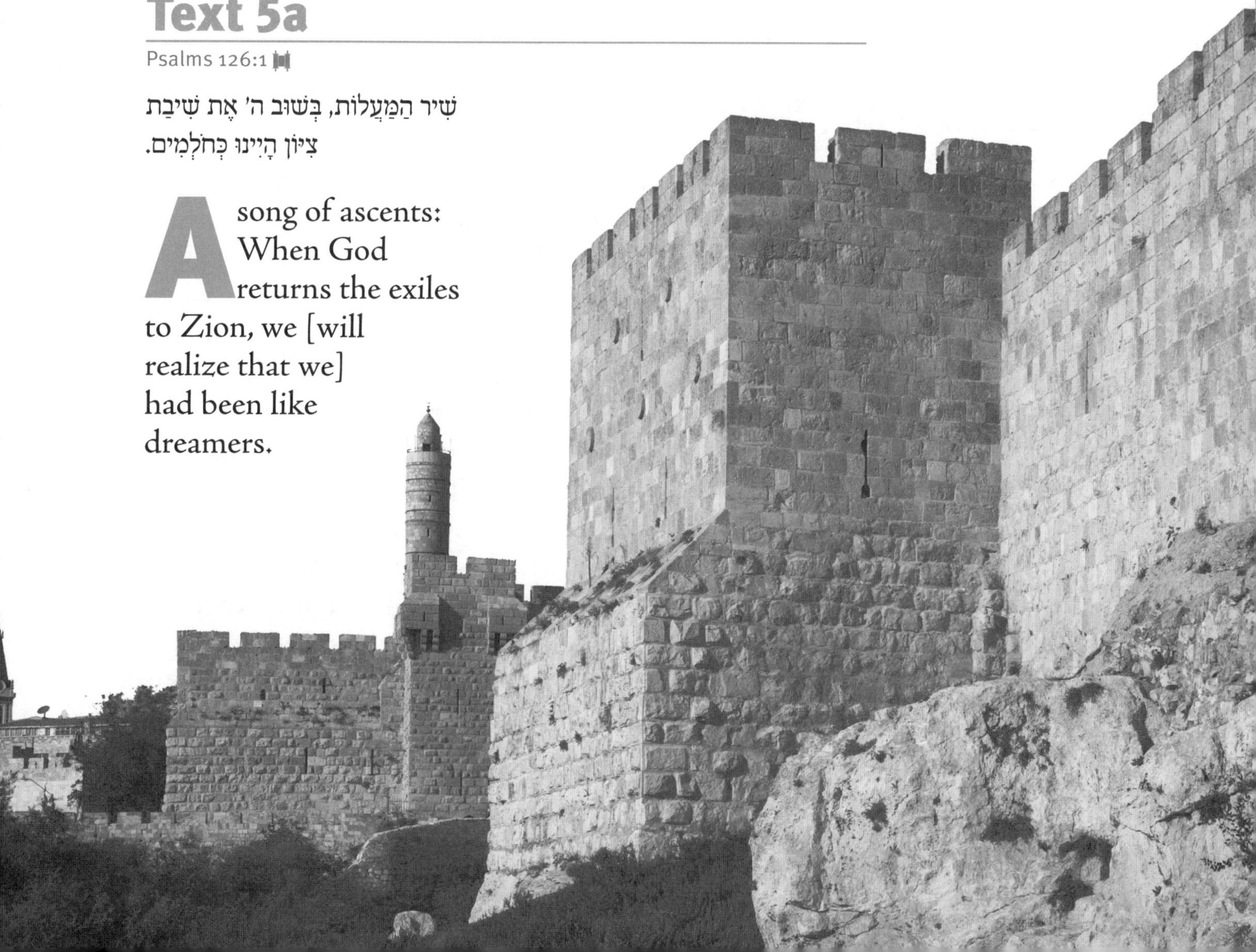

Text 5b

The Rebbe, *Torat Menachem* 5744, 4:2210–2211

ישנם כאלו שמתעוררת אצלם תמיהה ופליאה (אף שמטעמים מובנים אינם מעלים תמיהה זו על דל שפתם): היתכן, מהרהרים הם, שיושב לו יהודי לדבר ברבים, ובכל התוועדות והתוועדות מכריז ללא הרף ואינו מפסיק לדבר אודות נושא אחד – ביאת משיח צדקנו? . . . וכמו כן אומרים בכל פעם שינגנו "שיבנה בית המקדש במהרה בימינו", ומדגישים שאין הכוונה "במהרה בימינו" מחר, אלא היום ממש!

בודאי מאמין כל יהודי שמשיח צדקנו יכול לבוא בכל רגע – "אחכה לו בכל יום שיבוא", אבל אף על פי כן, מהרהרים הם, מהי פשר ההנהגה לדבר ללא הרף על ענין זה, ולהדגיש בכל פעם שברגע זה ממש יכול לבוא משיח צדקנו – דבר שקשה לפעול ברגש של האדם שיתייחס לכך כאל דבר מציאותי! בשלמא כאשר מזכירים פעם אודות ביאת משיח צדקנו – נו, סוף כל סוף הרי זה מעיקרי האמונה. אבל מהו פשר הדיבור והלהט בענין זה ללא הרף, בכל התוועדות והתוועדות, כאילו היו רוצים להכניס את הדבר בראשם של השומעים בכח? . . . אלא מאי, מסיקים הם, ענין זה הוא בגדר של "חלום", חלום טוב ויפה . . . אבל לא דבר מציאותי. ואם כן, טוענים הם, לשם מה צריכים לדבר אודות עניני "חלומות"? . . .

אמנם, לאמיתו של דבר – ההיפך הוא הנכון: . . . ה"חלום" הוא – לא הדיבור על הגאולה, אלא אדרבה: מציאות הגלות היא "חלום", שכן, מה ליהודי ולענין של גלות?! ואילו הגאולה היא – בהקיץ, זוהי מציאותו האמיתית של יהודי!

Torat Menachem

A Hebrew translation of the transcripts of the Rebbe's talks. This work also comprehensively cross-references and footnotes the material. As of 2014, more than 90 volumes have appeared in this series, covering the years 1950–1968 and 1982–1992. The Rebbe did not edit or review these publications for accuracy.

There are those who are incredulous (though, for obvious reasons, they do not articulate it) over the fact that there is a certain Jew with a large audience, who at every occasion and public gathering speaks about one topic without pause or let-up: the coming of Mashiach. . . . Moreover, at each of these gatherings, he requests that the assembled sing, "May the Temple be built speedily in our days," while emphasizing that the intent of "speedily in our days" is not tomorrow but *today*!

Certainly, every Jew believes that the redemption could happen at any instant. Nonetheless, they wonder, is it really necessary to speak ceaselessly about this matter, and to constantly emphasize that Mashiach could come at this very moment? It is difficult to relate toward the redemption as a practical reality! If we only mention the redemption occasionally, *nu*, what can anyone say? It is, after all, one of the principles of our faith. But the unceasing talk and passion at every single gathering is seemingly excessive; it seems as if he wishes to force the issue upon the listeners! . . . In the minds of these people, redemption is a dream, a good and beautiful dream, but not reality. That being so, they argue, why must he speak about dream-stuff?

However, in actuality, the opposite is true. The dream is not the talk about the redemption; quite the contrary, *exile is a dream*. Exile is a most unnatural dream-like state. The redemption is our "awake" state, our true reality!

Application Time

Text 6

Maimonides, *Mishneh Torah*, Laws of Repentance 3:4

צריך כל אדם שיראה עצמו כל השנה כולה כאילו חציו זכאי וחציו חייב,
וכן כל העולם חציו זכאי וחציו חייב . . . עשה מצוה אחת הרי הכריע את
עצמו ואת כל העולם כולו לכף זכות וגרם לו ולהם תשועה והצלה.

A person should always view oneself as equally balanced with merits and faults, and view the world, too, as equally balanced with merits and faults. . . . Therefore, if one performs but one mitzvah, he tips the balance—his own and the entire world's—and effects personal and global deliverance and salvation.

FIGURE 6.2

The Seven Noahide Laws

1. Acknowledge that there is only one God.	5. Respect the property of others.
2. Respect the Creator.	6. Do not cause unnecessary suffering to animals.
3. Do not murder.	7. Maintain a judicial system to enforce these laws.
4. Do not engage in illicit sexual behavior (e.g., incest and adultery)	

A World of Difference

Text 7

Midrash, *Shemot Rabah* 12:3

משל למה הדבר דומה, למלך שגזר ואמר: "בני רומי לא ירדו לסוריא, ובני סוריא לא יעלו לרומי".

כך, כשברא הקדוש ברוך הוא את העולם גזר ואמר, "השמים שמים לה', והארץ נתן לבני אדם" (תהלים קטו,טז).

כשבקש ליתן התורה בטל גזירה ראשונה ואמר, "התחתונים יעלו לעליונים, והעליונים ירדו לתחתונים.

A parable: A king decreed, "The Romans may not go down to Syria and the Syrians may not go up to Rome."

Similarly, when God created the world, He decreed, "The heavens are the domain of God, and the earth He has given to the children of Adam" (Psalms 115:16).

But when God sought to give the Torah, He nullified the original decree, and said, "Those below may ascend above, and those above may descend below."

Shemot Rabah

An early rabbinic Midrash on the Book of Exodus. The term "Midrash" is derived from the root *d-r-sh*, which means "to search," "to examine," and "to investigate." *Shemot Rabah*, written mostly in Hebrew, provides textual exegeses, expounds upon the biblical narrative, and develops and illustrates moral principles. It was first published in Constantinople in 1512 together with four other Midrashic works on the other four books of the Pentateuch.

Text 8

Zohar (*Ra'aya Mehemna*) III, 124b

Zohar

The most seminal work of Kabbalah, Jewish mysticism. The Zohar is a mystical commentary on the Torah, written in Aramaic and Hebrew. According to Arizal, the Zohar contains teachings of Rabbi Shimon bar Yocha'i who lived in the Land of Israel during the 2nd century. The Zohar has become one of the indispensable texts of traditional Judaism, alongside and nearly equal in stature to the Mishnah and Talmud.

ובגין דעתידין ישראל למטעם מאילנא דחיי, דאיהו
האי ספר הזהר, יפקון ביה מן גלותא ברחמי.

Because Israel in the future will taste from the Tree of Life, which is this very Book of Splendor, the *Zohar*, they will be redeemed with compassion from exile.

Text 9

The Rebbe, *Sefer Hasichot* 5752, 1:151–152

איצטער האלט מען שוין בא דעם מצב אז דער גוף הגשמי און
אפילו גשמיות העולם איז שוין אינגאנצן נתברר ונזדכך געווארן, און
איז א "כלי" מוכן אויף אלע אורות ועניינים רוחניים, כולל ובעיקר –
אורו של משיח צדקנו, אור הגאולה האמיתית והשלימה . . .

די איינציקע זאך וואס פעלט איז – אז א איד זאל אויפעפענען זיינע
אויגן כדבעי, וועט ער זען ווי אלץ איז שוין גרייט צו דער גאולה!

By now, we have reached the point where the physical body and even the materiality of the world is completely purified and refined and is ready to assimilate all sorts of spiritual matters, including and especially the light of Mashiach, the light of the true and complete redemption. . . .

The only thing that now remains is for us to properly open our eyes, and we will see how all is ready for the redemption!

LEARNING EXERCISE 2

The world today is a kinder, gentler place than it was a few decades ago, more reflective of its beautiful essence and more consistent with (its "blueprint,") Torah values.

☐ True

☐ False

☐ It's complicated because. . .

Text 10

The Rebbe, *Sefer Hasichot* 5750, 1:159–160

ישנם התמהים על המדובר בתקופה האחרונה שעומדים אנו בסוף זמן הגלות, עקבתא דמשיחא, ושואלים: היכן רואים זאת? הרי עולם כמנהגו מידי שנה בשנה **כרגיל** נוהג? – ולפלא הכי גדול שאינם מתבוננים בהמאורעות שמתרחשים בעולם, מאורעות הגלויים ומפורסמים!

בתקופה האחרונה (החל משנים הכי אחרונות, ומוסיף והולך מזמן לזמן) מתרחשים ברחבי העולם **מהפיכות קיצוניות**, מן הקצה אל הקצה, ובחסדי ה', מתרחשים מהפיכות אלה **בשקט**, כלומר, ללא מלחמות ושפיכות-דמים, רחמנא ליצלן, עד כדי כך, שחיי היום-יום (בעניני המסחר וכיוצא בזה) ממשיכים להתנהל על דרך הרגיל, כאילו עולם כמנהגו נוהג, למרות שמתרחשת מהפיכה קיצונית בהנהגת המדינה כולה, אלא שהיא מהפיכה **פנימית**, בדרכי פוליטיקא מדינית:

לכל לראש ומתחיל ממדינת רוסיא (המדינה שממנה בא כ"ק מו"ח אדמו"ר נשיא דורנו יחד עם תלמידיו ושלוחיו), אשה, לאחרי תקופה של שבעים שנות משטר **תקיף ואימתני** שהפיל חיתתו על כל תושבי המדינה, עד שאפילו עבור

התבטאות של ביקורת על המשטר היו עונשים להשלח לארץ גזירה (סיביר וכיוצא בזה) – נעשה לפתע, בפרק זמן קצר ביותר, **שינוי קיצוני** (על ידי העומדים בראש הנהגת המדינה) במשטר המדינה, ומתפשט גם בשאר מדינות דוגמתן.

ועל דרך זה במדינת סין – שבתקופה האחרונה מתרחשת מהפיכה בהנהגת המדינה בפנים וגם בנוגע לקשר ויחס עם שאר מדינות העולם, וכיוצא בזה, וכן במדינת הודו – שבפרק זמן קצר יחסית הוחלפו ראשי השלטון ששלט במשך תקופה ארוכה, ועל דרך זה מהפיכות קיצוניות בעוד כמה מדינות ברחבי העולם . . .

והמדובר אודות מהפיכות במדינות כאלו שיש בהם **ריבוי עצום** של בני-אדם, כלומר, מהפיכות בממשלות ומשטרים שמנהיגים **בליוני אנשים בכל רחבי העולם**, ועד לרוב האנשים שבכל העולם!

וה"נס" שבדבר – ולפלא הכי גדול שלא שמים לב לכל זה, "אין בעל הנס מכיר בנסו" – **שמהפכות קיצוניות**, שיש להם השפעה ישירה על רוב העולם, מתרחשות **בשקט ובמנוחה**, דבר שאין לו אח ורע בתולדות האנושיות כולה:

מהפיכות במשטר ושלטון של מדינות היו מלווים תמיד במלחמות עקובות דם שהתנהלו במשך תקופה ארוכה, שיבשו את מהלך החיים, הביאו הרס וחורבן רחמנא ליצלן. ואין צורך להרחיק לכת ולחפש בדברי ימי העולם בדורות שלפני זה, כיון שראינו בדורנו זה את החורבן הנורא במלחמת העולם השני', לא תקום פעמיים צרה.

ואילו בימינו אלה, מתרחשים מהפכות קיצוניות **גדולות יותר**, ברוב העולם, **ובחסדי ה'**, הרי זה ללא מלחמות, ללא שפיכות דמים, חס ושלום, אלא מתוך **שקט ומנוחה.**

There are those who are surprised at the recent statements asserting that we are standing at the end of exile, on the threshold of the redemption. They ask: "Where do we see this? After all, the world continues to run as normal, year after year." In truth, however, what is surprising is that these people do not contemplate current well-publicized events.

In the recent past, extreme and radical transformations have been transpiring around the world. Thanks to God's kindness, these upheavals are happening quietly, that is to say, without wars and bloodshed, heaven forbid, but through the paths of diplomacy. These changes are so quiet and peaceful, that daily life and regular routines (commerce and the like) continue unaffected, despite the extreme transformations taking place in the entire country.

This starts with Russia, the country from which my father-in-law, the Rebbe, emigrated, along with his students and emissaries. For seventy years, a powerful and fearsome regime cast its terror over all the inhabitants of the country, to the point that the slightest expression of criticism of the regime was punishable by exile to Siberia or similar places. Suddenly now, in the shortest period of time, a polar change took place in the country's government (led by the country's political leaders), and this change spread to other countries of the Soviet Bloc.

In China, similarly, this last period has seen an inner transformation in the governance of the country and also in the nature of its relations to the other countries of the world. Also in India, in a relatively short span of time, a government that had held sway for a long time was rejected in favor of a new one. There were similar extreme changeovers in several other countries around the world. . . . These are countries with enormous populations, governments and regimes that rule *billions of people all over the world*—a majority of the world's population!

It is an unfathomable wonder that people are not paying attention to all of this; even the beneficiaries of the miracles do not recognize their own miracle! The miracle in all this is that these extreme transformations, which directly influence a majority of the world, are taking place quietly and tranquilly, something that has no parallel or precedent whatsoever in all of human history.

Historically, regime changes have always been accompanied by bloody wars carried on over a long period of time, which dried up the course of life and brought ruin and destruction, God preserve us. There is no need to search too far into the history of previous generations, for we saw in our generation the awful ruin of the Second World War (may such trouble never recur).

But now, *even greater* transformations are occurring in most of the world, and thanks to God's kindnesses, they are without wars or bloodshed, God forbid, but are quiet and tranquil.

Text 11a

Isaiah 2:4

וְכִתְּתוּ חַרְבוֹתָם לְאִתִּים, וַחֲנִיתוֹתֵיהֶם לְמַזְמֵרוֹת.

לֹא יִשָּׂא גוֹי אֶל גּוֹי חֶרֶב, וְלֹא יִלְמְדוּ עוֹד מִלְחָמָה.

Nations will beat their swords into plowshares and their spears into pruning hooks;

Nation will not lift up sword against nation, and no more will they study warfare.

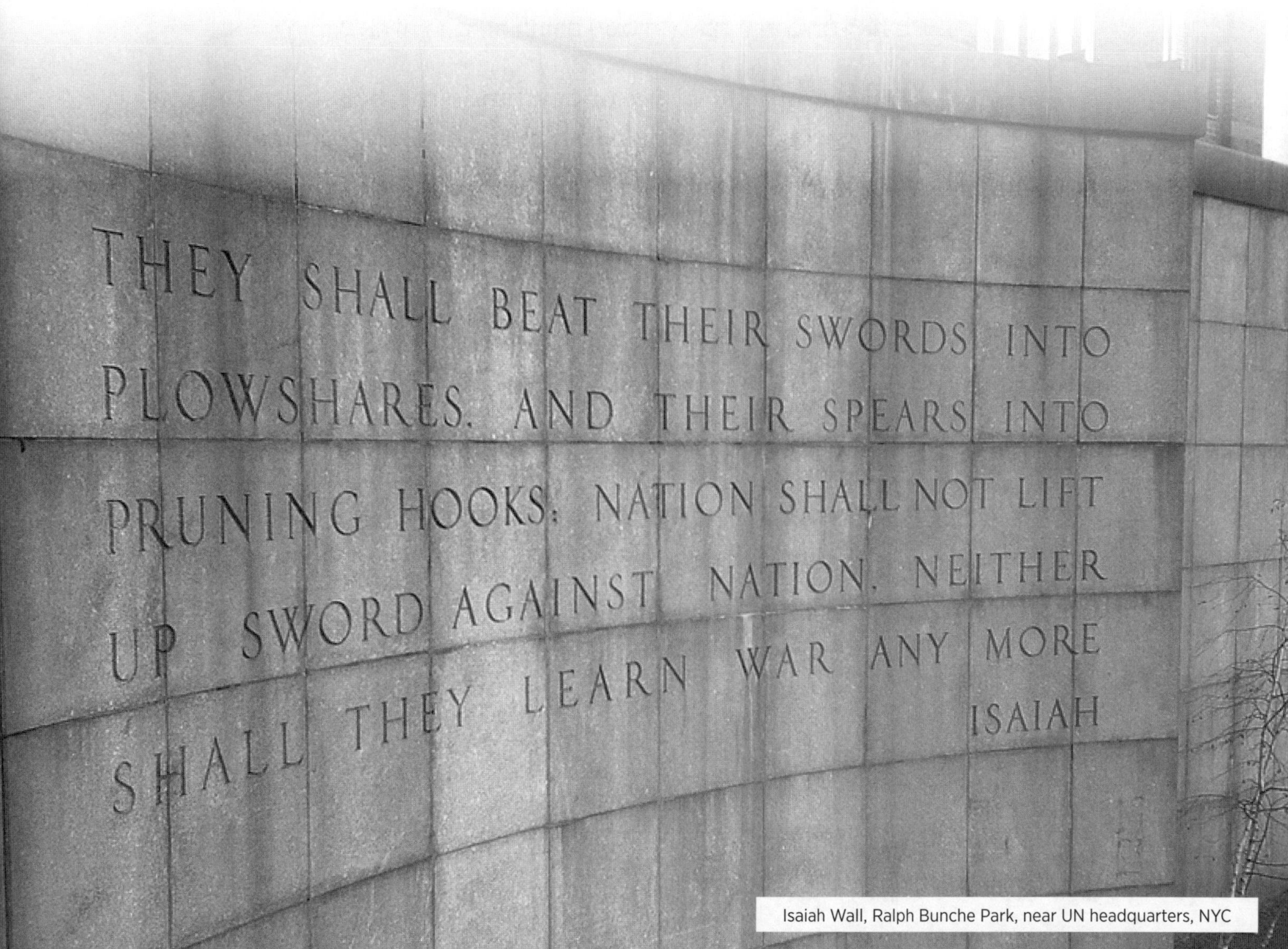

Isaiah Wall, Ralph Bunche Park, near UN headquarters, NYC

Text 11b

The Rebbe, *Sefer Hasichot* 5752, 2:368

"וכתתו חרבותם לאתים" הוא ענין המובן ומחוייב גם **בשכל האדם** ("משפטים"), שהרי, שכל אנושי מחייב קיומו של העולם על פי צדק ויושר, על ידי שלילת מלחמה שמביאה הרס וחורבן, רחמנא ליצלן, ועד שיביא לשבירת כלי המלחמה ("וכתתו חרבותם") והפיכתם לכלים שמביאים תועלת לישובו של עולם ("אתים").

ואף על פי כן, במשך כל הדורות התנהלו ריבוי מלחמות בין אומות העילם שגרמו הרס וחורבן בעולם – **בניגוד** להמתחייב בשכל האנושי!

ועל כרחך צריך לומר, שהסיבה **האמיתית** לכך שבתקופה האחרונה ניכרת השאיפה לגמר ולסיום תקופת המלחמות בעולם, והתחלת תקופה חדשה של קיום העולם על פי צדק ויושר, שלום ואחדות . . . [היא] מפני שמתקרבים להזמן שאודותיו הכריזה התורה ("מסיני") "וכתתו חרבותם לאתים".

The human mind understands the benefit of beating swords into plowshares. In fact, human logic *mandates* such behavior because it understands that the world must be conducted justly and uprightly, and absolutely rejects the notion of war, which brings ruin and destruction, may God preserve us. Logic also dictates the need to destroy weapons of war ("beat swords") and transform them into instruments that bring benefit to civilization ("plowshares").

Despite this, throughout the generations, many wars have been waged among the nations, wars that brought the world ruin and destruction—in defiance of plain logic!

We must conclude, then, that the true reason why the recent period has seen a multinational aspiration to end the era of war in the world and to begin a new era in which the world is conserved through justice and uprightness, peace and unity . . . is because we are approaching the time about which the Torah declared, "And they will beat their swords into plowshares."

Text 12

The Rebbe, *Sefer Hasichot* 5751, 2:661

ווי מ'זעט עס במיוחד בדורות האחרונים, וואס דער אויבערשטער האט געבענטשט אידן אז זיי זאלן באקומען זייער פרנסה מיט ווייניקער יגיעה, מתוך מנוחת הנפש ומנוחת הגוף (מער ווי ס'איז געווען בדורות לפני זה), דורך דעם וואס די וועלט אליין איז מסייע לזה.

Particularly in these last generations, we see that God has blessed us in that we attain our livelihood with less exertion, with tranquility of the soul and body, more so than in previous generations. The world itself facilitates this newfound tranquility.

Text 13

The Rebbe, *Sefer Hasichot* 5751, 2:692–693

למרות ה"שטורעם" שבדבר בתקופה האחרונה . . . רואים שישנו קושי ("עס קומט אן שווער") להחדיר ההכרה וההרגשה שעומדים על סף ימות המשיח ממש עד שיתחילו "לחיות" בעניני משיח וגאולה . . .

והעצה לזה – על **ידי לימוד התורה** בעניני משיח וגאולה, כי, בכח התורה (חכמתו של הקדוש ברוך הוא שלמעלה מהעולם) **לשנות** טבע האדם, שגם כאשר מצד הרגש שלו נמצא עדיין חס ושלום **מחוץ** לענין הגאולה (כיון שלא יצא עדיין מהגלות הפנימי), הרי על ידי לימוד התורה בעניני הגאולה מתעלה למעמד ומצב של גאולה, ומתחיל לחיות בעניני הגאולה, מתוך ידיעה והכרה והרגשה ש"הנה זה בא".

Despite the buzz and excitement over the redemption during the recent period . . . it is apparently difficult to instill within ourselves the recognition and feeling that we are really standing on the threshold of the redemption. It is difficult to bring ourselves to the point where we "live" with Mashiach and redemption. . . .

My advice, therefore, is to study in the Torah the topics of Mashiach and redemption, for it is within the power of Torah—God's wisdom that transcends the world—to change human nature. Even if we feel ourselves to be, God forbid, outside the realm of redemption (as we have not yet left our internal exile), by studying what the Torah says on the topic, we will be elevated to a state of redemption. We will then begin to live with these ideas, and with the knowledge, recognition, and feeling that the redemption is imminent.

Handing Over the Baton

Text 14

The Rebbe, *Sefer Hama'amarim Melukat* 6:134

שגם כשישראל נמצאים במצב של הרחבה, הרחבה בגשמיות וגם הרחבה ברוחניות, אלא שהם נמצאים בגלות . . . הם שבורים ונדכאים (כתית) מזה שהם בגלות, ועל ידי הכתית דישראל מזה שנמצאים בגלות, מגיעים להמאור.

Even when we enjoy conditions of plenty and abundance, both in material and spiritual matters . . . we are broken and crushed by our exiled state. And thus we arrive at the ultimate light.

Text 15

Simeon Bennett and Laura Marcinek, "Bill Gates Sees Almost No Poor Countries Left by 2035," *Bloomberg News*, Jan. 21, 2014

Bill Gates, the world's richest man, said that by 2035 no nation will be as poor as any of the 35 that the World Bank now classifies as low-income, even adjusting for inflation. . . .

"The facts are on the side of the optimists," Gates, 58, said today in a Bloomberg Television interview with Betty Liu. "It's actually dangerous that people are focusing on the bad news and not seeing the progress we've made. It means they don't look at the best practices, it makes them less generous." . . .

Almost all countries will be what are now called lower-middle income or richer by 2035, Gates said in the letter. They will learn from their most productive neighbors and benefit from innovations such as new vaccines, better seeds and the digital revolution, he said. "The belief that the world is getting worse, that we can't solve extreme poverty and disease, isn't just mistaken. It is harmful," Gates wrote. "By almost any measure, the world is better than it has ever been. In two decades it will be better still." . . .

"Headlines in a way are what mislead you because bad news is a headline and gradual improvement is not," Bill Gates said in the interview.

Text 16

Maimonides, *Mishneh Torah*, Laws of Kings 12:5

ובאותו הזמן לא יהיה שם לא רעב ולא מלחמה, ולא קנאה ותחרות, שהטובה תהיה מושפעת הרבה וכל המעדנים מצויין כעפר. ולא יהיה עסק כל העולם אלא לדעת את ה' בלבד . . . שנאמר (ישעיהו יא,ט), "כי מלאה הארץ דעה את ה' כמים לים מכסים".

During the Messianic era there will be neither famine nor war, neither envy nor competition, for all that is good will flow in abundance and all delights will be freely available as dust. The occupation of the entire world will be solely to know God . . . as it says, "The world will be filled with the knowledge of God as the waters cover the ocean bed" (Isaiah 11:9).

Text 17

The Rebbe, *Torat Menachem* 5744, 4:2212

הן אמת שברגע זה נמצאים עדיין בחשכת הגלות ממש, אבל אף על פי כן, מכיון שכללות ענין הגלות הוא "חלום" שענינו חיבור הפכים – הרי ברגע אחד יכול המצב להתהפך מל הקצה אל הקצה, היינו, שיוצאים מ"חלום" הגלות ובאים למציאות האמיתית – גאולה בפועל ממש!

It is true that at this moment we are yet in the darkness of exile. Nevertheless, because exile is a dream, in one moment, the situation can change from one pole to the other. That is to say, we can wake up from this dream of exile and immediately enter true reality—the redemption!

Key Points

1. Belief in a final redemption, an era of everlasting peace and goodness, and the anticipation of its arrival are fundamental to Jewish tradition and thought.

2. The redemption is an era when the beautiful and Godly essence of everything (the "*alef*") will be revealed to the naked eye. Redemption constitutes the ultimate reality, as opposed to our current dream-like state.

3. Considering that the central theme of the Rebbe's teachings is the importance of focusing on the pristine essence of every entity—the world, the human being, and so forth—it is no wonder that hastening the redemption, the day when that essence will be on full display, was the Rebbe's primary goal and lifelong vision.

4. We translate our yearning for the redemption into effective action by adding in deeds of goodness and kindness and by studying the topic of redemption in the Torah.

5. Many signs point to the historic role of our generation and the fact that we are on the cusp of redemption; it is up to us to seize the moment and make it a reality.

6. The Rebbe insisted that the world itself is already prepared for redemption and urged us to "open our eyes" to this reality. The Rebbe identified modern-day phenomena, such as the fall of the Iron Curtain, nuclear disarmament, and the development of advanced technologies, as "signs of redemption" and indications of the world's readiness for the Messianic era.

Appendix A

Talmud, Shabbat 31a

בשעה שמכניסין אדם לדין אומרים לו:

נשאת ונתת באמונה?

קבעת עתים לתורה?

עסקת בפריה ורביה?

צפית לישועה?

When a soul is brought to its [final] judgment, it is asked:

Did you conduct your business dealings in good faith?

Did you designate times for Torah study?

Did you endeavor to have children?

Did you eagerly await the redemption?

Babylonian Talmud

A literary work of monumental proportions that draws upon the legal, spiritual, intellectual, ethical, and historical traditions of Judaism. The 37 tractates of the Babylonian Talmud contain the teachings of the Jewish sages from the period after the destruction of the 2nd Temple through the 5th century CE. It has served as the primary vehicle for the transmission of the Oral Law and the education of Jews over the centuries; it is the entry point for all subsequent legal, ethical, and theological Jewish scholarship.

Appendix B

The Rebbe, *Sefer Hasichot* 5752, 1:192

המצוה שיש לה סגולה מיוחדת לקרב את הגאולה, היא מצות הצדקה – "גדולה צדקה שמקרבת את הגאולה" (בבא בתרא יו"ד,א). ומזה מובן שיש להוסיף עוד יותר במצות הצדקה, ומה טוב שההוספה בצדקה תהי' תיכף ומיד, כדי שגם הגאולה (שבאה על ידי מצות הצדקה) תבוא תיכף ומיד.

ובפרט שכיון "שאין גו' אתנו יודע עד מה" (תהלים עד,ט), הרי יתכן שהדבר היחיד שחסר להבאת הגאולה אינו אלא נתינת מטבעות אחדות לצדקה!

The mitzvah that has a unique power to hasten the redemption is *tsedakah* (charity)—"Great is *tsedakah*, for it hastens the redemption" (Talmud, Bava Batra 10a). We should therefore increase our charitable giving; even better, we should do so immediately, so that the redemption (which results from the mitzvah of *tsedakah*) will also come immediately.

In particular, because "None among us knows what [exactly is needed to bring the redemption]" (Psalms 74:9), it is possible that the one thing that is needed is the giving of a few coins to *tsedakah*.

Appendix C

Talmud, Yoma 9b

מקדש ראשון מפני מה חרב? מפני שלשה דברים שהיו בו: עבודה זרה, וגלוי עריות, ושפיכות דמים . . .

אבל מקדש שני, שהיו עוסקין בתורה, ובמצות, וגמילות חסדים, מפני מה חרב? מפני שהיתה בו שנאת חנם.

Why was the First Temple destroyed? For three things: idolatry, sexual immorality, and bloodshed. . . .

But during the time of the Second Temple there was Torah study, observance of *mitzvot,* and acts of kindness. Why then was it destroyed? Because of baseless hatred.

Appendix D

Torat Menachem 5747, 2:626

בנוגע לדיבור בענין שבע מצוות בני נח: מכיון שעומדים בזמן קרוב לגאולה, לאחר ש"כלו כל הקיצין", מובן שעתה הוא הזמן המתאים ביותר להכין את העולם כולו להיות ראוי לגאולה.

We speak about [influencing the nations of the world to observe] the Seven Noahide Laws because we are currently in the era close to the redemption; indeed, it is long overdue. Now is therefore the most appropriate time to prepare the entire world to be worthy of redemption.

SELECTED CORRESPONDENCE

OF THE REBBE

We've Seen Open Miracles

The following is a public letter issued by the Rebbe following the Gulf War of 1991. We bring you the letter in its entirety, minus the rich and copious Hebrew footnotes.

* * *

By the Grace of G-d
Motsa'ei Shabbat [Saturday evening]
25th of Adar,
Third day of the week, the day about which G-d twice said "It was good"
Parashat Vayikra, 5751 [March 11, 1991]
Brooklyn, N.Y.

To the sons and daughters of our people Israel, everywhere, G-d bless you all!

Greeting and Blessing:

We just celebrated Purim, a time of miracles G-d wrought "in those days at this season," and are approaching the festival of Passover when we celebrate the "Festival of Our Freedom," thanking G-d for the miracles and wonders that He wrought in connection with our liberation from Egypt.

It is now highly opportune to give our full attention to the miracles and wonders that happened just recently, around Purim time.

These were **revealed miracles**, not only for Jews but also for all nations. "All corners of the earth saw"—everyone saw—the great miracles that unfolded at this time.

It is well known that the miracles in the days of Mordechai and Esther were concealed in the natural order of events. Only if we connect the dots and perceive the various events as one continuous and connected sequence —the beginning of Achashverosh's reign, the third year of his reign, the seventh year of his reign, the month of Nissan in the twelfth year of his reign, Esther's banquets for Achashverosh and Haman—are we able to recognize the guiding hand of G-d.

This is one of the reasons why there is no explicit mention of G-d's name in the entire Book of Esther (one of the 24 holy books of the Bible). It is because the miracle of Purim occurred in a manner of "concealment of G-d's countenance," as alluded to in the verse, "I will hide My face on that day," which refers to the Miracle of Purim, a miracle that was "clothed" and concealed in a natural "garb."

By contrast, the events of recent months leading to the (middle of) Adar were clearly miraculous for the benefit of Jews and the benefit of the entire world. It was a conspicuous miracle before the eyes of all the nations.

* * *

When considering the natural conditions of the world, it seemed inevitable that not only would there be a declaration of war, etc., but that the war would engulf many nations and set off a new world war, G-d forbid. Yet, in a most extraordinary turn of events, not only was a world war avoided, but the war that had begun was over quickly.

All signs pointed to the outbreak of a massive war, requiring a huge army with massive weaponry of the most advanced technology. Although everything was duly assembled and in place for a long war that was expected to last weeks and months, victory came in a short order!

The victory was wondrous. Much bloodshed (which had been feared) was avoided, and prisoners of war were freed, including some that had been held from before.

(Our Torah teaches and directs us to guard against speaking negatively and predicting the occurrence of evil. We pray that henceforth there will be only good tidings, good that is revealed and obvious.)

Moreover, those who are "insiders," who know many details that were not publicized, appreciate so much more the marvelous miracles and wonders in our time, in these days.

* * *

Jews have designated the current year (5751) with the acronym: *ha'yah tehei shnat arenu nifla'ot*—"It shall surely be a year of revealed wonders." The preceding year (5750) was designated *ha'yah tehei shnat nisim*—"It shall surely be a year of miracles." During this year and the end of last year, we frequently emphasized the connection of the current events with our sages' prediction (in *Yalkut Shimoni*, Isaiah 499) concerning wars that would break out in that region of the world that will signal the near arrival of the true and complete redemption through our righteous Mashiach.

In light of the aforementioned events and miracles, one should become even more keenly aware that we are now living in an era of preparation for the fulfillment of the prophecy, "The kingdom shall be G-d's." All nations will recognize that "this world has a Master," and this will lead "all of them to call upon the name of G-d and to worship Him with one accord."

Specifically as we approach the month of Nisan, it is certain that G-d will show even greater miracles than heretofore. Nisan is related to the Hebrew word *nes*, which means "miracle." Moreover, as our sages point out, the spelling of "Nisan" (with two *nuns*) indicates multiple miracles (and "miracles within miracles").

[There is a relationship between the concept of "elevation" and the concept of a "miracle"—the Hebrew word *nes* connotes both of these.] G-d will particularly show us miracles when Jews increase their own efforts to elevate their daily Jewish conduct. Everyone, man and woman, should elevate and rise above their natural tendencies and habits in the area of Torah study and in being particular about doing *mitzvot* scrupulously. There should be multiple elevations, striving higher and ever higher.

There is an instruction at the very beginning of this week's Torah portion, (which in Hebrew is called "*sidra,*" which means "order"): "If any person brings an offering of you" (Leviticus 1:2). The Alter Rebbe taught a deeper meaning in this verse: Let the offering be of you, of yourself, by breaking out of your habits and constraints, in order to dedicate yourself fully to G-d.

Behaving in this manner of constant growth in a revealed way will hasten the fulfillment of the prophecy, "I will show you wonders as in the days of your liberation from Egypt." G-d will now fulfill His promise, "I have found David My servant, with My holy oil I have anointed him," followed immediately by the true and complete redemption through our righteous Mashiach.

With esteem and blessing for success, and with blessing for a kosher and joyous Pesach,

Paradigm Shift

ADDITIONAL READINGS

186 Putting Women in the Picture
Professor Susan Handelman

196 A Single Candle
Prime Minister Benjamin Netanyahu

197 Jewish Greatness
Professor Elie Weisel

198 The Rebbe's Inspiring Charge
Rabbi Lord Jonathan Sacks

202 Marching Orders
Rabbi Adin Even-Israel Steinsaltz

203 The Particular Path of the Seventh Rebbe
Rabbi Adin Even-Israel Steinsaltz

205 The Rebbe's Immense Spiritual Mission
Rabbi Adin Even-Israel Steinsaltz

209 Rebbe of the Abandoned and the Privileged
Rabbi Haskel Lookstein

211 Judaism's Mission to the World
Rabbi Joseph Telushkin

215 The Believer
MK Geulah Cohen

220 The Philosophy of Lubavitch Activism
Rabbi J. Immanuel Schochet

229 To Ignite the Soul
Ambassador Yehuda Avner

231 Where Change Begins
Gordon B. Zacks

235 Interview with the Lubavitcher Rebbe

239 The Rebbe and Viktor Frankl
Rabbi Jacob Biderman

242 A Visit with the New Lubavitzer Rebbe
Gershon Kranzler

246 The Lubavitcher Movement
Rabbi Herbert Weiner

257 The Rebbe and the Teenager
Rabbi Shmuel Kaplan

258 The Rebbe Said Thank You
Rabbi Yanki Tauber

260 What is a Rebbe?
Rabbi Tzvi Freeman

Some of these articles contain Hebrew or Yiddish words.
A glossary for these words can be found on p. 264.

PUTTING WOMEN IN THE PICTURE

THE REBBE'S VIEWS ON WOMEN TODAY

PROFESSOR SUSAN HANDELMAN

Let me begin with a story I heard from Robert Abrams, formerly the Borough President of the Bronx and District Attorney of the State of New York, and currently a practicing lawyer. As an influential New York politician he had several private audiences with the Lubavitcher Rebbe, Rabbi Menachem Mendel Schneerson, who was often visited by such figures. On one of his visits to the Rebbe, Mr. Abrams was accompanied by his wife, Dianne, who sat beside him in the Rebbe's office while the two men discussed current political and economic issues. Dianne Abrams is herself an accomplished lawyer and by her own account, "not a shy person at all." Assuming, however, that the Rebbe was only interested in conversing with her husband, she sat silently as they spoke. After some time, the Rebbe turned to her and said with a smile: "Why aren't you saying anything? These are the days of Women's Liberation...."

This little vignette summarizes the essence of what I want to say here, and my study of the Rebbe's writings, talks, activities in relation to women—and my own personal contact with him. I think he discerned the deeper meaning of what was occurring historically in relation to women. He saw within the stirrings of the Women's Movement a deep spiritual inner dimension and strong redemptive energies. He understood the need to use these energies for the good, and so encouraged women to speak, articulate their yearnings, and achieve their spiritual aspirations. And he himself worked very practically to implement all of this—from a global level down to encouraging one woman sitting in his office to speak her mind.

While I have written other essays that examine in depth the Rebbe's halachic and theological approaches to the status of women in Torah, this one will be somewhat different. It supplements those with a personal account from the point of view of an outsider/insider or participant/observer. There are many forms of knowledge, and there is a certain dimension of understanding one gains only through an insider's position, and through having known one's subject "face to face."[1] This is particularly true in relation to a "Rebbe," a figure who functions on many levels—not just as a thinker, writer, teacher, rabbi or public leader, but also as an intimate, personal counselor. So I hope to add a personal perspective to the literature about the Lubavitcher Rebbe's relation to women's issues.

While it is quite clear to me that the Rebbe understood and sympathized deeply with the yearnings and aspirations of women on many levels, it is important to first portray briefly here the larger theological-metaphysical framework in which he perceived their strivings, and their place in his over-all vision of Jewish history, the mission of the Jewish people and redemption.

The Rise of the Feminine Era in Kabbalah and Chassidism

Those familiar with chassidic philosophy recognize the idea that there are "sparks of holiness" (*netzutzot kedusha*) scattered throughout our lowly physical world, awaiting their redemption through our actions. Concurrently, there is the chassidic-kabbalistic principle the Rebbe also often cited that "everything that happens below has it source in what happens Above." I think he took this principle also to mean that there was a specific historical-theological reason why the Women's Movement was occurring in our times, and that our task was to infer what it signified for the current generation.

In an oft-quoted passage from a talk on Jewish education for women given in 1990, the Rebbe reinterprets the basic talmudic and halachic sources regarding women's Torah study, draws out the practical

[1] I have written in depth about this question in my essays, "'Knowledge Has a Face': the Jewish, the Personal, and the Pedagogical" in *Personal Effects: The Social Character of Scholarly Writing*, eds. David Bleich and Deborah Holdstein (Utah State University Press, 2002), pp.121-144 and "'Stopping the Heart': The Spiritual Search of Students and the Challenge to a Professor in an Undergraduate Literature Class" in *Religion, Scholarship and Higher Education: Perspectives, Models and Future Prospects*, ed. Andrea Sterk (Notre Dame University Press, 2002), pp. 202-230.

implications, exhorts women to increase their study and teaching, and asks for the community at large to support this endeavor. He further asks: why has this increase in Torah learning for women occurred specifically in the recent era? On the one hand, the Rebbe answers, there is the traditional idea that each generation further from the Divine revelation at Sinai is on a "lower" level; and so there is an increasingly greater need to bolster it. Nevertheless, he continues, the result has been a great good, an increase in Torah study; and this increase in Torah study by women he emphatically describes as one of the "*positive innovations* of the later generations."[2]

From another perspective, each generation further away from Sinai is also closer to the final Redemption and Messianic Era. And so, the Rebbe adds, we could say we have merited the increase in Torah study for women precisely because of that proximity: it is part of the preparation for—and already a taste of—redemption. A defining characteristic of the messianic era is a great increase in knowledge and wisdom; and so we now already have a "taste" of it, just as there is a halachah (Torah law) that before Shabbat one is to taste each of the special dishes to be enjoyed at the Shabbat meal.[3] (This also connects to the idea the Rebbe often repeated that different parts of Torah are revealed in the times appropriate for them. Hence, he explained, only in recent generations has the esoteric "soul" of Torah—kabbalah and chassidism—been revealed and become increasingly accessible to the masses. Even though these latter generations might be on a lower level than previous ones, they also have a greater responsibility, for they are to purify and complete the final *galut* (exile) and open the way to redemption. Hence the most sublime parts and secrets of Torah are revealed in the latter generations and they already begin to "taste" of the Torah of the messianic era.)

But there is an even deeper connection—continues the Rebbe in the above talk—of women to the messianic era. Kabbalistic and chassidic teachings have a special understanding of the role of the feminine in the Era of Redemption and the World-to-Come. Then, say the classical sources, all the "feminine" aspects of the world will emerge from their concealment and diminution in the unredeemed world and rise to the highest stature.[4] That is the deeper reason—says the Rebbe—that in our generation the innovations and increase in Torah study connect to and are emphasized in relation to women. The effect of their study is also great, for as the Talmud says in a well-known line: "In the merit of the righteous women of that generation the Jews were redeemed from Egypt."[5] And so, the Rebbe concludes, in the merit of the righteous women of our generation, may the full and complete redemption come.

Many other chassidic leaders and thinkers, including his own predecessors in the Chabad movement, write of the time of the redemption in these kabbalistic terms as the elevation of the "feminine" side (*Malchut* or *Nukvah,* as it is called in the literature). As far as I know, however, the Rebbe is the only one to specifically connect this long-held and abstract mystical idea to concrete sociological phenomena occurring in our time. He did not let it remain a metaphorical depiction of some coming future era far from us, unrelated to the current realities of women's lives.[6]

---

2 "*Al Devar Chiyuv Neshei Yisrael B'Chinukh u-veLimmud ha-Torah 5750* [1990]." *Sefer haSichot*, Vol. 2 (Brooklyn, N.Y.: Kehot, 1992), pp. 455-459.

3 See the Rebbe's discourse on the nature of chassidic philosophy and its innovations entitled *Inyananah Shel Torat ha-Chassidut* (and the appendix printed there, a discourse given on the Last Day of Passover, 1970) on the timing of revealing new insights and aspects of Torah. It is translated into English in the volume, *On the Essence of Chassidus* (Brooklyn, N.Y.: Kehot, 1978).

4 That is the deeper meaning of the famous verse from Proverbs (12:4), "A woman of valor is the crown of her husband" and from the prophet Jeremiah (31:21), "the woman will encircle the man." The crown, symbolizing the highest kabbalistic *sefira* (divine attribute) of *Keter*, sits on top of and encircles the head. Similarly, in the prophecy of Jeremiah, "the woman encircling the man," signifies the highest level of divine revelation, in the mode of a "circle" (*makkif*). In a circle, all points are also equidistant from the center, as opposed to the hierarchical structure of a line. A circle also symbolizes what encompasses and can't be contained and delimited. There are hints to this in the wedding ceremony where the bride indeed encircles the groom, and in the language of the wedding blessings. See further the chassidic discourse of R. Schneur Zalman of Liadi in his *Torah Ohr*, end of Parshat Vayigash, and his commentary on the Siddur and the wedding blessings for the relation of male and female in the messianic era and World-to-Come.

5 *Sotah* 11b.

6 Naftali Lowenthal adds, however, that "At the same time one cannot quite leave out what R. Yosef Yitzchak [the Rebbe's father-in-law and predecessor] was doing. His presentation (in his *Zikhronot*) of women secretly studying Talmud in the ancestry of R. Shneur Zalman, his setting up of *Achos HaTemimim* [a woman' study group] in Riga in the 1930s, and his statements about this, are very interesting in terms of a new view of womanhood. The messianic aspect is not stated, but then

This perspective paralleled his reinterpretation of the halachic obligations of women in the mitzvah of Torah study, and within Chabad, his encouragement of their dramatically increased public participation in Chabad outreach activities.[7] He also transformed the role of the *shluchah*—the wife of the *shaliach* or Chabad "emissary." The Rebbe sent thousands of young families to serve as his "emissaries" all over the globe to found Chabad houses and reach out to fellow Jews. He made the women's role independent in its own right. He instituted the *Kinus HaShluchot*, an annual conference in the Chabad Center in New York for these women emissaries, just as the Chabad male *shluchim* had all gathered from all over the world once a year in Crown Heights. The women came to New York for a long weekend of workshops, lectures, and had special gatherings with the Rebbe in the main synagogue; the men sat upstairs where the women usually sit for prayers, while the women sat with Rebbe downstairs.

My Personal Experience

My relationship with the Rebbe began when I was a graduate student in English literature in the 1970's and used part of a fellowship I had to research and study for six months in the Chabad world center in Brooklyn N.Y.—the place where the Rebbe had resided since coming to America in 1941. Over the years, I developed strong ties to the community and to Chabad Chassidism, and had personal contact with the Rebbe in many ways: participating in his *farbrengens* (public gatherings), corresponding and consulting with him, intensively studying his writings, and brief face-to-face encounters. I had ample opportunity to observe him up close and to experience personally his relation to women.

During my time in Crown Heights and afterwards, I wrote several essays about Chabad Chassidism, many of which were based on research into the Rebbe's writings, and several of which he edited personally. In 1978, while completing my Ph.D. work in literature, I also co-translated into English, with a Chabad rabbi, an important philosophical and hermeneutic discourse of the Rebbe's on the nature of chassidic thought, entitled *Inyanah shel Torat HaChassidut* (English title, *On the Essense of Chassidus*[8]). The manuscript was given to the Rebbe to be checked prior to its being published in honor of his seventy-fifth birthday. My rabbinical co-translator told me with a smile that it was reported to him that when the Rebbe was shown the manuscript for his comments, he did not question my participation or credentials, but instead that of my male colleague, who was well-known as a highly learned Torah scholar: "Since when does Rabbi G. know English so well?" asked the Rebbe.

At the suggestion of one of his secretaries, Rabbi Binyomin Klein, I had also consulted with the Rebbe about my Ph.D. dissertation topic. I was not the only one, of course, to be writing to the Rebbe for advice. The secretary told me that the Rebbe received and answered about four hundred letters a day. This was in addition to the endless phone calls and faxes that deluged his office in the course of any twenty-four hour period, along with the personal audiences he had with his followers and the many different people who came from all over the world to see him, and which lasted late into the night. I had at that time thought of two possible dissertation topics: one on Shakespeare, and one on literary theory and rabbinic methods of interpretation. I often like to ask people which topic they thought the Rebbe advised me to write about. Many answer, "Shakespeare." When asked why, they surmise he would not like me to mix rabbinic and secular studies, or would not think that

in general his intense messianism (seen in *Hakeriah veHakedushah*) is not expressed in his discourses and other teachings." Personal email correspondence with the author, August 19th, 2002.

7 See my essay "Women and the Study of Torah in the Thought of the Lubavitcher Rebbe" in *Jewish Legal Writings by Women*, eds. Micah D. Halpern and Chana Safrai (Jerusalem: Urim Press, 1998), pp. 143-178 for an explication of his technical halachic analysis of the mitzvah of Torah study for women. This analysis was printed in the Rebbe's *Likkutei Sichot*, Vol. 14 (Brooklyn, N.Y.: Kehot, 1978), pp. 37-44 and reprinted in *Chiddushim u-Viruim leShas*, Vol. 1 (Brooklyn, N.Y.: Kehot, 1979), pp. 217-223 . The Rebbe concludes through a careful analysis of the classical sources and *Shulchan Aruch HaRav* that the mitzvah of Torah study for woman is not based only on the need she has to know the laws pertaining to her—the classic justification—but acquires its own independent status as Talmud torah for its own sake, *leshmah*. On a sociological level there were also many "mivtzaim," public campaigns initiated by the Rebbe, that involved dramatically increased public participation of women both in their performance and promulgation. Among these were the campaign to have all girls from the age of 3 upwards light shabbat candles, and to spread and publicize in as many forums as possible public knowledge of the mitzvah of *taharat mishpacha*, the laws of family purity.

8 *Likkutei Sichot*, Vol. 4, (Brooklyn, N.Y.: Kehot), p. 1101.

as a woman, I had enough knowledge to pursue that topic. Those who choose the rabbinics option say they think he would want me to try to bring *Yiddishkeit* into the University, as part of the well-known Chabad emphasis on outreach. The answer was neither. The Rebbe's advice, as conveyed to me in the note typed by Rabbi Klein reproduced below was as follows:

> תלוי בההשערה–ע"ד יחס אלה שיבחנו עבודת ה Ph D
> שלה לדת וליהדות(שלא יהיו מנגדי–דת, שאז חשש שיפריעו
> לה וינגדו וכו').

My translation to English: "*It depends on what could be surmised about the attitude toward religion and Judaism of those who will be examining her Ph.D. work (that they should not be anti-religious, for then there would be some apprehension that they would disturb her and be opposed, and so forth).*" (Parentheses in the original; the Rebbe's answer was also phrased in the third person, in the formal European style of polite respect).

This response, I would say, was characteristic of the Rebbe. For as much as he was deeply immersed in the mystical traditions of chassidism and kabbalah, as much as he was forcefully engaged in a wide variety of campaigns to spread *Yiddishkeit* to every corner of the world, as idealistic he was about the "pure spark" in the soul of every Jew and about the ever-present potential of redemption, he was also very grounded, and pragmatic down to the last detail. The answer reflects an astute awareness of the politics of the university and of academic committees. It was very astute advice which I followed and which I now also give to my own graduate students: choose your academic advisor and dissertation committees very carefully. In the end I chose to pursue the topic of rabbinic interpretation and its relation to modern literary theory, which eventually became my first book, *The Slayers of Moses: The Emergence of Rabbinic Interpretation in Modern Literary Theory*.

The Rebbe Edits My Work

There were other very concrete and pragmatic ways in which the Rebbe assisted me in my writing and encouraged my academic work. One was connected to his active and intense interest in the activities of the Chabad Women's Organization, *Nshei Chabad*. One of the organs of this organization was a journal called *Di Yiddishe Heim*, "The Jewish Home." It is a small bilingual "in-house" magazine, half the articles written in Yiddish and half in English, and directed towards a lay audience of women of the Chabad community. When I came to study in Crown Heights in 1977 while a graduate student in English Literature, the feminist movement was in full swing. As a graduate of an Ivy League women's college at the forefront of the movement (Smith College, where my commencement address was given by Gloria Steinem), I was troubled by the issues feminism raised about the role of women in Judaism. As I learned more Chabad philosophy, I found very interesting talks and writings of the Rebbe and sources from previous rebbes which discussed the role of the "feminine." In order to help myself deal with these questions, I wrote an article based on these sources for *Di Yiddishe Heim* entitled, "The Jewish Woman: Three Steps Behind?"

Articles for the journal were written by both men and women, and the editor was a woman. I wrote the article and handed it in to her and she accepted it for publication. A short while afterwards, long before the article actually appeared in print, I wrote my first personal letter to the Rebbe to consult with him about something. After answering the personal issue he added the following words:

> נהנתי ממאמרה„בידישע – היים" הבע"ל,
> כן יצליחה ה' גם בשאר עניני'. "

Translation: "*I enjoyed her article in the forthcoming* Yiddishe Heim *and may G-d grant her success in all her other activities.*"

I was surprised, and did not know how the Rebbe would have known about the essay before it was published. So I asked the editor, who told me that although few people knew about it, after she had edited all the manuscripts, the Rebbe went over them again, editing them personally himself. And he took this time due to his great interest in the activities of women, and his desire to support and encourage them. I subsequently wrote several articles for this journal, many based on ideas from his published public talks and discourses, and as a favor to me and encouragement to write more, the editor gave my original manuscripts back to me with the Rebbe's corrections.

> Scientists, for example, have to deal with the "uncertainty principle", and the recognition that at a certain level of observation, the observer so interferes with his data that he can't attain any certain conclusions. Philosphers no longer attempt to explain the whys and hows of the universe, and restrict themselves mostly to analyzying language and logic--refusing to deal with "metaphysical"questions. Modern literature is extremely bleak, describing in painful detail the emptiness of the mind turning on itself, disconnected from the heart, and incapable of action.

In these corrections, one sees him relating with great care to the efforts of a young academic woman beginning to learn chassidic teaching and trying to relate it to current issues in philosophy, literature and politics. The extraordinary pains he took to read and edit my writing in English—including its typos, punctuation, and grammar as well as phraseology and ideas—astounded me and reminded me of the kind of the detailed, fatiguing reading and commenting I did for my own students when I taught intensive courses in English Composition. What follows are some representative examples from these manuscripts.

"One Sentence of Torah"

One essay I wrote was on "The Search for Truth—'Religion' and 'Secularism'" discussing the relationships among secular knowledge, Torah, and science—an issue with which I was concerned at the time. In the article, I wrote the following paragraph:

Scientists, for example, have had to deal with the "uncertainty principle" and the recognition that at a certain level of observation, the observer so interferes with his data that he can't attain any certain conclusions. Philosophers no longer attempt to explain the whys and hows of the universe, and restrict themselves mostly to analyzying language and logic—refusing to deal with "metaphysical" questions. Modern literature is extremely bleak, describing in painful detail the emptiness of the mind turning on itself, disconnected from the heart, and incapable of action. [Note: I must add here that this was written before the use of gender inclusive language became prevalent, so all the pronouns refer only to "he."]

The Rebbe edited this paragraph by

- deleting the extra words "so interferes with his data that he"
- changing "any certain conclusions" to "a certain conclusion"
- adding apostrophes to the phrase "why's and how's"
- correcting my typo in the word "analyzying" to "analyzing"
- changing the phrase "language and logic" to "events, phenomena etc."

In this essay, as well as others I wrote in an earlier time of more youthful extremism, he also qualified my large generalizations—as I often find myself now doing with the writing of my own students. Further on in the essay, I referred to a *sichah* ("talk") he gave about this subject[9] and I wrote:

...all secular sciences are limited and imperfect. They do not posses anything outside of themselves, or outside of reason—and furthermore, reason itself has its own inner limitations. Nevertheless, the Rebbe points out, it

[9] *Likkutei Sichot*, Vol. 4, (Brooklyn, N.Y.: Kehot), p. 1101.

is precisely these limitations that satisfy a person, because he can grasp the entire system and contain it. He feels the satisfaction of mastering a body of knowledge, and hence, secular knowledge leads to arrogance.

The Rebbe Shlite explains in a sicha (Likutei Sichos IV, p. 1101) that all secular sciences are limited and imperfect. They do not possess anything outside of themselves, or/of outside today's human reason--and, furthermore, reason itself has its own inner limitations. Nevertheless, the Rebbe points out, it is precisely these limitations that satisfy a person, because he can grasp the entire system and contain it. He feels the satisfaction of mastering a body of knowledge, and hence, secular knowledge very often leads to arrogance.

The opposite is the case with the study /of Torah, which is absolutely true, and contains all wisdom; it is unlimited, infinite, and contains no defects (ח"ו) whatsoever. Thus one can never contain all the content of even one Dvar (sentence of) Torah, master it. One a person always feels how far he is from grasping the whole of it and fathoming its infinite depth. Therefore, he doesn't become arrogant, but on the contrary--humble. And the more he learns, the humbler he becomes, and the greater is his thirst for learning Torah.

In this paragraph, the Rebbe,

- deleted the word "all" in the first line, so it then read instead "secular sciences are limited and imperfect"

- inserted the words "today's human" to the next line, which now read "or outside today's human reason"

- qualified my sweeping generalization in the last line by inserting the adverb "very often" to the phrase "secular knowledge leads to arrogance" to now read "secular knowledge very often leads to arrogance"

The essay continued with my writing in the next paragraph that the opposite was the case with the study of Torah, which is an unlimited, infinite wisdom:

Thus one can never contain Torah, master it. A person always feels how far he is from grasping the whole of it and fathoming its infinite depth. Therefore, he doesn't become arrogant, but on the contrary—humble. And the more he learns, the humbler he becomes, and the greater is his thirst for learning Torah.

The Rebbe here, in what is my most favorite revision of his, inserted the words "all the content of even one <u>Dvar</u> (sentence of)" in the first line. It then read: "Thus one can never contain all the content of even one <u>Dvar</u> (sentence of) Torah, master it." Yet he was indeed one of the masters of Torah in our generation. I remember attending his *farbrengens*"public gatherings the Rebbe would hold. The large synagogue in Brooklyn would be packed with a thousand or more people. If it were a weekday, he would start to speak at around 9:30 P.M. and often give several *sichot* or "talks," each lasting about forty minutes. Without a note, he would speak into the early hours of the morning, for five or more hours, citing liberally from memory and constructing innovative interpretations intricately woven from of the whole corpus of Jewish literature—Bible, midrash, Talmud, the classic commentaries, Kabbalah, Jewish law, chassidic philosophy.

There are also the many personal stories of scientists and mathematicians who corresponded with and spoke to the Rebbe about the technicalities of their work, and which he corrected as well. In the essay I wrote on Torah and science, I went on to paraphrase a well-known talk of his given on Parshat Noach 5738,[10] in which he speaks of the pre-eminent truth of Torah that "G-d is One" as also meaning the following:

Unity is more true than diversity; the real truth is the interdependence of all things into a unity, the Unity of

[10] *Likkutei Sichot*, Vol. 15, pp. 42-48.

G-d. The multiplicity of creation is no contradiction to the Unity of G-d; indeed this multiplicity comes from His Unity, as Chassidut explains at length.

The Rebbe has pointed out that science is approaching the same realization, so to speak. He explains that it was once thought that every natural force was an independent power, that the substance of every being was composed of many different elements. With the growth and progress of science, however, man is coming more and more to realize that this multiplicity and separation of elements is something external—merely the

> out that
> The Rebbe has pointed science is approaching the same realization, so to speak (<u>Likutei Sichos</u>, "Noach," 5738). He explains (ibid.) that it was once thought that every natural force was an independent power, that the substance of every being in the world was composed of many different elements. With the growth and progress of science, however, men are coming more and more to realize that this multiplicity and separation of elements is something external--merely the manner in which parts combine, the way they are broken down or expanded. Science has more and more reduced the number of essential elements until it has come to realize that the essence of the existence of the world consists in the <u>unification</u> of two apsects:"quality and quantity," or "energy and mass"; everything is a unity of these two aspects. What science does not yet realize or admit is that this unity is from G-d and is an aspect of His Unity.

manner in which parts combine, the way they are broken down or expanded. Science has more and reduced the number of essential elements until it has come to the realization that the essence of the existence of the world consists in the <u>unification</u> of two aspects: "quality and quantity," or "energy and mass"; everything is a unity of these two aspects. What science does not yet realize or admit is that this unity is from G-d and is an aspect of His unity.

His corrections to this paragraph were:

- to change the phrase "composed of many different elements" to "composed of essentially different elements"
- to delete the word "external" from the phrase "this multiplicity and separation of elements is something external"
- to insert the phrase "has made it it's goal to" to the beginning of the sentence, "Science has more and more reduced the number of..."
- to invert the word order of "more and more reduced" to "reduced more and more"
- to change the phrase "essential elements until" to "basic elements and forces until"
- to change the phrase "the <u>unification</u> of two aspects : 'quality and quantity'" to "the two ultimate aspects: quality and quantity"
- to qualify my sweeping generalization, "What science does not yet realize" to "What some scientists do not yet realize"

Women's Unique Powers of Eliciting Holiness

There was a case, however, in which the Rebbe intensified a large generalization I had made, one specifically about Jewish women.

In another essay I wrote entitled, "Judaism and Feminism: Our G-d and the G-d of Our Mothers," I explicated some of his writings on the nature of feminine spiritual power in the light of chassidism and kabbalah. The focus, in particular, was on the relation of the two *sefirot* (the divine attributes in kabbalistic thought which also are the superstructure of the world) *chochmah* and *binah*, "wisdom" and "understanding." These are also called "Father" and "Mother," and he discussed their relation to the "Fathers" and "Mothers," i. e. the Patriarchs and Matriarchs of Israel, and the powers they bequeathed to the Jewish people. To summarize briefly: in commenting on the parshah (Torah reading) of *Chayei Sarah* (Gen. 23-25:18),[11] the Rebbe discussed the quality of *binah*, and the ability of the feminine "attributes" to more closely affect the physical world and bring what is actual out of what is potential—both in the kabbalistic schema, and on the parallel psychological-physical plane of our mundane world of male and female.

In the essay, I prefaced the idea by explaining a foundational notion in chassidic thought, and wrote that before the giving of the Torah at Mount Sinai, the physical and spiritual "realms had been separated from each other and not connected." To this sentence, the Rebbe inserted the adverb "perfectly"—"had not been perfectly connected." He had further elaborated the idea in the *sichah* that the mitzvot performed by the Patriarchs and Matriarchs who lived in the pre-Sinaitic era helped prepare the way for the stronger, more perfect connection that would occur later, but their mitzvot could not affect the physical world as strongly as those we perform after the giving of the Torah.

Here he had made a very interesting distinction between the kinds of *kedushah*, "holiness," the Patriarchs and the Matriarchs respectively brought into the world. The Matriarchs of Israel brought a different kind of *kedushah* into the world than did the Patriarchs, he maintained. The Patriarchs could draw into the world a "holiness" that would remain in the physical object after the mitzvah they performed was fulfilled—but *only* in that part of the physical which had a connection to the Patriarchs themselves. For example, the mitzvah of circumcision which Abraham was commanded, drew *kedushah* into the body that fulfilled the *mitzvah* but not into the world outside. However, through Sarah, the first Matriarch, *kedushah* was drawn into a part of the world *outside of her*, and this power she bequeathed to all Jewish women. (For a further analysis of how and why this is so, see the original *sichah).*

In another *sichah,*[12] the Rebbe wrote of another distinctive trait Jewish women possess more than men, which is indicated by G-d's giving of Rosh Chodesh (the first day or days of the Jewish month) as a special holiday to Jewish women in all generations and into the World-To-Come as a reward for their not participating in the sin of the Golden Calf. The Rebbe describes this special female attribute as a certain unshakeable attachment to and deep faith in G-d that helped the Jewish women in the desert resist the trials to which the Jewish men succumbed. Although this feeling of pure faith is rooted in the heart of every Jew, male and female, he adds, it can become covered over or concealed due to various difficulties, and its effect on daily life and behavior no longer be visible. Jewish women, he asserts, have however a special strength in not permitting concealment of this feeling, and its effects on behavior. As I summed up these ideas in my essay, I wrote:

The Rebbe points out that the reason why this great reward is given to all Jewish women in all times, till the coming of the Messiah and after (and not just to the women of that one generation [who left Egypt and contended with the Golden Calf]*) is because the power to withstand such a great test which even the men could not endure comes from an innate superior trait that all Jewish women in all ages possess.*

In the original version, I myself had twice underlined the word "all" in the first line, but not in the last part of the sentence where this adjective is used again. Here, however, the Rebbe intensified my generalization by underlining once again the last two uses of the word "all": all Jewish women in all ages. And then once more again later on in the essay, where I summed up and wrote, "Every Jewish woman, in every time and every place, has inherited the special powers of the matriarchs," he underlined the first word "Every."

"There Must Also Be A Girl In The Picture"

Around 1980, the Rebbe initiated a campaign to encourage children to take more part in the overall public activities and initiatives of Chabad, and become part of *Tzivos HaShem*, "The Troops of G-d." Many pamphlets were produced for this campaign, and the chassidim who were in charge of it founded a journal for children called *The Moshiach Times*. Several highly interesting editorial comments and corrections to

[11] *Likkutei Sichot*, Vol. 5, pp. 336-353.

[12] *Likkutei Sichot*, Vol. 8, pp. 317-319.

this magazine were also made by the Rebbe. One of the later staffers of the journal, Dr. David Sholom Pape, compiled a series of these.[13] He relates that on the cover of the very first issue there was a drawing of two rows of children—one of boys and above it another of girls, each child carrying a banner with a letter on it , which all together spelled the words *Ahavat Yisrael*, "Love of a fellow Jew" (figure 1).

35 cents
The Moshiach Times
VOL. I NO. I SHEVAT, 5741 JAN. 1981
ואהבת לרעך כמוך
אהבת
ישראל
LOVE YOUR FELLOW JEW AS YOURSELF!

Figure 1

One of the older chassidim on the staff balked and wondered if it was "modest and *chassidish* for boys and girls to be on the same cover." The younger members of the staff argued that since it was a magazine for both boys and girls, it was indeed appropriate. To resolve the dispute, the cover was sent to the Rebbe for his instructions on the matter. The Rebbe, however, did not instruct the staff to remove the girls from the cover.

The matter arose again when the second issue was prepared for Purim, and the cover had a boy and girl in Purim costumes, dressed as Mordechai and Esther blowing bubbles in which were images of the mitzvot of Purim (figure 2). Again objections were raised that such an image of a boy and girl playing together in proximity was against chassidic ethics; the previous cover had had the boys and girls separated in row, but now the boy and girl were next to each other! The cover was again sent to the Rebbe, who simply returned it with a check indicating it was fine to print.

Figure 2

The third issue was designed for Passover and had a cover sketch of a boy looking into a stamp album, each stamp depicting one of the fifteen steps of the Passover seder. The angle of the drawing and size of boy's head and the album left no room for an image

[13] Dr. Pape printed them in the *Souvenir Journal: Celebrating the Wedding of Bentzion and Rochie Pape 30 Adar 1, 5760*—a private illustrated gift volume distributed at the wedding of his son. I am grateful to R. Shlomo Gestetner of the Maayanot Institute in Jerusalem for locating this source for me.

of a girl as well. Since the other two covers had been sent in, this cover was also sent to the Rebbe for approval and the answer came back:

Tzarikh lihiot gam na'arah—"There also needs to be a girl."

The artist redrew and redesigned the cover to add the head of a girl on the left side and the boy on the right side (figure 3), and by then a custom had been established to send the covers in to the Rebbe for all the issues.

Figure 3

A few years afterwards in 1984, a cover was prepared by a well-known cartoonist for the Elul issue, portraying a boy returning home from summer camp to his room, carrying his sports equipment. The room is portrayed as filled with holy objects, equipment for a soldier in the *Tzivos HaShem*— *chumash, siddur,* charity box, and so forth, and he is wearing a *kippah* and *tzitzit*. The cover was sent into the Rebbe who returned it with two comments: "The *tzitzit* should be seen" and "There must also be a girl in another corner."

Figure 4: First draft of cover (left) and actual cover drawn after the Rebbe remarked, "There must also be a girl in another corner"

I conclude with these stories since I think this directive, "there must also be a girl in the picture" summarizes what I have been saying throughout. On the broadest theological-metaphysical level, the emergence of the aspect of the "feminine," of *malchut*, was also the deepest question of Redemption. And the Rebbe connected the most abstract speculations and concepts in kabbalah and chassidism to the most practical and detailed endeavors in daily life.

I think this stance was also related to how he saw himself in the role of the seventh Lubavitcher Rebbe. His mission was to continue and expand all the work of the previous rebbes, but especially that of his father-in-law, the sixth Lubavitcher Rebbe, Rabbi Yosef Yitzchak Schneerson—to widely diffuse, develop and bring the latter's work completely into concrete reality. There is a Chabad chassidic idea that each of the seven Rebbes paralleled a different *sefirah*. In this schema, the sixth rebbe, Rabbi Yosef Yitzchak , paralleled the *sefirah* of *yesod*, and Rabbi Menachem Mendel, the seventh, was *malchut*—the last *sefirah* in the kabbalistic schema which is on the "feminine" side of the *sefirot*. Malchut, the last *sefirah*, receives and channels all flow from the preceding configurations of *sefirot*, and connects and implements them in the physical world. It is also called "sovereignty" or "kingship" as defined by the notion of a king whose power only comes by virtue of the people, and whose life is given over to serve the people, and implement physical action in the world.

The Rebbe would often vigorously end his public discourses with the words *"u-lematah me-assarah tefachim, b'karov mamash!"* ("Below ten handbreadths, soon and really!"). In other words, to bring all the wishes for good for the Jewish people, for redemption, for *tikkun* of the world—to bring this all down from abstract concepts and spiritual ideas to "below ten handbreadths." "Ten handbreadths" is the halachic measurement for a "private domain" on Shabbat, but more to the point, a reference to the rabbinic saying that "the *shechinah* (divine presence) never descended below ten handbreadths."[14] In other words, bring this all completely down to earth, to the ground, to our collective and individual literal, historical, physical, daily, mundane existence. And this, too, I believe, is what he tried to do in putting women "into the picture" of Jewish life, not just in theory, but pragmatically and actually—"soon and really"!

Bread and Fire: Jewish Women find God in the Everyday [Jerusalem: Urim Publications, 2008], pp. 343–356

Forthcoming in *The Chabad Movement in the Twentieth Century* [Ramat-Gan: Bar-Ilan University Press]

Reprinted with permission of the author

A SINGLE CANDLE

PRIME MINISTER BENJAMIN NETANYAHU

The following is an excerpt from Prime Minister Benjamin Netanyahu's speech at the United Nations General Assembly, Sept. 23, 2011.

Ladies and gentlemen, Israel has extended its hand in peace from the moment it was established 63 years ago. On behalf of Israel and the Jewish people, I extend that hand again today. I extend it to the people of Egypt and Jordan, with renewed friendship for neighbors with whom we have made peace. I extend it to the people of Turkey, with respect and good will. I extend it to the people of Libya and Tunisia, with admiration for those trying to build a democratic future. I extend it to the other peoples of North Africa and the Arabian Peninsula, with whom we want to forge a new beginning. I extend it to the people of Syria, Lebanon and Iran, with awe at the courage of those fighting brutal repression.

But most especially, I extend my hand to the Palestinian people, with whom we seek a just and lasting peace.

Ladies and gentlemen, in Israel our hope for peace never wanes. Our scientists, doctors, innovators, apply their genius to improve the world of tomorrow. Our artists, our writers, enrich the heritage of humanity. Now, I know that this is not exactly the image of Israel that is often portrayed in this hall. After all, it was here in 1975 that the age-old yearning of my people to restore our national life in our ancient biblical homeland—it was then that this was braided—branded, rather—shamefully, as racism. And it was here in 1980, right here, that the historic peace agreement between Israel and Egypt wasn't praised; it was denounced! And it's here year after year that Israel is unjustly singled out for condemnation. It's singled out for condemnation more often than all the nations of the world combined. Twenty-one out of the 27 General Assembly resolutions condemn Israel—the one true democracy in the Middle East.

Well, this is an unfortunate part of the UN institution. It's the—the theater of the absurd. It doesn't only cast Israel as the villain; it often casts real villains in leading roles: Gadhafi's Libya chaired the UN Commission on Human Rights; Saddam's Iraq headed the UN Committee on Disarmament.

You might say: That's the past. Well, here's what's happening now—right now, today. Hezbollah-controlled Lebanon now presides over the UN Security Council. This means, in effect, that a terror organization presides over the body entrusted with guaranteeing the world's security.

You couldn't make this thing up.

[14] Talmud, *Sukkah* 5a.

So, here in the UN, automatic majorities can decide anything. They can decide that the sun sets in the west or rises in the west. I think the first has already been pre-ordained. But they can also decide—they have decided that the Western Wall in Jerusalem, Judaism's holiest place, is occupied Palestinian territory.

And yet even here in the General Assembly, the truth can sometimes break through. In 1984 when I was appointed Israel's ambassador to the United Nations, I visited the great Rabbi of Lubavich. He said to me—and ladies and gentlemen, I don't want any of you to be offended because from personal experience of serving here, I know there are many honorable men and women, many capable and decent people serving their nations here. But here's what the Rebbe said to me. He said to me, you'll be serving in a house of many lies. And then he said, remember that even in the darkest place, the light of a single candle can be seen far and wide.

Today I hope that the light of truth will shine, if only for a few minutes, in a hall that for too long has been a place of darkness for my country. So as Israel's prime minister, I didn't come here to win applause. I came here to speak the truth....

JEWISH GREATNESS

PROFESSOR ELIE WEISEL

Some of you are aware of my admiration, not only for the Rebbe, but also for his education and work. The fact that he knew whom to send where, to G-d-forsaken places, simply to bring a word of faith and the word of the Law to youngsters who otherwise would have been lost, is to me probably one of the elements that give hope to a generation.

As a Hasid I can tell you a Hasidic story tonight. It's about a very great hasidic master called Reb Naftoli of Ropshitz. He was a great speaker, endowed with a superb sense of humor. One Shabbat HaGadol, he came home from the synagogue. Customarily, the rabbi of the town must deliver a speech on that Sabbath about charity, about the need to help poor people who don't have enough money to celebrate the Seder.

When he came home, his wife asked him, "Nu, how was it?" He said it was okay. "Well did you accomplish anything?" He said, "Only half." She said, "What do you mean?" He said, "I managed to convince the poor to receive."

The Rebbe manages to convince the rich to give and the teachers to teach, and the students to study. The Rebbe manages to do things that normal human beings wouldn't even dare to dream of undertaking....

How does one measure greatness? I mean, what criteria does one use in evaluating human greatness? In the case of the Lubavitcher Rebbe, the answer is easily obtained. I know of no one who has left the Rebbe, even after a moment of *yehidut* (one-on-one meeting), without being deeply affected, if not changed, by their encounter.

I hope I will always remember what I felt when I was first introduced into his study, some thirty years ago, and what we said to one another. Time in his presence begins running at a different pace. You feel inspired, you feel self-examined, you are made to wonder about the quest for meaning which ought to be yours. In his presence nothing is superficial, nor is it artificial. In his presence you come closer in touch with your inner center of gravity.

But what is great about the Rebbe is that not only those who have met him are affected, but even those who haven't. Somehow the presence of the man in our midst sends out an emanation of mystical quality that touches people who have never heard of him, and this, probably more than anything else, is what makes the Rebbe so unique.

It is due to his influence, to his presence, that Jewish awareness and Jewish education have reached unprecedented heights on almost every continent. Is there a place under the sun where the Chabad emissaries have not carried his word of tolerance rooted in Ahavas Yisroel, in the love for Israel, which really, by extension, means love for humanity? Wherever Jews dwell and work, they somehow become exposed to the Rebbe.

Thanks to him, a Jew, anywhere and everywhere, cannot but feel that he or she belongs to an ancient people whose tradition emphasizes the greatness of its task more than the prerogatives of its condition. Thanks to the Rebbe, a Jew becomes a better Jew, thus a better human being, thus making his fellow human beings more human, more hospitable, open to a greater sense of generosity. So this is where the Rebbe's greatness also lies.

Now some of us were lucky and we heard his lessons; we joined him in study, in song. We have seen him with his disciples, we have witnessed his accomplishments. Therefore, I feel, with a deep sense of devotion, affection and admiration, that we should lift our glasses to say "L'Chaim" to this generation's *Admor* (master, teacher and rabbi), whose life and work have been a blessing to so many of us, indeed to all of Israel and the world.

So, to the Rebbe in Brooklyn, what could we say except, we are your disciples, we are your followers because like you, and with you, we believe in study, we believe in prayer. We believe in prayer as a link between one human being and the other. We believe in study as a link between one generation and the other. And we believe in an added measure of solidarity that must always be present in whatever we do for ourselves, for our people, and for each other...

Excerpted from an address given by Nobel-laureate Elie Wiesel on April 7, 1992, at a congressional dinner held in Washington on the occasion of the Rebbe's 90th birthday

THE REBBE'S INSPIRING CHARGE

RABBI LORD JONATHAN SACKS

Throughout Jewish history there were great leaders, but I know of no precedent for one who transformed, visibly and substantively every single Jewish community in the world—including many parts of the world that never had a Jewish community before.

And let me tell you a little story that sums it up:

It happened forty one years ago, Elaine and I were on our honeymoon. We decided to go to the Swiss Alps—I had never been to mountains before. We went, we arrived. It was brilliant sunshine. The view was magnificent.

The next morning I opened the window and said, "Who moved the mountains? They're gone!" Then I looked again and I saw they were covered in very long clouds. What to do? We'd come all this way to climb a mountain, and we couldn't go back without climbing a mountain. But we couldn't see more than two or three feet in any direction. We didn't know where we were going, we didn't know how, [if] we got wherever we got, we'd get back.

So I said to Elaine, "It is very simple. We will sing Chabad niggunim."

She said, "Why are we singing Chabad niggunim?"

I said, "Very simple. Because if a Jew is lost, anywhere in the world, Chabad will find them."

And all of this, because of the Rebbe, [Rabbi Menachem Mendel Schneerson,]zechusoh yagen aleinu [of righteous memory]. So it was, and so it is....

Friends, Rabbi Kotlarsky asked me to tell you a little story, a personal one, of how the Rebbe changed my life. And I've agreed, not because I think my story is special, it isn't. But it is by telling such stories that we remind ourselves of what Chabad is about and what makes it special.

It is a story in three acts; the first took place in 1968, when I was a second year student, a sophomore, at university. I had already encountered Chabad, because Rabbi Shmuel Lew and Rabbi Faivish Vogel visited Cambridge. They were among the very first to go out to university campuses and I was one of the very first beneficiaries. They came that summer, '68 and I came to America to meet great rabbis of the day, and every one of them, every single rov [rabbinical leader] I met in America said, "You must see the Rebbe! You must see the Rebbe."

So I went to Eastern Parkway, 770, I came in; I said to the first Chassid I met, "I'd like to speak to the Rebbe, please." He fell about laughing.

He said, "Do you know how many thousands of people are waiting to see the Rebbe? Forget it!"

I said, "Well, I'll be traveling around America, here is the phone number of my aunt in Los Angeles, if it's possible phone me."

Weeks later, I was in Los Angeles, came motzoei Shabbat, the phone went, it was Chabad, "The Rebbe will see you on Thursday."

I had no money in those days, and all I had was a Greyhound bus ticket, if you've ever ridden from Los Angeles to New York on a Greyhound bus… Seventy two hours nonstop I sat on this bus.

I came to 770, and eventually the moment came when I was ushered into the Rebbe's study. I asked him all my intellectual, philosophical questions; he gave intellectual, philosophical answers, and then he did what no one else had done.

He did a role reversal, he started asking me questions. How many Jewish students are in Cambridge? How many get involved in Jewish life? What are you doing to bring other people in?

Now, I hadn't come to become a Shliach [Chabad-Lubavitch emissary]. I'd come to ask a few simple questions, and all of a sudden he was challenging me. So I did the English thing. You know, the English can construct sentences like nobody else, you know? They can construct more complex excuses for doing nothing, than anyone else on earth. (laughter)

So I started the sentence, "In the situation in which I find myself..." —and the Rebbe did something which I think was quite unusual for him, he actually stopped me in mid-sentence. He says, "Nobody finds themselves in a situation; you put yourself in a situation. And if you put yourself in that situation, you can put yourself in another situation."

That moment changed my life.

Here I was, a nobody from nowhere, and here was one of the greatest leaders in the Jewish world challenging me not to accept the situation, but to change it. And that was when I realized what I have said many times since: That the world was wrong. When they thought that the most important fact about the Rebbe was that here was a man with thousands of followers, they missed the most important fact: That a good leader creates followers, but a great leader creates leaders.

That's what the Rebbe did for me and for thousands of others.

Friends, that particular episode had an unusual ending: I was due to leave the States, go back to England, on my charter flight on a Sunday at the end of August, beginning of September, I can't remember exactly when. So the day before, on Shabbos, there was a big farbreng[en], and the Chassidim told me, "You're going back to England? Take a bottle of vodka, go up to the Rebbe in a niggun, during the farbrengen, and he'll zog a le'chaim, and you'll take it with you and that'll be the Rebbe's vodka."

So in the middle of the farbrengen, thousands of people there, I went up to the Rebbe and asked him to say a le'chaim, and he looked at me with surprise. He said, "You're going?"

I said, "Yes."

He said, "Why?"

I said, "I have to get back to Cambridge, the term is beginning."

He turned to me and he said, "But the Cambridge term does not begin until October."

I never knew then, I still don't know today how he knew it, but he was right! He said to me, "I think you should stay for Rosh Hashanah." So he said a le'chaim; I went back.

Everyone around me wanted to know, "What did the Rebbe say to you? What did the Rebbe say?" So I told them what the Rebbe said. I didn't know—if the Rebbe says stay, it's the polite thing, you say thank you very much—I didn't realize; if the Rebbe said stay, you stay. So I stayed.

As a result of which, I heard the Rebbe on Rosh Hashanah blow shofar. Quite the most remarkable experience I ever had. The purity of those notes, the sight of all the Chassidim hanging from every surface, trying to catch sight of the Rebbe blowing shofar. And I heard a sound in which heaven and earth touched. And the echoes of that shofar have stayed with me ever since. That was the challenge he threw down. A challenge to lead.

That didn't immediately change my life. I went back to University, although I still felt the power of the Rebbe's challenge. So in 1969 after getting my degree, I went to study in Kfar Chabad, where I learned with Rav Gafni, and it was a wonderful experience. In 1970 I came back, got married, started teaching philosophy, writing a doctorate, but I still felt I hadn't done enough to meet the Rebbe's challenge. So I studied for smicha. I qualified as a rabbi, and I thought that's it. I've grown a little as a Jew, and now I'm ready to get back with the rest of my life.

That was when I made the second great mistake—I went back to see the Rebbe again. (laughter)

January 1978: My friends in Lubavitch told me exactly what to do. You put your question in writing, you give the Rebbe options; one, two, three, and the Rebbe will tell you, the one or two or three. So I set out my options. I said to the Rebbe, "I have a career in front of me, I have three choices." Number one, maybe I would like to be an academic—halevai one day I would be a professor or maybe a fellow of my college in Cambridge. Or number two—I went to university initially to study economics—I'd like to be an economist. Or number three, I'd like to be a barrister, an advocate. I was a member of one of the Inns of Court, the Inner Temple where you study to be a lawyer.

I went in to the yechidus [private audience] not knowing what the Rebbe would answer, would it be one, would it be two, would it be three? The Rebbe looked at me and he went through the list; not one, not two, not three.

I thought, "Hang on, this is against the rules!"

The Rebbe did not give me time to reply. He told me Anglo Jewry was short of rabbis, and therefore he said to me, "You must train rabbis." He specified Jews College, where rabbis were trained in Britain. And then he said, you yourself must become a congregational Rabbi, so that your students will come and they will hear you give—I still remember the way he pronounced the word—"sermons." They will hear you give sermons and they will learn. He said you say you will train rabbis and you will become a rabbi. Well, I was a little *farblonged*—a word I've introduced into the English language courtesy of the BBC—but if the Rebbe says do it, I did it. I gave up my three ambitions, I trained rabbis, I taught in Jews College, eventually I became head of Jews College, and I became a congregational rabbi, in Golders Green and Marble Arch.

You know, a funny thing happened.

Having given up all my three ambitions, having decided to walk in the complete opposite direction, a funny thing happened. I did become a fellow of my college in Cambridge. I did become a professor. In fact, this year I have three professorships; one in Oxford University, two in London University. I did deliver Britain's top two economics lectures, the Mais lecture and the Hayek lecture, and Inner Temple made me an honorary barrister and invited me to give a law lecture in front of six hundred barristers, the Lord Chancellor—the highest lawyer in Britain, and Princess Anne who's the Master.

You know, you never lose anything—by putting yiddishkeit first.

And I learned something very deep: Sometimes the best way of achieving your ambitions is to stop pursuing them, and let them pursue you.

And that was act two. Act three was in 1990. Anglo Jewry was looking for a new Chief Rabbi. It was clear that I was going to be one of the candidates. But I wasn't sure that I was right for the job or the job was right for me. And so, I sat down with my family, with Elaine, with my children, and they agreed to permit me to write to the Rebbe and ask his advice.

I set out the tzdodim lekan u'lekan—the pros and cons of the job, and the Rebbe wrote a most extraordinary reply, a brilliant reply, without using a single word.

You know that the Rebbe, before he was Rebbe, ran the Chabad publishing house—Kehot—and as a result he knew—I've written twenty four books and I don't know these things yet, but he knew the typographical symbols that are used by proofreaders. So towards the end of the letter having set out the pros and cons, I wrote the sentence, "If they offer me the job, should I accept?" This was the Rebbe's reply: The typographical symbol for reverse word order. Instead of saying, "Should I?" The answer is, "I should."

So, thirteen years to the day after I became a congregational rabbi I became Chief Rabbi, and in that job I have tried to the best of my ability—if I succeeded I don't know—but I tried to do what I know the Rebbe would have wanted me to do: To build schools, to improve Anglo Jewish education, to reach out, and to make—not followers—but leaders....

Think about this—the Rebbe, like every Rebbe, set it his goal to mekarev the geula and to bring Moshiach. But the Rebbe was different from other Rebbeim, because the Rebbe did so with particular urgency, and although he never specified why, I've speculated on this, and I thought this—maybe I'm wrong, but I think not—because he was the first Rebbe to become Rebbe after the Holocaust.

And how can you redeem a world that had witnessed Hitler? And the Rebbe did something absolutely extraordinary; he said to himself: if the Nazis searched out every Jew in hate, we will search out every Jew in love.

This was the most radical response to the Holocaust ever conceived and I don't know if we still —if the Jewish world still—understands it. . . .

Friends, forty two years ago, one of the great Jewish leaders of all time, took an unknown student from thousands of miles away, and lit a light in his soul that has burned from that day to this, and he did it not just for him, but for ten thousands of thousands of others. And we are his Shluchim.

We will never manage to do it fully, but we will do our best to walk as he walked, eat as he ate, shluft as he shluft, which was pretty nearly never.

And you know, you know what I know, and this, in the silence of our souls we can hear what the Rebbe would be saying to us now. He would be saying, "You think you've done enough? You must be as a light is on Chanukah, mosif veholech—always doing more. Mailin bakodesh, v'ein moreidin—in kedushah, you always climb, and there is always more of the mountain to climb."

And he would be saying to us: number one, live, breath, and sleep ahavas yisroel; number two, become leaders who turn other Jews into leaders; and number three, be madlik mener le'ner, take your light and make light others. And together, let us light a flame in the hearts of other Jews, and together let us light up the world. Amen.

Excerpted from an address given at the 2011 gala banquet of the International Conference of Chabad-Lubavitch Shluchim

MARCHING ORDERS

RABBI ADIN EVEN-ISRAEL STEINSALTZ

"On the day that our father Abraham passed away, all the great men of the nations stood in a row and eulogized him."[1] The moment memorialized forever in this Talmud text bears a striking similarity to the aftermath of the passing of the Lubavitcher Rebbe. In considering both Abraham and the Rebbe, the difference is not so very large. After Abraham passed away, the great people of all the nations felt that something terrible had happened, and they came to deliver eulogies. They said, "Woe to the world that lost its leader. Woe to the ship that lost its captain." And as well as having lost its leader, Chabad, too, has lost its captain.

There is a difference in nuance between losing a leader and losing a captain. A leader is necessary, important, helpful. A world without a leader is a confused place. The people are waiting for someone to make decisions, to take the lead. However, it is worse when a ship loses its captain. A ship at sea is not anchored to something stable. The people on board cannot sit and wait. The captain has to steer while, with every passing minute, conditions are changing. He has to navigate constantly, holding or correcting the course of the ship. The ship does not go by itself to its destination, so who, without the captain, will set that course and maintain it? Who will tell the sailors to slow or to increase speed, to change course whatever degree to starboard or to port? Who will decipher the stars? Who will know what lies beyond, and be able to show the sailors the way?

We may think of the famous Walt Whitman poem about Abraham Lincoln: "O Captain, My Captain." But for Chabad the situation has been more perilous; the Rebbe's ship has not reached port. It has not come to rest at the end of its intended course. While in the middle of the sea, it lost its captain. So what is the crew to do? What do people do in such a time? In this case, fortunately, the captain did set the intended *course* toward a destination. He prepared the charts. He showed the way. The crew has only to plot their progress along those lines, trying to stay the course until the journey is completed.

It may be best to think that the Rebbe did not leave a legacy. Instead, he left marching orders—an entirely different concept. He did not leave just a revered memory and a collection of books, videos and speeches. Of far greater value, he left a task to be completed. The Rebbe led the Chabad movement for more than forty years. His message became far clearer, far more prominent, with every passing year. That message: Prepare, do the work, because the Mashiach is coming. He also left the guidance that will enable those who follow to carry out that task.

It seems to many of us that we do not live in hopeful times. In the past century, we have seen power and force displayed as blatantly as a naked iron fist. At no other time were so many people killed, all over the world, for so many obscenely wrong reasons. And still, the Rebbe was saying that he *saw* the coast lying ahead. Israel's former president Zalman Shazar told me that once—while he was in the midst of a mundane conversation with the Rebbe—the Rebbe suddenly said, "You see, just as I know by my watch that you will be leaving in half an hour, so I know that the Mashiach is coming." The Rebbe warned that we may see terrible waves on the way—and there is indeed a terrible storm. The winds are blowing relentlessly. And yet he saw that the coast is close by, that the Mashiach is coming. Just now.

Now? Many have spoken about the Rebbe as a saintly person. His saintliness was apparent not only from time to time: it was his very essence. People also spoke about, and will speak about, the Rebbe as one of the great Judaic scholars of the time, perhaps the greatest. His grasp of technology was strong as well, and his knowledge of events unfolding throughout the world even stronger. He himself had lived through some of the most momentous upheavals in living memory. Knowing the world and its myriad troubles, how is it at all possible that he could insist that the Mashiach is coming soon? How could he even speak about it?

1 Bava Batra 91a.

And yet the Rebbe repeated that one central thought of his again and again in his last years. Sometimes he couched it as an order, sometimes as a request. He would say, "Open your eyes." Open your eyes and see. We see the power in the world and we are overwhelmed by it. Yet... what is that power, really? It stands on feet of clay. The smallest push may topple it. The Rebbe was seeing into the fog of the future. He was one of the first to predict that that mighty power addicted to brutal force, the Soviet Union, would collapse. It did not collapse under a rain of atomic bombs; it collapsed because it had feet of clay.

In telling people to open their eyes and see the world as it really is, the Rebbe had in mind a much grander—yet more subtle and sensitive—message. It was not so much about structures of power as it was about structures of *life*. In essence he said: So you think this is a world in which people are interested in only sex or money? You are mistaken. What they really want is a little bit of love. Those who seem to be striving only for power and for possessions are really striving for comfort and to hear a good word. When we open our eyes and see through the fog, beneath the husks—this harsh, Hobbesian exterior—we can understand that people are not as they appear to be. It is the end of those ages of ideologies, so many of which have already faded away. It is even the end of the ages in which people thought that power or money could solve all problems. It is a time in which many, in their inner hearts, have already prepared for faith. We have only to open our eyes and see how life is developing, how faith is unfolding.

The Rebbe's message was not only for Jews. He said the same thing to humanity in general. The Rebbe spoke about the Children of Noah, all humankind. He turned to all the peoples of the world to say: You can become free. You just have to allow yourself to do it. You can be better. It is not as arduous as climbing a big mountain. It is just allowing your soul to speak. Which, then, is the real folly, and which is the more realistic: a dream of the worldly triumph of some ideology driven by brute force? Or the age of Mashiach, the reign of the spirit?

That is why the Rebbe would say, "Open your eyes." Open your eyes inwardly, but open your eyes to the world as well, so that you can relay the supreme secret: we all have to change. The Rebbe conveys this truth to the simplest of the simple, to the most ignorant, and also to the most erudite: you may be whoever you are, but you can be better. And—almost unbelievably—when you do begin to change, you will find with growing confidence that you can do it.

When the *tzaddik* passes away, his presence is felt far more widely than when he lived in this world. He sees all these things, and believes in all these things. He knows that even though a captain may no longer be at the helm, those left on board can do it, should do it, and shall do it: just sail a little farther on the proper course... and arrive at port.

My Rebbe [Jerusalem: Maggid Books, 2014], pp. 191–194

Reprinted with permission of Maggid Books, a division of Koren Publishers Jerusalem

THE PARTICULAR PATH OF THE SEVENTH REBBE

RABBI ADIN EVEN-ISRAEL STEINSALTZ

In a famous Jewish story, a man once came to a rabbi and complained that his wife, his children and his mother-in-law were all stuffed into a small apartment. He was practically suffocating. The man also mentioned that he had a goat. The rabbi said, "Bring the goat into your apartment." The man did as he was told—but the goat took up room and also smelled bad.

The man returned to the rabbi and complained again. The situation was worse and they were more crowded than ever. The rabbi then said, "Take the goat out." A few days later, the man returned and reported, "Now we have some space."

When Chasidim complained to the Rebbe that they were overworked, he said in effect "bring the goat in," that is, take upon yourself another responsibility. Yet unlike the story, the Rebbe never told his Chasidim to take the goat out. The complaints were irrelevant to the Rebbe, who would always demand an increasing workload. Reducing complaints was not the point; the point was to accomplish more. Eventually, there were more than ten mitzva campaigns, Chabad outreach operations. The Rebbe never ended any of them; he just added new ones. Similarly, the Rebbe would add new subjects to the Chasidim's daily study schedule. None ever ended; new ones were always added.

In my last letter to the Rebbe, I told him I was holding down three full time jobs: scholarly writing, outreach work in Russia, and a network of schools in Israel. Since it all seemed like too much for one person, I asked him what to focus on. His answer was typical of him, that I should "continue to do all these things and to do more things and work even harder."

When someone does "more and more"—as the Rebbe would say—we worry that he is being stretched too thin. In our daily routines, we seem to be at the limits of the human condition. However, the Rebbe believed that by doing more, we could change the very nature of reality. The science of physics has such a law: when one applies massive amounts of pressure to an object, the molecules collapse and the very nature of the object changes. The white dwarves of astronomy are small stars, the size of the earth, sometimes even smaller. The mass they contain is many times that of the sun. Each cubic centimeter weighs many tons. Matter has collapsed and become something else; the laws of nature themselves changed.

In a way, this was what the Rebbe wanted to do. He wanted to change the very nature of human matter, human behavior, the very way the human being operates. With everybody he encountered, he tried to change their nature into something completely different. They weren't people anymore, they became something else.

There could never be enough, because the Rebbe believed that there are no theoretical ideas in Judaism. Every verse in the Torah, every idea in the Talmud and every word in the chasidic teachings was an instruction for the Rebbe. Everything had to be applied.

It seemed as if the Rebbe was measuring everyone else on his own scale. Even the rebbetzin was heard saying to herself, as she listened to the Rebbe's *farbrengens* via telephone: "He thinks everyone cares about Mashiach as much as he does," and, "He thinks everyone is as close to God as he is."[1] What he expected of himself, he expected of his Chasidim: to make the utmost effort to the best of their abilities, and to carry out his directions.

The Rebbe was focused on the idea that one should never be satisfied. While he had a calm temperament, his plans drove him further and faster. He needed his Chasidim to keep up with him in order to fulfill his dreams.

Rabbi Herbert Weiner, who led Temple Israel in South Orange, New Jersey, wrote a number of articles about the Rebbe for *Commentary* magazine. They were very friendly and Rabbi Weiner interviewed him more than once; he and I would often exchange notes. Rabbi Weiner once asked the Rebbe how he could give orders to his Chasidim and expect them to be followed. The Rebbe replied: "I never tell a person to do what I think he is neither willing nor able to do."[2] The Rebbe was saying that he never demanded the impossible. While it might seem that his requests were far beyond his Chasidim's abilities, he actually took their capabilities and limitations into account. The Rebbe only asked of them the nearly impossible, which he believed they were capable of fulfilling.

My Rebbe [Jerusalem: Maggid Books, 2014], pp. 73–75

[1] From the memoirs of the assistants at the Rebbe's house.

[2] Personal conversation.

THE REBBE'S IMMENSE SPIRITUAL MISSION

RABBI ADIN EVEN-ISRAEL STEINSALTZ

From childhood, the Rebbe had dreams about the coming of the Mashiach. In a letter to Israel's second president, Yitchak Ben-Zvi, the Rebbe wrote: "From the day I went to *cheder* [religious primary school] and even before, the picture of the final redemption started forming in my mind—the redemption of the Jews from their last exile, a redemption in such a way that through it will be understood the sufferings of exile, the decrees and the destruction…"[1]

As we have seen, the Redemption is the coming time in history when humankind comes closer to God. Through this spiritual closeness, the world will be rid of sin, pain, suffering, calamity and warfare. In the redeemed world, care for spiritual concerns will be paramount. Each of us will care for the other as much as we care for ourselves. Redemption begins with each of us: humanity through its deeds and behavior will bring it about.

It is true that redemption demands *tikkun olam*—repairing the world. Yet *tikkun olam* cannot be an end in itself. When we say "*letaken olam bemalchut Shadai*,"[2] we accept the mandate to perfect humanity under the kingship of the Almighty. We acknowledge that God is our king, and like every king He has rules and laws. We understand that we should be changing the world as He directs us. This is the difference between "I'm for a revolution" and "I'm for the *Communist* revolution." "I'm for a revolution" has no substantive meaning, no real call to action. The declaration, "I'm for the Communist revolution," however, begins to take on meaning.

Based on kabbalistic concepts, *Chasidut* believes that repairing the world is an urgent task. It means both the pursuit of social justice and the universal acceptance of God's laws. In a chasidic metaphor, these actions create a home for God in this world.[3] In the chasidic worldview, the task of bringing the Mashiach belongs to the entire world: people, animals, even inanimate objects. Each of our actions, when done for good, uncovers a Godly spark. Each deed, each aspect of our life, can be connected to holiness and to becoming closer to God. This is true when we use wheat to make bread, and when we treat our fellow with respect. We elevate inanimate objects when we use them to fulfill God's will—when we use parchment to write a Torah scroll, when we make a blessing over the food we eat, when we use our money for charity. This great mission requires collectivity. Each individual is of paramount importance, because without each of us, a collective cannot exist.

The steps we take to bring the Mashiach foreshadow the perfect world of the Redemption. Redemption is a progressive process, involving the ongoing, successive actions of individual men and women. Each of us clears the path, so to speak. The aggregate result of our actions brings the world closer to God, so that one day we will all sense Godliness in every aspect of our lives. As we change the world in small or larger ways, we help create a redeemed world that culminates in the messianic age.

It was the Rebbe's absolutely unsparing commitment to bring redemption to the world through actions. For the Rebbe, bringing the Mashiach was not a mystical or kabbalistic maneuver; it was supremely practical. He believed that bringing the Mashiach would depend entirely on wholehearted Torah study and observance of *mitzvot*. Toward this end, he organized the mitzva campaigns so that his Chasidim could bring this message to Jews everywhere.

As the Rebbe made his life's work to bring the Mashiach, he focused both on the individual and on the collective. He cared about both the little girl who lights Shabbat candles and the struggle to end the Communist regime in the Soviet Union. For the Rebbe, each deed was a repair of reality and a stone in the vast mosaic of human behavior that would bring the Mashiach.

1 The Rebbe, *Iggrot Kodesh*, vol. 12, p. 414.

2 The *Aleinu* prayer.

3 Tanya, chapter 36.

In the aftermath of the Holocaust, Rebbe Yosef Yitzchak had begun to focus on the coming of the Mashiach. The Rebbe continued this theme in the very first *ma'amar* he delivered when he took over the leadership of Chabad. "It is this generation's task," he said, "to bring the Mashiach."[4] The *ma'amar* was his blueprint for his life mission.

As the years went on, the Rebbe's statements about the coming of the Mashiach came more often—and were ever more intense. The Rebbe would remind his Chasidim that the Mashiach could come at any moment. At *farbrengens* he encouraged the Chasidim to sing "We want Mashiach now." He once said, "They say about me that I am crazy about Mashiach—and that is indeed true."[5]

In the two years before his first stroke in 1992, the Rebbe seemed to speak almost solely about the coming of the Mashiach. The Rebbe said, "Redemption is at the threshold. It is waiting for every man and woman to open the door and pull it in."[6] Asked by a CNN reporter what he would want to tell the world about the Mashiach, the Rebbe replied, "Mashiach is ready to come now. The only thing left to do, on our part, is something additional in the realm of goodness and kindness."[7]

On April 11, 1991, the Rebbe gave a talk that still resonates in the hearts of his Chasidim. With great passion he explained that he had done what he could, but that it had been insufficient. Now he was placing the messianic mission in their hands.[8] It was at this moment when all of the Rebbe's talk about the Mashiach moved from the theoretical to a concrete and physical drive. Previously, the Chasidim might have had some sympathy for the Rebbe's passion; now he was asking them to take actual steps forward. I saw this speech as the Rebbe's desperate move to make a substantive change while he still could. If he did not push for the Mashiach now, the opportunity would be lost.

4 *Torat Menachem*, vol. 2, p. 195.

5 To Rabbi Elimelech Noiman. Heard from Rabbi Leibel Groner, the Rebbe was speaking to Rabbi Elimelech Noiman.

6 *Torat Menachem* 5752, vol. 1, p. 242.

7 *Living Torah*, disc 34, program 135.

8 *Torat Menachem* 5751, vol. 3, p. 119.

Later that year, at the annual *sheluchim* conference, the Rebbe directed the *sheluchim* to help the world greet the Mashiach.[9] A few weeks later he urged: "We just have to open our eyes and see that everything is here for the Redemption."[10]

For the Rebbe, the twentieth century had experienced the rumblings before a huge upheaval. It underscored the urgency of his mission and pointed to the likelihood that the Mashiach is near. The Rebbe's century was a time of great changes, events that radically upended the world.

The twentieth century was witness to earthshaking revolutions. Totalitarian dictatorships or military juntas in Russia, Germany, Italy, Spain and Japan emerged, grew, achieved hegemony—and all collapsed. The face of greater Europe, Africa and Asia changed. And two world wars devastated much of the planet.

There were also changes in the spheres of thought and knowledge. The new disciplines of psychology and psychoanalysis made a lasting impact on general culture. Abstract art, new forms of literature and computerization brought entirely new images and ideas and new means of transmission into human experience. Our advanced grasp of biology brought about a tremendous shift in our understanding of how we grow and change, and opened the possibility of genetic engineering. The theory of relativity was a remarkable insight, changing the world's age-old perception and understanding of itself, a position to which it can never return. The same can be said of quantum mechanics. Work on atomic physics begat nuclear weaponry and power generation. These developments, and so many others, still hover over us as both threats and opportunities.

Within the Rebbe's century, Jewish life underwent three major transformations. The first unfolded over an extended period of time; its impact, while not immediately evident, was quite far-reaching. Following a very long stretch of history during which many if not most Jews had been more or less religiously

9 Ibid., 5752, vol. 1, p. 286.

10 Ibid., p. 354.

observant, there began a clear trend away from Orthodoxy. By the end of World War I, most European Jews were non-observant.

A second change: One-third of the Jewish people was lost in the Holocaust. Men, women and children—perhaps the most vibrant, animated elements of the Jewish people—six million of them, and possibly more, were slaughtered. Finally, there was the establishment of the State of Israel: another unprecedented event, a further tremendous change for world Jewry in particular. Each of these three factors alone represents a dramatic alteration in the history and life of the Jewish people. And each factor reinforced the effect of the others. Nothing on their combined scale had happened in the previous two millennia.

As the political world changed, as the intellectual world changed and as the Jewish world changed, the Rebbe was there. He survived the pogroms in Russia as a child, was a young man at the time of the Russian Revolution and escaped from Europe during the Nazi hegemony. In his work, the Rebbe drew on considerable stores of both spiritual and scientific wisdom—of physics, biology, literature and knowledge of human nature.

The coming of the Mashiach and Redemption were not vague dreams for the Rebbe. As I understand it, this was not only some heavenly vision; the Rebbe based his thinking on concrete observations of how the world was developing, on the changes he had witnessed. He viewed the suffering and pain that he had seen in his lifetime as presaging a major event. The Rebbe saw all the change and distress throughout the century as labor pains heralding an impending birth.

The Rebbe himself pointed to the positive events of the last decades of his life as signs that the Mashiach would soon come. As the Soviet Union began to fall, the Rebbe commented, "Some wonder about what I have been saying recently, that we are now at the end of the Exile, and ask, 'How do we see that? The world looks just the same.' It is a great wonder that they do not observe the different events that have occurred in the world recently, events publicized everywhere!"[11] The effective end of the Cold War: the fall of the Berlin Wall in the same year as the Beijing protests, the reforms in Poland and Hungary, the Velvet Revolution in Czechoslovakia and more—these were the events that sparked the Rebbe's enthusiasm. In broad strokes, he saw the world's events moving toward less oppression, fewer wars and greater care for suffering nations.

In 1991, during the Gulf War that reclaimed Kuwait from Saddam Hussein's Iraq, the Rebbe delighted in an ancient midrashic source that the Mashiach will come after a battle involving Arab kings in the area of the Persian Gulf.[12] In January 1992, there was another sign for the Rebbe: the first-ever United Nations Security Council summit meeting, with the heads of all fifteen member nations in attendance in New York City. This meeting was followed by a report of the United Nations Secretary-General titled "An Agenda for Peace," a document urging that funds must be invested in projects that promote peace, and not in ever more weaponry. The Rebbe spoke about this meeting at length.[13] It reminded him of Isaiah's prophecy about the days of the Mashiach: "And they shall beat their swords into plowshares and their spears into pruning hooks; nation shall not lift sword against nation, neither shall they learn war anymore."[14]

Since talmudic times—and through the generations—there have been respected nominees for the role of Mashiach. The Talmud records that students were not shy about pointing to their own teachers as the possible Mashiachs of their generations.[15] Maimonides, in his *Epistle to Yemen,* thought one candidate in his own time was incompetent, but highly respected another. Drawing on these ancient traditions, Rabbi Ovadia of Bartenura, a famous fifteenth-century Italian rabbi, taught, "In every generation, there is a *tzaddik* who has the potential to be Mashiach."[16]

11 Ibid., 5750, vol. 1, p. 420.
12 See, for example, ibid., vol. 4, p. 179.
13 Ibid., 5752, vol. 2, p. 267.
14 Isaiah 2:4.
15 See Sanhedrin 98b and Rashi's commentary ad loc.
16 In his commentary to Ruth.

Jewish philosophy holds that there is nothing wrong with considering oneself to have the potential of messianic greatness. Many great rabbinic figures have hinted that they could wear this mantle—from Rav Nachman in the third century CE[17] to Rabbi Chaim Ben Atar, the "Or HaChaim," in the modern period.[18] Trouble came only when false messiahs proclaimed heretical views and led their followers out of the mainstream. It was the national trauma inflicted by Shabbetai Tzvi, the false messiah of the 1660s, that stifled all discussion of the likelihood of redemption after the seventeenth century.

The question of whether the Lubavitcher Rebbe could be the Mashiach consumed many of his followers and onlookers for decades, and intensified as the Rebbe spoke of the Redemption with increasing passion in his later years. During his lifetime, his Chasidim believed that he was the chief candidate of his generation; what happened after his death will be discussed in the following chapter. Did the Rebbe himself believe that he was the Mashiach? And does it matter?

The acceptance of the Rebbe as the Mashiach of his time was almost universal among the Lubavitchers of the late twentieth century. Some acted on the idea, while others kept it to themselves. In most homes, it was not much discussed—it was simply an article of faith. Others, however, felt the need to broadcast their beliefs of the Mashiach's identity. As early as 1965, one Chasid leafleted all of Israel with the news. Hearing about this, the Rebbe told him to retrieve them all.[19]

While he never said so outright, I think that the Rebbe considered it possible that he might be tapped to become the Mashiach—and that he could bring the Redemption. Chasidim could pick up on the hints that the Rebbe left about his messianic role. However, he never made the claim outright and tried to quash all speculation. At a 1991 *farbrengen*, just a few months before his first stroke, some of the Chasidim began a song which clearly named the Rebbe as Mashiach. The Rebbe stopped them quickly and said, "I cannot leave here now, but after hearing such a claim I should leave this room as a protest."[20]

While he was alive, I believed that he could be the Mashiach. That is, I believed in the potential of his candidacy. The Rebbe repeated often that each Jew has the messianic spark, but I have not seen anyone else with similar capability. His piety and saintliness, his wisdom and his leadership all seemed to qualify him for the role.

The Rebbe remarked that the identity of the Mashiach is unimportant.[21] He thought that the bearer of the title is of far less concern than that the Redemption begin. In saying this, he was swimming against the tide. Public imagination often needs a human face, a symbolic figure, around whom to rally. It was much harder for the Chasidim to speak about a faceless Mashiach than to have an impressive, memorable figure as the focus. For the Rebbe, however, it was the preparation for the Mashiach that was key. This is how we can best understand his insistent calls for action, the mitzva campaigns and the relentless waves of *sheluchim* around the world. Here is where he devoted his energies—to opening the door so that the Mashiach could walk in.

My Rebbe [Jerusalem: Maggid Books, 2014], pp. 171–178

17 Talmud, Sanhedrin 98b.

18 As hinted in his commentary to Deuteronomy 15:7, and as his famed student the Chida understood from his letter.

19 See the biography of that chasid by E. Wolf, *Echad Haya Avraham* (Kfar Chabad: Eshel-Kfar Chabad, 2001), p. 98.

20 *Sichot Kodesh* 5752, vol. 1, p. 259.

21 In a handwritten note, a few weeks before the first stroke. Menachem Mendel Schneerson, *Tzadik LaMelech* 7 (New York: Tzadik LaMelech, 1994), p. 239.

REBBE OF THE ABANDONED AND THE PRIVILEGED

RABBI HASKEL LOOKSTEIN

Who sat *shiva* for the Lubavitcher Rebbe? Technically, no one; in reality, almost everyone.

Due to a technicality—a tragic one, at that—there was no formal *shiva* for Rabbi Menachem M. Schneerson, the Lubavitcher Rebbe, of blessed memory.

He left no family and, therefore, no obligated mourners.

He did, however, leave a bereaved Jewish world, which lost a man of great spiritual and intellectual intensity, a heroic human being of incalculable strength but, most of all, an uncompromising and unconditional lover of Jews individually and the Jewish people as a whole.

Most of what has been written and said since the Rebbe's passing focused on what will happen after: How will Chabad chassidism survive? What will be the fate of the Lubavitcher movement? Will there be another Rebbe and, if so, who?

In the period of mourning, however, our focus ought properly to be on what we lost and, therefore, what he was.

What he was is epitomized by the following story.

One of his great admirers and devoted followers, George Rohr, who created and conducts the beginners service in our congregation, Kehilath Jeshurun, came to the Rebbe three years ago, right after Rosh Hashanah.

Rohr told him proudly, "Rebbe, you will be pleased to know that we had 180 people for Rosh Hashanah services, Jews with no background." The Rebbe's eyes flashed and he responded: "You're wrong; they have a background. Go tell them that they are the children of Abraham, Isaac and Jacob, Sarah, Rebecca, Rachel and Leah!"

This response encapsulates a worldview with love of your fellow at its core.

The Rebbe saw every Jew as family, as having the same background, that of our Patriarchs and Matriarchs, and, therefore, as having the same potential for a full Jewish life.

To help each of us realize that potential, the Rebbe reinvented outreach, a philosophy that is fundamental to Chabad chassidism—"And you shall expand outward to the west and east, to the north and south" (Genesis 28:14)—and made it into a powerful movement which literally moved people all over the world.

The Rebbe's outreach, which spawned a variety of similar efforts by various Jewish groups, expressed itself on four levels.

The first was outreach to the abandoned. The Rebbe sent emissaries all over the world to Jews who otherwise would have been forgotten.

These emissaries went simply because the Rebbe told them to go.

They entrenched themselves in communities and usually brought about the most blessed results.

I saw three of those emissaries 10 years ago in Casablanca; they had been there for between 25 and 30 years.

It is impossible to imagine Jewish life in Morocco without these three rabbis and their families.

I saw Lubavitcher emissaries in Russia during the early days of the Soviet Jewry movement, working feverishly to bring about a spiritual revival.

These were people who under other circumstances would have left to go to Israel or other places. They remained because the Rebbe told them to remain.

I saw Lubavitcher emissaries creating a religious life in Ladispoli, outside of Rome, where tens of thousands of Russian Jewish émigrés passed through on their way to the West or to Israel.

They literally had no background except for their own origin with Abraham, Isaac and Jacob.

The Lubavitchers created a school and a network of social and educational institutions to bring to these people for the first time in their lives the knowledge, the feeling and the spirit of Judaism.

On a visit with the UJA Rabbinic Cabinet to Ladispoli, one of my colleagues from another movement expressed annoyance that the Lubavitchers seemed to have a monopoly on Jewish life there.

I asked him: "Are there Reform rabbis here? Are there any Conservatives? How about Modern Orthodox? No one is here," I said, "except the emissaries of the Rebbe."

It was the Rebbe who reached out to the abandoned.

The second level of outreach was to the uninformed and the uninitiated.

The Rebbe created "mitzvah tanks" which roamed the streets of New York and other places. How many of us were stopped on Fifth Avenue and asked, "Did you put on *tefillin* today? Did you make a blessing on the *lulav* today? Would you like to come in to our mobile *sukkah* and make a blessing?"

There was a philosophy here, a philosophy which said that it is our job to get a Jew to do one mitzvah. One never knows the infinite significance of one righteous act, and where it will lead—and it led many people to a much fuller expression of their Judaism than before.

The outreach to the uninformed and uninitiated was extended to the college campuses where Chabad Houses are frequently found, campuses which we all know constitute a disaster for Jewish continuity. Lubavitch is in El Paso, the Hamptons and the far-flung reaches of America.

Sometimes, these outposts create problems in the community. Not always do they bring people together. Occasionally, they even create divisiveness. No movement is without its failures and blemishes. But, on the whole, Chabad is where Jews are and, particularly, Jews with little background except for Abraham, Isaac and Jacob, Sarah, Rebecca, Rachel and Leah.

A third level of outreach is to the religiously committed.

To this group the Rebbe called for greater commitment.

Learn the *Rambam* (Maimonides), he said, and he started a whole program to achieve it. Write Torah scrolls. Give charity.

He was once known to tell an observant Jew that he should think about G-d while engaged in business during the week.

The Jew was surprised. "How can I think about G-d while I am working in business?" The Rebbe, with his wonderful sense of humor, responded, "Many people don't seem to have a problem thinking about business while they are in synagogue. Why not think about synagogue and G-d when in business?"

There was hardly one of us who was not touched and inspired by the Rebbe's call and outreach to the committed religious community.

Finally, there was his personal outreach.

Beyond the movement, beyond the calls to action, there was a man who was ready to meet any Jew, day or night.

How many of us were privileged to stand before him, if only for two minutes, and see those deep blue, sparkling eyes focus on us individually, somehow to see through our masks, understand, and offer a word and a dollar for charity, to give us comfort, encouragement and inspiration.

I remember such an opportunity on a Sunday morning, the first day of the Jewish month of Sivan.

There were 3,000 people on line waiting to meet the Rebbe.

What I only learned afterwards was that it was reportedly the practice of the Rebbe not to sleep Friday nights or on the night of the first day of the month.

Therefore, when he stood and focused on me and my needs and was preparing to do the same for 3,000 others, he had not slept for over 48 hours.

He was 87 years old at the time.

This was nothing short of an heroic act of strength on the part of a man who was inspired by his unquenchable love for all Jews—the abandoned, the disaffiliated, the affiliated—all Jews, a love expressed in his programs, his policies and most of all, his person.

Who sat *shiva* for the Rebbe? Technically, no one; in reality, almost everyone.

This article first appeared on www.chabad.org
Printed with permission of the author

JUDAISM'S MISSION TO THE WORLD

RABBI JOSEPH TELUSHKIN

"We are not two sides. We are one side. We are one people living in one city under one administration and under one God."

In 1990, Geoffrey and James Davis, two African American communal activists in Brooklyn (James Davis later became a New York City councilman), founded an organization, Love Yourself: Stop the Violence, with the goal of increasing self-esteem and lowering violence in American life, particularly within the black community.

In a 2012 interview[1] Geoffrey Davis revealed that the initial inspiration for much of his work, and even his organization's name, was the Rebbe: "Our whole life career-wise was because of a lot of the teachings that he taught us." As Davis related, he and his brother grew up on Brooklyn Avenue, a block from the Rebbe's house. The two boys used to play ball in the street, and the Rebbe, walking home from synagogue, would often stop to chat with them: "We embraced him because he embraced us," Davis remarks of their frequent, informal conversations. He recalled one incident in particular when he was about twelve, and he and his brother were arguing over a ball game. The dispute was growing heated and at that moment the Rebbe walked by. After telling them, "Behave yourselves," he immediately added words that Davis insists forever changed his and his brother's life: "Love your brother as you love yourself. And love yourself as you love your brother, because you're one, so love yourself."

At the time these encounters occurred, starting in the mid-1970s, neither brother knew just who this man was, only that he was "a nice friendly man" who always spoke to them warmly and used to give each boy a dollar. They eventually learned that he was the "Grand Rebbe" of Chabad, and some fifteen years lat-

[1] Mr. Geoffrey Davis in an interview on March 21, 2012, conducted by JEM, and available at Chabad.org/2139959.

er, when they founded the organization Love Yourself: Stop the Violence, it was the Rebbe's words that framed their goal: "We have his picture hanging in our house not because he was a Grand Rebbe, but because he was our friend, somebody who took a liking to two children. He didn't look like us, but he opened the door for us to communicate and to embrace all human beings."

Is this story unusual? It would be nice to say that it isn't, but this tale of a prominent rabbi befriending and deeply influencing two non-Jewish children is not a common one. Yet, it represents the sort of world the Rebbe wanted to help shape. His love of Jews, intense as it was, did not come at the expense of others. Indeed, when dealing with correspondence, the Rebbe usually responded first to letters addressed to him by non-Jews: "My Chasidim will understand the delay; others might feel slighted."[2] In a remarkable and infrequently commented-upon encounter with David Dinkins, New York City's first black mayor, the Rebbe told Mayor Dinkins: "I hope that in the near future, the 'melting pot' [of America] will be so active that it will not be necessary to underline every time [when speaking of others], 'They are Negro,' or 'They are White,' or 'They are Hispanic,' because they are no different. All of them are created by the same God and created for the same purpose, to add to all good things around them."[3]

Not surprisingly, the Rebbe's embracing attitude and behavior influenced those around him. We have related elsewhere how the Rebbe requested, as a birthday present for himself, that David Chase pray daily, and Chase agreed to do so. Some time later, Chase, a successful businessman and philanthropist, was vacationing on his yacht. Each morning he would ask the captain in which direction—north, south, east, west—the boat was heading. After several days of such questions, the captain, a man named Dick Williams, asked Chase, "Are you studying navigation? Are you trying to learn how to run a boat?" Chase answered no. The reason he needed to know the ship's direction was because each morning he prayed, and the Jewish tradition is to face east, in the direction of Jerusalem, while praying. He told Winters: "I don't want to start up facing east and wind up facing south because the ship is turning."

The captain asked Chase how much time he needed for his prayers. Chase told him twenty minutes, and Winters assured him that during those twenty minutes he would not change course. That way, Chase could face east without trepidation.

A few days later, Sunday morning, the boat pulled into Black Island and Winters came to Chase with a request to leave the boat for an hour or two. Chase answered yes and asked the captain where he was going. "I would like to go to church," Winters answered. "You pray to your God every morning, and you're making me feel guilty that I don't follow my faith. So I want to go to church and say my prayers."

At his next visit to 770, Chase told the Rebbe about this incident. The Rebbe, to quote Chase, "got a big kick out of it," and the businessman learned that the Rebbe shortly thereafter spoke of this event at a public lecture; he wanted his Chasidim to know that their behavior could encourage non-Jews, not just Jews, to come closer to God.

Bringing non-Jews closer to God was not a goal that would have occurred to, let alone preoccupy, many Jewish leaders. Indeed, throughout the Jewish people's millennia-long history in exile, they generally did little to make known their religious teachings to the non-Jewish world. As a rule, Jews encountered so much hostility in the societies in which they lived that their primary hope was simply that the non-Jewish world would leave them alone. And so the Jewish people generally made no effort to discuss the notion of God and His demands of human beings with non-Jews. Therefore, when the Rebbe launched his campaign in 1983 to bring knowledge of the sheva mitzvot b'nai Noach (the Seven Noahide Laws) to the non-Jewish world, many Jews, particularly in the Orthodox world, were surprised and some were upset.

[2] See Schneerson, *The Letter and the Spirit*, 17. Mindel was the secretary in charge of the Rebbe's English-language correspondence, and therefore in a position to know the Rebbe's priorities in responding to mail.

[3] From a conversation between the Rebbe and Mayor David Dinkins on Sunday, September 1, 1989. A video of this encounter is available at Chabd.org/604940.

Indeed, if going out into the world with religious teachings was a value, they wanted to know, why do we not find efforts by earlier Chabad Rebbes, scholars such as the Alter Rebbe, the Tzemach Tzedek, and the Rebbe's own father-in-law, the Frierdiker Rebbe, to educate non-Jews about God's expectations of them.[4] The Rebbe's response was that his program did not represent a change in ideology but a recognition of a change in historical circumstances. God, he asserted, has always wanted Jews to reach out to the non-Jewish world—He is, after all, the God of all humankind, not just of the Jews—but until now there was no opportunity to do so; the environments in which Jews lived were too hostile. In Czarist Russia where Chabad originated, the government orchestrated pogroms against the Jews and sometimes organized campaigns to convert Jews to Russian Orthodoxy. In such a society, there was no openness on the part of non-Jews to Jewish teachings. And in Communist Russia, the successor government to the Czars, the government's decades-long campaign to wipe out Judaism (and other religions as well) would have made any Jewish effort at educating non-Jews about God a suicide mission.

But America, the Rebbe concluded, was different.[5] A nation of high ideals—the Rebbe routinely referred to the United States as a "government of kindness" (malchut shel chesed) —he saw America as perhaps the first society in which there was a hope of carrying out Judaism's universal mission: not to make the whole world Jewish but to bring the world, starting with the United States, to a full awareness of One God, Who demands of human beings moral behavior. The Rebbe was deeply impressed by the fact that the country's currency carried the words, "In God we trust," and he was struck as well by yet another of America's foundational principles, e pluribus unum ("from many, one"). At yet another meeting with Mayor Dinkins, during a tense period following anti-Jewish rioting in Crown Heights in which a Jewish man, Yankel Rosenbaum, had been murdered in the aftermath of a car accident in which a black child, Gavin Cato, had been killed, the Rebbe expressed the hope that the mayor would be able to bring peace to the city. "To both sides," Dinkins responded. The Rebbe replied, "We are not two sides. We are one side. We are one people living in one city under one administration and under one God. May God protect the police and all the people of the city."[6] For the Rebbe, and he emphasized this on different occasions, "From many, one" and "In God we trust" were the bedrock of the United States' power and specialness.

This is why the Rebbe reacted with such concern and upset when the Supreme Court outlawed all prayers and any acknowledgment of God in the country's public schools; the United States, he feared, would be in danger of great moral deterioration if the next generation was not raised with a belief in a God before Whom each individual was responsible (see chapter 18).

The Rebbe's vision of how to safeguard the values that defined America and all moral societies was best articulated in a speech prepared for presentation at the United Nations on October 21, 1987, by Dr. Nissen Mindel, the Rebbe's secretary, and the man in charge of all of the Rebbe's English-language correspondence (unfortunately, in the end, the UN speech did

4 There is one unusual, and hardly typical, story in which the Alter Rebbe offered a lesson in biblical ethics to a non-Jew. There are several versions of the story, in all of which the basic facts are the same. While the Alter Rebbe was in prison, facing a possible death sentence, an official in the prison, possibly the head of the prison guards, approached the Rebbe, whom he had been informed was a religious scholar, with a question about the Bible: "Why is it," he wanted to know, "that after Adam sins by eating of the Tree of Knowledge of Good and Evil, and he hides in the Garden of Eden, God calls out to him, 'Where are you?' *[ayekah;* Genesis 3:9]. God is all-knowing. How could he not know where Adam was?" The Alter Rebbe answered: "This is God's question to man in every generation: 'Where are you? What are you doing with your life? Where do you stand and what do you stand for?'"

5 The Rebbe's recognition that America was vastly different from other nations in which Jews had lived was in no way a repudiation of his father-in-law's oft-cited aphorism, "America is not different." What the Frierdiker Rebbe meant by that statement—which he coined upon arriving in the United States in 1940—was that even though people had been warning him that strict observance of Jewish laws was alien to American Jews, and would not catch on here, America and American Jews, in his view, were no different from all other Jews, and there would be openness among American Jews to leading a life of Jewish commitment. It was in this regard that he believed "American is not different." However, what became increasingly apparent to the Rebbe and to Lubavitchers in general was that in terms of openness to Jews, America was very different from Europe; in recent years, it has become even more so. To cite just one example: In 2012, both the Democratic and Republican parties invited rabbis to deliver prayer invocations at their conventions, an act that would have been quite inconceivable in Eastern Europe, Ger many and the Arab world, the three societies from which the large majority of American Jews descend.

6 See Todd Purdum, *New York Times,* August 26, 1991.

not happen). Mindel based the draft of the speech on the Rebbe's teachings, and the speech itself was edited by the Rebbe (all citations are drawn from a copy of the speech that contains the Rebbe's handwritten emendations).

Early in the text of the speech, Mindel raised the issue of ongoing problems of lawlessness and violence throughout the world and then posed the question: "Is there perhaps a basic universal moral code that would be acceptable to all nations, all of humankind?"

There was indeed such a code: "We are talking about a G-d-given moral code which has served as the foundation of human society from its very inception ... the Seven Noahide Laws," the ordinances that Jewish tradition teaches that God gave to Noah and his children in the aftermath of the biblically recorded flood ("children of Noah" is the rabbinic term for non-Jews; "children of Abraham" is the rabbinic term for Jews): "These [seven laws] were to serve as the minimum set of Divine injunctions for all mankind in order that [the world] not degenerate into a [a place of lawlessness and violence]."

The Seven Laws of the Children of Noah:

1. Prohibition of idolatry
2. Prohibition of blasphemy
3. Prohibition of homicide
4. Prohibition of incest
5. Prohibition of robbery
6. Prohibition of eating the limb of a living animal
7. Institution of courts of justice (Sanhedrin 56a, based on Genesis 9)[7]

The text continues, "The Jewish people were assigned the task and the obligation of disseminating and promoting the Seven Noahide Laws in their immediate society and in the world at large."

Mindel's draft of the speech made reference several times to the "Gentile world" and the obligation of the Jews to bring God's teachings to them. The Rebbe repeatedly crossed out the word "Gentile"; he was not interested in emphasizing a Jewish/Gentile dichotomy but in establishing that God's message is directed to all humanity.

Similarly, the fundamental factor motivating the launching of the 1983 Seven Noahide Laws (Sheva Mitzvot) campaign was to make God and his ethical demands known to the world. When Jews are spoken of as "the Chosen People," the Rebbe believed, it is this mission—to bring knowledge of God into the world—for which they were chosen. (Whether or not one believes that the Jews were in fact chosen by God for this mission, it is historically undeniable that it is through the Jews that the concept of One God became known to humankind.)

Making God and His moral demands of human beings known to non-Jews was regarded by the Rebbe as equal in significance to promoting knowledge and practice of the commandments (mitzvot) among Jews, a universalist position that one does not find, to say the least, echoed widely in traditional Jewish circles.[8]

Perhaps the cause with which the Rebbe became most associated in the American mind was with his emphasis on education. In the late 1970s, the Rebbe's shliach Rabbi Avraham Shemtov organized a campaign to help establish the Department of Education as a separate cabinet-level position (until then, education was subsumed into the Department of Health, Education, and Welfare), which President Carter subsequently did. In honor of the Rebbe's involvement in this cause, the president declared the Rebbe's seventy-sixth birthday in 1978 as the first Education Day U.S.A. Since then, Education Day U.S.A., commemorated on the Rebbe's birthday, has become a part of the American calendar, and has been signed into effect every year by the president.

In the Rebbe's thank-you letter to President Ronald Reagan for declaring the 1987 Education Day U.S.A., the Rebbe noted that the proclamation itself, issued by the American government, spoke of "the historical tradition of ethical values and principles which

[7] The laws actually come to far more than seven, as they include entire categories of prohibited acts. Thus, the ban on robbery, for example, includes prohibitions of theft, extortions, and withholding or delaying payment of an employee's wages. It is estimated that the laws come to about sixty in number, perhaps more.

[8] Cited in Menachem M. Schneerson, *The Letter and the Spirit* 2:21.

have been the bedrock of society from the dawn of civilization when they were known as 'The Seven Noahide Laws.'"

The Rebbe's role in the focus on education was acknowledged in a talk given in honor of the third anniversary of his death by Richard Riley, then serving as secretary of education under President Bill Clinton. In speaking of the creation of the Department of Education, Riley noted that the Rebbe helped "make it happen. So I owe my job to him" (emphasis added).

But the truth is, while the Rebbe prized intellectual achievements, the education in which he was most interested was moral education. Having attended university in Germany in the late 1920s and early 1930s, he knew firsthand that academic excellence in and of itself is no predictor of moral behavior: "For it is precisely the nation which had excelled itself in the exact sciences, the humanities, and even in philosophy and ethics, that turned out to be the most depraved nation in the world."

The Rebbe wanted education, and not fear of police or of incarceration, to foster morality. As he emphasized in the speech composed for the U.N.: "Respect for law and order will not be instilled by fear of punishment, especially when the delinquent juvenile or adult may feel that he can outsmart the cop and the judge. What will make a human being a better and more decent person is awareness that there is 'an eye that sees and an ear that hears,' an awareness of always being present in the presence of a Supreme Being—our Heavenly Father who cares how every one of his children conducts himself or herself, and before whom every one of us will have to account for our every action, word, and thought."

Rebbe: The Life and Teachings of Menachem M. Schneerson, the Most Influential Rabbi in Modern History [New York: HarperCollins Publisher, 2014], pp. 156–162

THE BELIEVER

MK GEULAH COHEN

The following are excerpts from an account by Israeli activist, writer and former Knesset member, Geulah Cohen, of her meeting with the Rebbe. The original Hebrew version was published in the Israeli daily, Maariv, *December 18, 1964.*

I have been in the company of wise men, men of great learning and intelligence, men who were superior artists. But sitting opposite a true believer is quite a different matter. After having met a wise man you remain the same as before—you have become neither less of a fool nor more of a sage. The education of the man of learning hardly rubs off on you, nor does the artist endow you with any of his talents or inspiration. Not so with a believer. After having met him you are no longer the same. Though you may not have accepted his faith, you have nevertheless been embraced by it. For the true believer believes in you as well.

The Lubavitcher Rebbe, Rabbi Menachem Mendel Schneerson, of Brooklyn, the spiritual leader of the world Chabad movement, is both wise and learned, but above all he is a man of faith. And if faith be the art of truth, he is also an artist whose creation is the army of believers that he commands, the army of the Jewish faith, of the G-d of Israel and the people of Israel.

What about the belief in the Land of Israel?

To ask the Rebbe this question I first had to get to him. Jewish legend says nothing about how exactly the angels were received in audience by the L-rd, but had it wanted to it might well have taken its inspiration from the manner in which I managed to be received by the Lubavitcher Rebbe.

First of all, as with every ordinary mortal, there is, of course, the secretary with fixed reception hours and a long waiting list, except that here the secretary does not ask you what you intend to discuss with his boss. That is a matter between you and the Rebbe himself.

Here, even if you may sometimes have to wait for days on end, anybody and everybody is eventually admitted. And the reception hours are not in daytime, but at night—all the night through. The day is for learning, the night for talking.

"At 11 o'clock at night?" I repeated, when told by Rabbi Hodakov, the Lubavitcher Rebbe's secretary, that this was the time of my appointment, for I was sure I had not heard right.

"Tomorrow, at 11 p.m.," came the laconic reply over the line connecting me with the Rebbe's court in Brooklyn.

"And why not in the daytime?" When I posed this question to one of the Rebbe's followers, he looked at me as if I had come from the moon.

"During the day the Rebbe studies," came the answer, in a tone that left no room for further questions.

And indeed I found myself wondering whether this was not as it should be; whether at night the heavens and the hearts of men might not be more open, more disposed to listen; at night, when the barriers are down and man is closer to the truth....

Perhaps the very fact that my thoughts were turning this way was already due to the incipient effect of the secret drug that begins to work on you, whether you want it or not, long before you actually meet the Rebbe, possibly from the moment that you decide you want to see him. However rationalistic you may be, all your skeptical questions begin to blush with shame...

The Rebbe's Court

I don't remember a single preface in any book I have read that I did not skip. But from the long preliminaries I had to go through until I actually met the Rebbe, I learned that there are some preambles one cannot do without for the simple reason that they already constitute the beginning of the story. What the Rebbe has to say may be important, but still more important, perhaps also for the Rebbe himself and the Chassidic lore of the Chabad school, is to whom, when and where he said what he did. The atmosphere around him is no less relevant than what he actually says. The "how" may matter no less and perhaps even more than the "what." The Rebbe starts off where his court begins. His parlor begins at the porch. His followers are no less part of his personality than, as the Chassidim believe, all human beings form part of G-d. My interview therefore began the moment I entered the Rebbe's court and met his disciples.

The young men who crowded the premises, studying the Talmud, can hardly be referred to as students or disciples. Although they were sitting in front of an open book they did not look like people learning something they did not know before. They seemed more like people in a laboratory who are experimenting with the spirit and its manifestations just as others experiment with matter: combining and decomposing, designing and synthesizing. And all this is accompanied by their melodious humming. Much has been written about the Chassidic melodies, and much more will still be written about them. For they are tunes which have no end and no beginning. They seem to perpetuate the song which you sing so that someone else may continue it after you. Hearing that tune, it occurred to me that the Ten Commandments, the foundation of mankind, could never have been written and spoken according to a Chassidic melody. But it also occurred to me that mankind may not have been able to comply with this severe code had it not been for this softening melody....

Those who were not leaning over their books were standing about and talking among themselves. Perhaps they were talking about everyday things, but the expression on their faces was enough to indicate that they were like frontline soldiers exchanging a few whispered words before going into action. The commander might have been invisible, but his presence made itself felt through and through. No orders were being issued, but they might be at any moment, and everybody was ready to listen and obey.

The Rebbe's Peace Corps

I, too, was waiting, for my orders to go in to the Rebbe. The time was a quarter past eleven, half past eleven ... when will it be my turn to be called in? I was just about to ask one of the young men in the court office when a well-dressed young woman came in, with a patter of high heels, her blonde hair streaming out beneath her kerchief. Before I could see her face I could hear her half-choking voice: "Have you got an answer yet?" Instead of answering her the young man she had addressed went over to a pile of letters, pulled out the one she had written, and told her that the Rebbe's answer was right in there. The woman snatched it away, opened it and read it on the spot. For a moment her eyes froze over. There might have been tears as well of joy or of sorrow, who can tell? Leaving without a goodbye, she was back again as soon as she had gone.

"I have another question. May I ask the Rebbe another question?"

"Of course," she is told. "At any time and about anything you may wish."

Her face lights up with happiness.

"Poor woman," says the man to me after she has left. "All her life she's been going to psychiatrists, and they didn't help her at all. How could they help her if all they have is knowledge and no faith? They don't love her; they love only their books. How can one help without love?" I became curious about this young man.

He was about twenty-five, and it transpired that he had only recently returned from a trip to Australia undertaken on the Rebbe's behalf. "What am I doing here? What do you mean? I have a wife and a family but one day the Rebbe told me to go on a trip and I asked no questions about where and why. Nobody questions the Rebbe. His every word is an order. He doesn't say things that might have remained unsaid or could have been said otherwise. So I took my family and went. What did I do in Australia? Whatever I was told. There are people being sent round the world to distribute food and money among the Jews, but what the Jews really need is spiritual food, a bit of love, of Yidishkeit. The Rebbe's orders were for me to go and give them love, to encourage them, to bring a little Jewishness into their souls. There is social assistance and there is First Aid for physical ailments, but we are concerned with First Aid for spiritual ills. Of course we are concerned with people's physical well-being, too. Have you heard about the 'Maccabees' who organized the defense of the Brooklyn Jews during the riots? The man who organized them, Rabbi Shraga, is one of ours.... It was a great honor for me to have been sent on a mission by the Rebbe but I am only one of many hundreds and thousands. We have a whole army here, our Peace Corps. This is our headquarters. From here the Rebbe dispatches his soldiers to the various fronts. Wherever there is a single Jew there is a front for us to fight on, with the Holy Scriptures in our hands and the love of Israel in our hearts. These are our weapons. If there is some Jewish corner in the world that is inaccessible by car, we go there on donkeys. There is nothing that can stop us. All we have in mind is that the Rebbe's orders should be carried out to the full, that we should be able to come back and report to him: 'Mission accomplished.'"

But the Peace Corps, as I am informed by the office manager, is only one of the many ramifications of the Lubavitcher court.

The Sun Never Sets Over the Lubavitch Empire

"People used to say that the sun never sets over the British Empire, but it is already going down. Not so with the Lubavitch empire. We are growing stronger from day to day," he said. "Have you heard about our publishing house? It is the biggest publisher of Jewish writings in the world, issuing books in over ten languages. We also have hundreds of yeshivos with some 30,000 students. Do you know our village in Israel? There'll be many more such communities. Once a week we publish an information bulletin, circulated by the ITA News Agency.

"Who are the people who come to see the Rebbe? Well, who doesn't? Chassidim and Misnagdim, men and women, tradesmen and scholars, young and old, Jews and Gentiles, leaders and statesmen; including the present President of Israel—did you know he was one of ours? As for his correspondence—again, with whom doesn't he correspond? Even with Ben Gurion. What about? That is the Rebbe's own affair. Nobody opens the letters that are addressed to him. He himself opens them all, and answers them, too.

"What do Jews ask about as a rule? About matters of religion and how to make a living, about their personal affairs, and about politics. In short—about everything. There is no question he cannot answer. Where there is faith, one is able to answer every question. For him there are no important and unimportant questions. Every question calls for a true answer.... Excuse me a minute."

I hadn't heard the bell ringing, but the secretary jumped over to the phone and immediately left the room. Unwittingly I found myself adjusting the kerchief I had tied over my head in anticipation of my interview with the Rebbe. I was just in time, for the next moment the secretary was back to tell me, with the air of one presenting a most marvelous gift: "That's it now; come along with me."

He may have said some more, but I no longer heard him because I was too busy covering up for my sudden palpitations, telling myself not to be a fool, that there was no need to get excited, that this wasn't my first midnight appointment...

Midnight Appointment

When the door closed behind me and I remained alone with the Rebbe the time was twelve midnight, but the Rebbe rose from behind his desk to receive me with a smile that spelled noon rather than midnight.

If that is what you are interested in, you may see a handsome face with a kind and gracious expression, a black hat above and a gray beard below. Alternatively you may see nothing but a pair of eyes fixed upon you not in order to see but in order to discover and reveal. Then it won't be so pleasant for you if you have something to hide, if your intention was to deceive. You try to button yourself up anew, because you feel some of your buttons may have suddenly burst. Is it because the Rebbe really has magic eyes or is it because you have brought the magic along with you as a result of your nighttime experience and the purge administered by the Rebbe's disciples? But the question of cause and effect no longer matters. What matters is to try and remember why one has come in the first place. And so I start by introducing myself.

Except that it isn't necessary. He knows more about me than I might be able to tell him. He knows not only what I have done but what I ought to have done, not only what I am doing now but what I am not doing and should do. His disciples had told me that he reads the papers every day and took a lively interest in Israel, but it was a little frightening nevertheless.

"I understand that you are writing for the press now. Well, that's all right, but it isn't the main thing. The young generation, that is the main thing. One has to talk to youngsters, not write for them. Why aren't you talking to them? Why is nobody talking to them? They are waiting for someone to talk with but nobody does. They are being addressed in lofty speeches, but nobody talks to them, and then people are surprised that they remain indifferent."

The Rebbe does not speak with me in Yiddish but in Hebrew. His accent may not be the purest Sephardi, but his language is the language of the Bible. And however exciting his words, his voice remains level and calm.

"What the youth is waiting for is an order which must be given in the same voice and tone in which all the great commands were issued to the people of Israel. They may obey or they may not, but that is what they are waiting for. But there is no commander to issue that order. Where are they all? No salvation can come from those who walk in the beaten path, but only from those who break new ground. What has happened to all those who were once burning with the holy fire of a holy war that they are now dealing with such bagatelles as whether people should pay a little more or a little less income tax instead of thinking about the urgent concerns of the Jewish people as a whole? Where are those who at one time knew how to issue commands? I believe physics: that energy can never disappear. Forces that have once existed will exist forever. Therefore I believe in the everlasting force of the Jewish people. Whatever forces there may once have been in its youth still exist and need only be evoked. Once there were those who knew how to evoke them—where have they gone?

"Everybody is in a rut, following a course of dull mediocrity. And, as you know, there is nothing worse than conformity. To be carried away by the current is very much like dying. Creativity begins by swimming against the current. What is needed is someone to start swimming against the current. I am not preaching, G-d forbid, revolt, only protest against the set pattern of conformity. If the present set-up has turned into a prison, one must find ways to break away from it. That does not mean breaking the law, but fighting against the law. Yet everybody, the entire Jewish nation, is conforming to the set pattern, and there is no one to lead the way out..."

The Rebbe's voice is filled with deep despair, but without pathos. "Have you ever calculated how many precious youth-hours are going to waste every day? The use of every such hour could work wonders. Instead of giving orders the leaders make speeches and the young people go to cafés and waste their precious irretrievable time. Do you remember them during the Sinai campaign, how they rose like one man because there was a commander whose orders were such as they had been waiting for, even if they did not know it beforehand? Just give them an order as was done during the Sinai campaign—never mind the particulars, all that matters is that it should ignite some spark as it did then—and you will see how all the latent forces will rise up again...

"It would hardly matter if everything were as it should be in the Land of Israel and in the Diaspora. But it isn't. All the 'ideals' and all the 'panaceas' have failed and only very, very little has so far been accomplished. Never in the 3,500-year history of the Jewish nation was there a period without any prospects; sometimes the chances were used and at other times they were allowed to escape. But never in the whole history of the Jewish people has there been a period which offered as many opportunities as the present, and never has there been a period when so few were utilized."

The Torah Also Needs a Commander

Until I suddenly heard the sharp ringing of a bell I had not realized the vast silence that dwelt in this room. The ringing came from outside, from the office, presumably. I gathered that my time had run out. But it did not occur to me to get up, and I went on sitting there as if there had been no ringing. Despite the repeated exhortation of the bell, the sound of the Rebbe's voice assured me that this was not yet the end.

"Every day that goes by is a tremendous loss. What it takes ten years to do in the Diaspora can be done in ten days in the Land of Israel, provided one gets down to the latent spark. A fire can go out, but a spark never. Our youth are asleep without knowing it, and those who address it with speeches are surprised at their not hearing. Unless they hear their own words, they are not aroused.

"What exactly are the words of our youth? I cannot tell. The words will follow with the inner force of the imperative. They must come from deep inside. The main thing is the awakening, the pioneering spirit. Once the vanguard is there, the banner may follow. Now there are many banners, but what are they all worth without anybody to walk ahead of them and carry them? Take those boys in Israel who throw stones on people who desecrate the Sabbath—I believe they have the spirit, there is something they really care about. I am not suggesting that they should throw stones, G-d forbid, but I feel that they care, that there is something burning inside them, and that is the main thing. Then I can try to convince them that they are using the wrong means, to divert their fire into the right channels...

"On the other hand the young people who are coming from the Land of Israel to study at foreign universities—they are not pioneers. What can they learn abroad that they cannot learn in the Holy Land? If a man leaves his home to go to the North Pole or climb a mountain at the risk of his life to satisfy his thirst for knowledge one may call him a pioneer. A young man who goes from Brooklyn to the Negev and risks his life on the border may be called a pioneer. But leaving Israel to study at a university in Brooklyn—that is mere hankering after comfort, not pioneering.

"Take our yeshivah students—they study, too. But in order to teach they go everywhere in the world where there are Jews, not to sit there in a yeshivah but to open new academies. They knock on every door. They find their way to non-religious kibbutzim in Israel and to assimilated homes in the Diaspora. The spirit of Judaism is the one ideal that has not failed like all the rest. Only the values of religion persist unscathed and unaltered. So far nothing has been found to replace them. And that is precisely why no compromise is possible in this respect. Everything may be done to facilitate its teaching, but nothing to facilitate its observance. Attempts to compromise will only alienate our youth rather than bring them closer to our religion. Israel's youth want no compromises. But here, too, no leader has been found, no commander who will issue the order, as in the Sinai campaign."

I Shall Come when the Messiah Arrives

It is getting close to two o'clock. The bell has stopped ringing. It has probably given up. But ringing in my own ears was the redoubled sound of my question:

"Why won't you come and give the order?"

"My place is where my words are likely to be obeyed. Here I am being listened to, but in the Land of Israel I won't be heard. There, our youth will follow only somebody who has sprung up from its own ranks and speaks its own language. The Messiah will be a man of flesh and blood, visible and tangible, a man whom others may follow. And he will come."

"He has been on his way for quite a while," I found myself saying.

"But he is very near and we must be prepared for him at any moment, because he may have come just one moment before."

THE PHILOSOPHY OF LUBAVITCH ACTIVISM

RABBI J. IMMANUEL SCHOCHET

Introduction

Over the past few decades Lubavitch has become well-known in Jewish communities throughout the world for its intense offensive toward a greater observance of Torah and *mitzvot*. Numerous young men and women move to dozens of cities and countries, often far away from their own places of origin, on *shlichut* (mission) to establish new, or fortify already existing, educational institutions and to fill responsible positions involving spiritual or educational needs. Their sole objective is to strengthen Jewish consciousness and religious awareness in their new surroundings. Many more, holding a variety of positions over the whole spectrum of professional occupations, seek, each in his or her own way, to achieve the same objective in their different environments.

A profound spirit of activism pervades the whole community of Lubavitch. Thousands of Jews from every kind of background have been exposed to an experience and influence of classical Judaism causing them to reorient their lives toward their historical identity and traditional values. And many of those who found the way back to their roots are now themselves active in the frontlines guiding other back.

Lubavitch seems to be an anachronism in this day and age. As early as a century ago already, professional historians, anthropologists and sociologists, wrapped up in their precisely calculated statistics and natural laws of causality, wrote off Hassidism as a passing relic and idiosyncrasy of an age long past. But it seems that no one informed the Hassidim of these prognostications. They defy and frustrate these prophets of doom by their tenacious, continuing survival. Verily, even after the terrible, decimating tragedy of the holocaust which, proportionally, struck the Hassidic community more than any others, Hassidism today enjoys a renaissance which staggers the imagination. Like the *chol*, the legendary phoenix-bird which constantly rises again in youthful freshness from its own ashes, Hassidism blossoms again, vibrantly alive and persistently spreading.

Many are perplexed: whence this strength? Whence this miraculous courage? Whence this unbelievable steadfastness and power in this day of counter-culture? In the midst of this very world Lubavitch not only stands its own ground but successfully broadens it.

The following is an attempt to formulate, more or less systematically, the philosophy of Lubavitch activism which inspires the Hassid to pursue his ideals unaffected by his environment. It is taken from the writings and talks of the present Lubavitcher Rebbe, R. Menachem M. Schneerson, *shelita*, most of which have already appeared in print in the course of time. (Most of the quotations are freely translated and adapted from the original Hebrew or Yiddish.) In these sources it will seek the answer, and its philosophical rationale, to the general questions:

1. What is a Hassid? 2. What is the Hassid's mission? 3. How is he to go about realizing it in the context of Lubavitch activism? 4. What is the role of the Rebbe?

More specific questions, like what is the rationale behind the Chabad principles of disseminating the mystical lore of Hassidic teachings and what is the basic concept of a Rebbe *per se* in Hassidism, are outside the present frame of reference. Though ultimately these two aspects are intimately related to the point of unity, we shall deal here only with the exoteric face of Lubavitch rather than with the esoteric one.

I.

The foundation-stone of Hassidism is the Zoharic dictum of the unity of God, Torah and Israel.[1] Thus the Ba'al Shem Tov taught: the essence of worship this day is that man bring himself to an all-encompassing love of God, love of Torah, and love of Israel.[2] And the very first proclamation the Lubavitcher Rebbe issued on the day he assumed Hassidic leadership was to the effect that these three loves are wholly and inextricably one:

> One cannot distinguish between them, for they are truly one, like unto one essence. The Ba'al Shem Tov states in the name of earlier sages that when seizing but a part of essence one seizes it in its totality.[3] Hence, as the three loves are essentially one, every one of them contains all three; for when seizing a part of essence one seizes it all. Where there is love of God but no love for Torah and Israel, that love of God is clearly defective.[4] In turn, where there is a true love of Israel then, notwithstanding the fact that this itself is one of the 'rational commandments' which reason alone already obligates,[5] ultimately one will arrive at love of Torah and God.
>
> And this must be made known: when seeing a Jew who has love of God but no love of Torah or Israel, he is to be told and made to realize that it cannot endure. In turn, when seeing a Jew who has but love of Israel, he must be brought to love of Torah and love of God. One must further see that his love of Israel should not consist of merely providing food for the hungry and water for the thirsty, but that on account of his *Ahavat Israel* (Love of Israel) he is to bring fellow-Jews to love of Torah and love of God.
>
> Where these three loves shall be united they will form the "threefold cord that is not quickly broken" (Eccles. 4:12). And that, too, shall bring the ultimate redemption. For just as this last exile was caused by the opposite of *Ahavat Israel*,[6] so by means of *Ahavat Israel* will occur the redemption from this exile speedily in our days.[7]

1 Zohar III: 73a; cf. Tikunei Zohar XXI:60b.

2 *Butzina Denehura*, quoted in R. Sholom Mendel's comprehensive anthology. *Sefer Ba'al Shem Tov* (2nd ed. Landsberg 1946), vol. II, p. 68.

3 *Toldot Ya'akov Yosseph*, Vitro: VI (ed. Jerusalem 1960, p. 1 82a). See also ibid., *Chaye Sarah*: III (p. 69a) where this maxim is cited in relation to the *mitzvah* of *Ahavat Israel. Sefer Ba'al Shem Tov*, vol. II, pp. 134 ff.

4 See *Mekhilta* on Exodus 15: 7;. *Sifre* on Numbers 10:35; *Pessikta Rabati*, *Ki Tissa*, (ed. Friedmann, p. 39b). And thus the Ba'al Shem Tov taught: "Love of Israel is love of God. 'You are the children of the Eternal your God' (Deut. 14:1) —when one loves the Father one loves His children;" R. Menachem M. Schneerson, *Hayom Yom* (Kehot: New York 1961), p. 81.

5 See *Yoma* 67b; R. Saadiah Gaon, *Emunot Vede'ot* III: 1ff.

6 See *Yoma* 9b; *Zohar Chadash*, *Yayeshev* 29d.

7 R. Menachem M. Schneerson, *Likutei Sichot* (4 volumes, Kehot: New York 1962-64), II: p. 499f. Cf. also ibid., pp. 298 and 800.

The Ba'al Shem Tov interpreted the dictum "All Torah that is without work ends in failure"[8] to mean that in order that the Torah endure it must be accompanied by work in and preoccupation with Ahavat Israel.[9] Every one must work on Ahavat Israel to influence a fellow-Jew to become better. Indeed, this will be to his own benefit as well, as our sages commented[10] on the verses "the poor man and the man of substance meet together, and the Eternal enlightens both their eyes" (Proverbs 29:13) and "the rich and the poor meet together, the Eternal is the Maker of them all" (Proverbs 22:2). For just as it is with the poor and rich in the material sense so it is with the poor and rich in the spiritual realm – that when the rich endows the poor, the Eternal endows the rich also.[11]

Only he that surrenders himself with complete self-sacrifice to Ahavat Israel can be sure of himself that he will be whole.[12] Thus R. Schneur Zalman of Liadi taught that the commandment "and you shall love your fellow-man like yourself" (Levit. 19:8) is a means and prerequisite to the commandment "and you shall love the Eternal your God" (Deut. 6:5);[13] and that by the act of material and spiritual charity is effected that "*tzedakah* exalts a nation" (Prov. 14:34)[14] – i.e., that his own mind and heart become purified infinitely beyond what they were.[15]

II.

This concept of "spiritual charity" is a constantly recurring theme. In one of his first pastoral letters the Rebbe writes:[16]

> Man possesses a body and soul. And just as there is material poverty (in food, clothing, shelter) so there is spiritual poverty where the deficiency is in spiritual things: knowledge of Torah, observance of *mitzvot*, and the practice of good deeds.

The Rebbe refers to the Rabbinic interpretation of Isaiah's statement of the ordinances of righteousness that draw nigh unto God – "is it not to deal your bread to the hungry and that you bring the cast-out poor to your house! When you see the naked that you cover him and that you hide not yourself from your own flesh" (Isaiah 58 :7):

> The hungry refers to him that is famished of Torah, and bread refers to the Torah.... If there be a person that understands Torah he is to provide others, too, from his Torah... How are we to understand "when you see the naked," etc.? Surely in the sense of when you see a man lacking in the knowledge of Torah, take him into your house and teach him to say the *Shema* and prayers, and teach him daily one verse or one law, and encourage him to fulfill the *mitzvot*. For none is naked in Israel but he that lacks Torah and *mitzvot*.[17]

The constant emphasis on "spiritual charity" is not to belittle in any way the plain sense of the *mitzvah* to render material assistance: One of the ways to befriend and bring nigh a fellow man is by extending a helping hand to offer physical and material succor. While this is an essential part of the obligation of *Ahavat Israel*, obviously it will also help to bring him nearer spiritually. But one is not to wait and make material aid dependent on the spiritual, but do so absolutely and unconditionally.[18]

III.

The preoccupation with *Ahavat Israel*, of which the Ba'al Shem Tov taught that it applies even to a Jew at the furthest end of the world whom one has never seen,[19] and of which the Maggid of Mezeritch said that it means to love even a totally wicked person just like a completely righteous man,[20] relates especially

8 *Avot* 11:2.

9 *Cf. Yevamot* 105a and 109b "Whoever says that he has nothing but Torah—he has not even Torah; rather, one must be engaged with Torah and the performance of kindness."

10 See *Temurah* 16a.

11 *Likutei Sichot* I:p. 260; *cf.* ibid., p. 134.

12 *Ibid.*, p. 105.

13 *Ibid.*, II:p. 298.

14 R. Schneur Zalman, *Torah Or*, Bereishit 1bf. *Cf. Tanchuma* on *Ex. 22:24.*

15 *Likutei Sichot*, I:p. 262.

16 Dated 18 Elul 5710; reprinted in *Outlines of the Social and Communal Work of Chabad-Lubavitch*,. (Kehot: New York 1953) p. 48. *Cf. Likutei Sichot*, IV: p. 1059.

17 *Eliyahu Rabba*, ch. 27. *Cf.* also *ibid.* ch. 13; *Pirkei de R. Eliezer* ch. 19; and *Shulchan Arukh, Yoreh De'ah* 245:3, and commentaries *a.l.*

18 *Likutei Sichot*, I:p. 262. *Cf. ibid.*, p. 133f.

19 *Ibid.*, II:pp. 435 and 686.

20 *Ibid.*, p. 299. *Cf.* R. Moses Cordovero, *Tomer Devorah*,. ch. 2; and J. I. Schochet, "Ahavath Israel," *The Jewish Home* IX:1 (New York, Summer 1967), p. 18 and note 56.

to one whom Divine Providence has led to a place where Torah and *mitzvot* are weak. Should such a one claim that he needs to protect himself and seek to escape from this kind of place saying "I save my own soul," he should know that this is a matter of *pikuach nefashot*—saving lives.[21] And in cases of *pikuach nefashot* one is not permitted to make such calculations.[22] As Divine Providence has led him there, it placed upon him a mission and endowed him with the abilities to convert that place to one of Torah and *mitzvot*. To teach us this very truism the Talmud[23] relates how Rav came to Babylon and '"found there an open field" —i.e., places where the people were ignorant and negligent in the observance of the laws of Sabbath, dietary laws, etc., "and he put a fence around it" – i.e., he instituted enactments to prevent them from further transgressions.[24]

Also, the Talmud[25] relates of R. Chanina bar Pappa that he wished to experience what R. Joshua ben Levi had attained. But notwithstanding that there is not anything written in the Torah that he had not observed, and, indeed, when his soul passed to its eternal rest a pillar of fire formed a partition between him and the world,[26] he was unsuccessful. For R. Chanina could not answer affirmatively the question put to him "have you attached yourself to the sufferers of *ra'atan* (a contagious disease with extremely repugnant symptoms) and engaged thus in Torah?" Many *Amoraim*, the Talmud relates there, had distanced themselves from people afflicted with this disease. R. Joshua ben Levi, however, attached himself to these sufferers and studied the Torah. He sought to disseminate Torah everywhere, even among the sufferers of *ra'atan*, and that is why he merited what he did. And that, too, is the instruction of R. Joshua ben Levi, in *Perek Kinyan Hatorah*,[27] that one must be occupied with Torah, i.e., not just learn for oneself but disseminate Torah even unto the very lowest level of the "sufferers of *ra'atan*."[28]

However, this principle is by no means to be understood in terms that one is to neglect oneself and go out of his way to be preoccupied with others only. For one thing, the above-cited *locus classicus* of Isaiah 58 ends with the exhortation "hide not yourself from your own flesh," i.e., you may not ignore, and must work on, your own fleshness, your own involvement with the mundane.[29] Moreover, one should for sure not force oneself of oneself into "narrow straits." To be sure, there is always a lot to be achieved, but at the same time "all roads are presumed to be dangerous,"[30] —thus why expose yourself intentionally to danger!

If, however, it be (that he went down into Egypt compelled) by decree,[31] i.e., that he was told to and sent there, or that he finds that Divine Providence has led and brought him to that particular place, then all these arguments fall by the side; after all, it is "by Divine decree."[32] He must know that when he comes there by decree, then as for himself he is under compulsion, going only because of the decree, and hence he must do so joyfully and is assured that "I will also surely bring you up again" (Genesis 46:4) and in the end he will come out "with great substance" (Genesis 15: 14) spiritually as well as materially.[33]

IV.

The previous Lubavitcher Rebbe, R. Joseph Isaac (1880–1950) once recalled[34] a thought-provoking conversation that took place between his father R. Sholom Ber (1860–1920) and a Hassid:

21 *Cf.* Midrashim on *Numbers* 25:17, and *Sifre* Deuter. 252 (*ed.* Friedmann, p. 120a). See also *Zohar* II:139a and the next note.

22 See *Yoma* 82a ("There is nothing that stands before the duty of saving life," etc.). *Cf. Sanhedrin* 73a ("The following must be saved from sinning... Whence do we know that if a man sees his fellow drowning, mauled by beasts or attacked by robbers, he is duty-bound to save him," etc.) and *ibid.* 74a. ("R. Shimon bar Yochai said," etc.).

23 *Eruvin* 6a and 100b, and *Chullin* 110a; see Rashi *ad loc.*

24 *Likutei Sichot*, I:p. 262.

25 *Ketuvot* 77b.

26 The *Gemara ad loc.* explains that this happens only to the one, or at most two, most outstanding men in a generation.

27 *Avot* VI:2.

28 *Likutei Sichot*,. IV:p. 1239.

29 *Ibid.*, p. 1059.

30 *Yerushalmi. Berakhot* IV:4.

31 *Hagadah*; see Genesis 46:3 and commentaries *ad loc.; Zahar* II:53a.

32 This follows the principal Hassidic doctrine with respect to an all-embracing, particular Divine Providence. Thus the Ba'al Shem Tov interpreted the verse "A man's goings are established by the Eternal," etc. (Psalms 37:23) to mean that wherever man happens to be, and for whatever personal reasons he happens to have gone there, it is really Divine Providence that has brought him to that particular place in order to carry out some spiritual task. See *Sefer Ba'al Shem Tov*, vol. I, p. 219*f.*, and *Hayom Yom*, p. 104.

33 *Likutei Sichot*, IV:p. 1220.

34 *Sefer Hasichot* 5701 (Kehot: New York 1964), p. 136*f.*

The Hassid asked: "Rebbe, what is a Hassid?"

R. Sholom Ber answered him: "A Hassid is a street-lamp lighter. A street-lamp lighter has a pole with fire; he knows that the fire is not his own, and he goes around lighting all lamps on his route."

The Hassid asked: "But what if the lamp is in a desolate wilderness?"

The Rebbe answered: "Then, too, one must light it. Let it be noted that there is a wilderness and let the wilderness feel ashamed before the light."

"But what if the lamp is in the midst of a sea?"

"Then one must take off his clothes, jump into the water and light it there!"

"And that is a Hassid?"

The Rebbe thought for a long moment and then said: "Yes, that is a Hassid."

The Hassid persisted: "Rebbe, I see no lamps!"

"That is because you are not a street-lamp lighter."

'"How does one become such?"

And R. Shalom Ber replied: '"One must be *sur mera* (avoid evil). When beginning with oneself, cleansing oneself, becoming more refined, then one sees the lamp of the other. When, Heaven forefend, one is crude—one sees but crudeness, but when himself noble one sees nobility."[35]

When the present Rebbe recounted this conversation, he added: The lamps are there but they need to be lit. It is written "The soul of man is a lamp of the Eternal" (Proverbs 20:27) and it is also written "A mitzvah is a lamp and the Torah is light" (Proverbs 6:23). A Hassid is he that puts his personal affairs aside and goes around lighting up the souls of Jews with the light of Torah and *mitzvot*. Jewish souls are in readiness to be lit. Sometimes they are around the corner; sometimes they are in a wilderness or at sea. But there must be someone who, disregarding personal comforts and conveniences, will go out to put a light to these lamps. And that is the function of a true Hassid.[36]

Hassidism in general demands that one disseminate Torah and *Yiddishkeit* all over and seek to cause good to a fellow Jew, and as R. Sholom Ber put it another time: "A Hassid is he that surrenders his self to seeking the welfare of another."[37] Over and beyond that Chabad demands *pnimiyut* (inwardness; essence), i.e., that all things be done not just superficially, as a mere act of faith, but with inner conviction, with the soul faculties of Chabad,[38] to the point of involving even the rational faculties of the animal soul and even the physical brain of the body; this is the mystical concept of the Divine soul entering the physical body.[39]

V.

To this point we have a clear definition of what it means to be a Hassid and what the Hassid's task and mission in life is. But how is he to set out to realize his ideal? The answer to this question is found in the following quotations from the Lubavitcher Rebbe:

> The essential features of the attitude and policy of Lubavitch are not to content ourselves with defensive tactics. That is to say, not to wait until a position of *Yiddishkeit* is attacked in order to rally to its defense. This has been the erroneous attitude of American Orthodox Jewry and also of Jewries in certain European countries. The proper attitude is to employ offensive and preventative methods through the widest possible dissemina-

35 This again reflects typical Hassidic thought. The Ba'al Shem Tov (in comment on *Avot* IV:1; *Nega'im* II:5; and *Kiddushin* 70a) teaches that what man sees in another is a mirror-reflection of himself: as he is himself so he sees the other. See *Sefer Ba'al Shem Tov*, vol. I: pp. 86-89.

36 Sichot 13 *Tamuz* 5722 (in *Ms*); *cf. Likutei Sichot* II:p. 315*f.*

37 *Sefer Hasichot* 5700 (Kehot: New York 1956), p. 33.

38 *Chokhmah* (conceptual wisdom), *Binah* (comprehensive understanding), *Da'ath* (penetrating knowledge and conscious awareness of the *chokhmah* expanded by *binah*, to the point of bringing it to its logical conclusion in actual implementation)—*Tanya*, ch. 3—the key concepts underlying the psychological and philosophical system of Lubavitch-Hassidism which, therefore, is referred to as Chabad-Hassidism.

39 *Likutei Sichot*, III:p. 800*f.*

tion of, and propaganda for, those high ideals for which classical Orthodoxy stands. As a logical corollary of this attitude it follows that we cannot remain content with activity confined to our own, immediate circle. Propaganda for true Orthodoxy must be directed at all strata of Jewry.[40]

In a private conversation in the summer of 1951, the Rebbe dealt with this same point at greater length:

> Orthodox Jewry has unfortunately concentrated upon defensive strategy. We were always worried lest we lose positions and strongholds. And indeed we had all reason for worry. One Jewish bastion after another has fallen into the hands of the non-religious. Had Orthodox Jews, instead of waiting to defend, taken the offensive and sought to widen their influence and create more and better bastions for Torah *Yiddishkeit*, the situation would be quite different and the non-religious would not, as is now the case, dominate Jewish communal affairs. The lesson to be drawn from this is obvious. To discharge ourselves of our duty we must take the initiative and wage an offensive. This, of course, takes courage, planning, vision and the will to carry on despite all odds.
>
> But that has always been the true Jewish approach, the Torah perspective on life and the ways of Divine Providence. If we were to count the odds and weigh the chances, we would be lacking in *Bitachon*, faith in the ultimate affirmation of the right and justification of the just. Weakness, lack of power and influence should never deter us from the path prescribed by the Torah. We must not be frightened by the fact that only a minority of the millions of Jews gathered in this country are to be counted as Torah-conscious Jews. We must know only one thing: our task and our will to do it. Success is not up to us; it is in higher hands.
>
> The thing we have to fear most at this moment is the defeatism and the defection that has gripped some of our best elements in this country in the face of the growing effects of so-called "inter-faith" movements, of the watering down of the very content of our religion to a point where our children will no longer know whether they are Jews or not. This defeatism is even worse than the limitation to defensive tactics. Charity begins at home. We cannot talk of assuming responsibility for the rest of the Jewish world, of building new centers for Torah and *Yiddishkeit* elsewhere, even in Eretz Yisrael, when right here in our midst our brothers and sisters are being engulfed. More than that, we have no right to teach and lead others if at home we neglect the very thing we want to make others do.[41]

The offensive for Torah-Judaism that the Rebbe speaks of is directed at all Jews, regardless of their background and present status. For one thing, all Jews in unison are one body, the individual members of which interact and are most intimately related one to another. The acts and affectations of any one of them affect directly every other one as well.[42] Also, there is not a single Jew, as far as he may seem or thought himself to have drifted from the center of Yiddishkeit, who does not have some good point, some particular mitzvah which by nature or inclination he may promote. This spark of "good" in each soul can and must be utilized for the good of the Jewish community, and, in turn, for the good of the person who does it.[43] Each individual counts, because each individual may perhaps become a leader or the father of many generations to be gained for the Torah, or God forbid—to be lost.[44]

According to the Rebbe, the non-Orthodox are to be not only the objects but also the subjects of the call to arms for Torah *Yiddishkeit*.

---

40 Quoted in Charles Raddock, "Bridging the Gap between East and West," *The Jewish Forum*, December 1953.

41 Quoted in G. Kranzler, "A Visit with the New Lubavitcher Rebbe," *Jewish Life*, Sept.–Oct. 1951.

42 *Likutei Sichot*, II:pp. 297-301, *398ff.* and 435. See *Mekhilta de'Rashb'y* on Exodus 19:6 (*ed.* Epstein-Melamed, p. 139): "They are as one body and one soul . . . if one of them is afflicted all of them feel it," etc. See also the celebrated simile of R. Shimon bar Yochai in *Levit. Rabba* IV:6 and *Zohar* III:122a; J. I. Schochet, *op. cit.*, ch. VII-VIII.

43 Kranzler, *op. cit.*

44 *Ibid.*; *cf. Sanhedrin* 37a ("Whosoever preserves a single soul of Israel," etc.).

> For example, take the danger of mixed marriages; if we can use even those of our people who do not believe in any other of the 613 *mitzvot* than the preservation of the purity of our families, we must definitely call on them in order to be able to stem such defections from our faith and with it from our nation. Not always does it matter who does the "doing" as long as it is done. The accomplishment counts for what it achieves objectively and for what it does to the one involved. (The same would apply to Jewish education—that whoever has the power and the will to contribute some aspect, some particular skill or capacity towards the offensive for Jewish education must be drawn upon.)[45]

VI.

The obvious questions that rise now are: how does one approach non-religious Jews to become involved and more observant? Even while allowing for individual gains to be made, what realistic hopes are there for the success of such an offensive for Torah *Yiddishkeit*? At times it would seem that for every one won over, the Hassid probably meets up with perhaps two disappointments as well. How, then, does one retain the courage and enthusiasm to carry on if the odds are so heavily weighted against?

The Rebbe states that it is a well-known empirical fact that where matters of Torah and *mitzvot* are concerned every Jew, no matter how estranged, is generally found responsive.[46] To be sure, one Jew may more readily respond to this particular mitzvah or idea, while another one to that. It is all a matter of experience and approach. But where the approach is right no Jew is wholly unresponsive! For no Jew is absolutely stripped of every vestige of Jewishness.[47]

It would serve no purpose to approach the non-observant with demands for immediate, full ascent to the Torah way of life. But through a pleasant, understanding and helpful approach a good many of these straying souls can be brought back partially, and gradually even completely. But this is possible only if we take the offensive and if we do not fall into the trap of overlooking the trees because of the forest.[48]

The most important thing is "no compromise," according to Lubavitch. Compromise is dangerous because it sickens both the body and the soul. A compromiser who tries to mediate religion and environment is unable to go in either direction and unable to distinguish the truth.[49] The great fault of Conservative and Reform Judaism is not that they compromise but that they sanctify the compromise, still the conscience, and leave no possibility for return (*teshuvah*).[50] The Rebbe states that

> It is important to know that one must do everything, but at the same time we welcome the doing of even a part. If all we can accomplish is to save one limb, we save that. Then we worry about saving another.[51]

This strict adherence and allegiance to the principles and precepts of Torah in the perspective of the historical tradition of classical Orthodoxy by no means implies that Orthodoxy in general, and Hasidism in particular, are to be seen as a fossilized conservatism. The Rebbe says that:

> I don't believe that Reform is liberal and Orthodox is conservative. My explanation of conservatism is someone who is so petrified he cannot accept something new. For me Judaism or Halakhah or Torah encompasses all the universe, and it encompasses every new invention, every new theory, every new piece of knowledge or thought or action. Everything that happens in 1972 has a place in the Torah, and it must be interpreted, it must be explained, it must be evaluated from the point of view of Torah even if it happened for the first time in March of 1972.[52]

45 Kranzler, *loc. cit.*

46 See Maimonides, *Hilkhot Gerushin* II:20, where this maxim is stated in Halakhic context. And hence the oft-cited principle in Chabad-Hassidism that "it is innate to every Jew that he does not will, nor is he able, to be separated from Divinity," see R. Menachem M. Schneerson, *Kobetz Yud Shevat*, (Kehot: New York 1968), p. 22*f*.

47 Raddock, *op. cit.*

48 Kranzler, *op. cit.*

49 Quoted in H. Weiner, "The Lubavitcher Movement—II," *Commentary*, April 1957, p. 327.

50 *Ibid.*, p. 318.

51 *Ibid.*, p. 327.

52 Quoted in *New York Times*, March 27, 1972, p. 39.

The distant future does not seem to be the immediate concern of the Hassidim. As the Rebbe put it:

> We can see only what is going on right now, in the present, and on the surface. The patterns of Providence are not unveiled to us till later. Our task, and in particular that of Jewish youth, is to do and want to do. The rest is not up to us. But, to cite the late Lubavitcher Rebbe (R. Joseph Yitzchak) of sainted memory, we have two basic assurances. The first is: every action is worth more than a thousand sighs. And secondly: no action for a good purpose has ever been done in vain. In the long run it will succeed and pay its dividends. These must be our guiding principles.[53]
>
> We ourselves do not count. It is our task, our sacred mission, that matters. And if we but want to carry it on, our goal will not remain unachieved.[54]
>
> If all the *mitzvot* of the Torah must be carried out with vigor, then, *a fortiori*, the mitzvah of *Ahavat Israel*, the very foundation of the Whole Torah.[55] One must speak with fellow Jews about Torah and *mitzvot*, and, if unsuccessful, speak again. Even if he should object adamantly, be not impressed. On the contrary, his opposition only proves that he is affected.[56] Thus one must speak to him again and again until he accedes.[57] One must go about this strongly. To be sure, the discussion must be in a pleasant manner to make it acceptable, but with convincing strength. With this combination of pleasantness and vigor one will succeed. When not successful at first, one is to know that the fault lies not with the other but within yourself. The other is good, but because your own words "do not come from the heart" that is why "they do not enter the heart."[58]

In the perspective of this goal and sense of responsibility, odds just do not count and may not count.

VII.

What is the role of a Rebbe in this context? If such comparison be permissible, it would seem to be that of a "chief street-lamp lighter." Every Jew has the "soul of man that is a lamp of the Eternal," though there are some among them that wait until it be lit for them. And that is the function of the *Nesi'ey Yisrael* (the Leaders of Israel; the Rebbes) —to light this Divine lamp in every Jew. Just as in the Menorah (Candelabra) there are seven different branches, so too, there are seven general groups of Jews,[59] each with its own peculiar traits, needs and approach, —and the Rebbe's role is to light them all.[60]

In a similar, though differently worded way, the Rebbe once answered a group of students that had asked him this very question:

> The Jewish people are referred to as *Eretz Heifetz* (a land of delight, or a land of treasure, Mal. 3:12). In the earth lie concealed many treasures, but they are not visible on the surface and one must dig deeply in order to find them. However, not all know the right places where to dig for them. Some explore and in the end find only swampy waters and mire, as happened, for example, to Freud when he delved into the labyrinth of man's psyche. Others again wind up with nothing but rocks, as happened, for example, to Adler who found but a striving for superiority directed toward strength and dominance. Only an expert knows where to dig so as to find the truly precious treasures: silver—symbolic of the love of God; gold—symbolic of the awe before God; and diamonds—which allude to the essence—faith. To find these treasures that is the task of a Rebbe.[61]

53 Kranzler, *op. cit.*

54 *Ibid.*

55 *Shabbat* 31a; *Sifra* on Levit. 19:18; *Tanya*, ch. 32.

56 For as long as some reaction is evoked this is an indication that the person is affected and impressible. The indifferent, impassible person is beyond reach. See R. Sholom Ber, *Torat Shalom*, (Kehot: New York 1957) p. 10*f*.

57 "Whence do we know that if a man sees something unseemly in his fellow he is obliged to reprove him? Because it is said: 'you shall surely rebuke' (Levit. 19:17). If he rebuked him but he did not accept it whence do we know that he must rebuke him again? The text states 'surely rebuke'—anyhow," (*Arakhin* 16b) even a hundred times (*Baba Metzia* 31a) until the reprover be beaten (*Arakhin ad loc.*). See Maimonides, *Hilkhot De'ot* VI:7 *et passim*).

58 *Likutei Sichot*, I:128*f*.

59 For this homily see at length R. Schneur Zalman, *Likutei Torah*, *Beha'alothekha*: p. 32d. Its source can be traced to the Ba'al Shem Tov. See *Toldot Ya'akov Yosseph*, *Beha'alothckha* and *Chukath*.

60 *Likutei Sichot*, II:315*f*.

61 *MS*, and *Ma'ariv*, 16 January 1970, p. 29.

The role of a Rebbe thus is that of a soul-geologist who manifests the latent powers and treasures concealed in all, who seeks to awaken in everyone the potential he has. He is the generator that charges and a beacon that guides in whom all the above is succinctly crystallized. His role as mentor and counselor, whose advice and blessing is sought in matters spiritual and material, is seen in the same context: the context of responsibility toward his people. When asked how he can possibly reply to the multifarious concerns ranging from questions of theology and meta physics to family- and business affairs as well as medical problems, the Rebbe replied that, for one thing, he is not afraid to answer "I do not know." But above all—

> If I know, then I have no right not to answer. When someone comes to you for help and you can help him to the best of your knowledge, and you refuse him this help, then you become a cause of his suffering.[62]

But even while the Rebbe's role is central, at no times should his presence give rise to some form of personality-cult. Hassidim are not to rely for themselves on the Rebbe's efforts: Chabad Hassidism demands that a Jew attain all positive qualities by means of personal effort.[63] One must not be content even with natural goodness, i.e., with that which comes to man naturally and easily. Everyone must exert himself in the service of God, both physically as well as spiritually, and as it is written "man is born to toil" (Job 5:7).[64]

The objective of every individual must be to act and to actualize, though not just simply act but to do so with the effort which the Torah refers to as *amal* (toil). Only then does man raise himself from the level of *adam* (man)—"dust from the *adamah* (ground)" (Genesis 2:7), to the level of *adam*—"*e-dameh* (I will be like) the Most High," (Isaiah 14:14)[65] as it were.[66] And as the Rebbe proclaimed the day he assumed leadership:

> Chabad has always demanded that everyone must act himself and not to depend on the Rebbe.

[This is the difference between Polish Hassidism and Chabad: the former base themselves on the principle of "The *Tzadik yichyeh* by his faith" (Habak, 2:4). Do not read *yichyeh* (lives) but *yechayeh* (animates).][67]

Thus all of us need to act personally, with the 248 organs and 365 limbs of the body and the 248 "organs" and 365 "limbs" of the soul... Each one must convert to holiness the folly of the "opposing forces" and the vehemence of the animal soul. Moses could have built the sanctuary all by himself, but he wished that all Jews have the merit of participating. Thus it is self-evident that in fulfilling our duty to establish an abode for Divinity here on earth *all of us, and all Jews*, must partake. Everyone must act himself and carry out his mission.[68]

And in a paraphrase of the maxim that "everything depends on the will,"[69] the Rebbe says:

62 *New York Times, ad loc. cit.*

63 In fact this, too, reflects classic Hassidic thought, i.e., the original teachings of the Ba'al Shem Tov and R. Dov Ber, the Maggid of Mezeritch. They refer to the Patriarchs as models from whom we are to learn not to rely on faith and tradition alone: Isaac did not rely on the tradition of Abraham alone, nor did Jacob rely simply on the heritage from his predecessors. Each exerted himself to understand his heritage, to arrive at his knowledge and beliefs through personal labor and efforts. That is why, in our prayers, we refer to "God of Abraham, God of Isaac, and God of Jacob" (rather than compounding all three together). The Maggid (in the footsteps of the earlier commentators) states "*Know* the God of your father" (I-*Chron*. 28:9) and do not just accept it simply as a tradition, as a matter of habit. See *Sefer Ba'al Shem Tov*, vol. I:pp. 183, 196*f*., and 252: and the Maggid's *Or Torah, Tehilim* (on Psalms 92:3), and *Likutei Amaram*, *ed*. Jerusalem 1962. p. 24a.

64 *Likutei Sichot*, III:p. 800*f*; *cf. ibid*., II:p. 485.

65 An etymological interpretation of *adam* frequent in mystical literature. See R. Isaiah Horowitz, *Shnei Luchot Habrit, Toldoth Adam* (*ed*. Jerusalem 1963, vol. I:p. 3b): "If (man) attaches himself to Above and likens himself unto Him, blessed be He, by walking in His paths (see Deut. 13:5 and *Shabbat* 133b, etc.). he is then called by the essential name *adam* which is an idiom of *edameh le'elyon* (Isaiah 14:14) . . . But if he separates himself from the attachment he is then called *adam* in relation to *adamah* (ground, soil) from which he was taken—dust he is and unto dust he shall return. The principal purpose, however, is for the term *adam* to indicate *edameh le'elyon."* See also *ibid*., *Tzon Yosseph*, vol. II:p. 29a: "The name *adam* originally, indicated *edameh le'elyon*, but after Adam sinned it indicates the earthly character of 'dust from the ground.'"

66 Pastoral Letter of 11 Nissan 5732; *cf. Hayom Yom*, p. 48.

67 This radical difference between reliance on the *Tzadik* and personal efforts by every individual was a principal point of disagreement between R. Schneur Zalman of Liadi and his Chabad-school on the one side. and R. Shlomo of Karlin and his school on the other side. See at length R. Joseph Isaac, *Likutei Diburim*, (Kehot: New York 1957). vol. I:p. 282. See also the correspondence between R. Abraham of Kalisk on the one hand and R. Schneur Zalman of Liadi and R. Levi Yitzack of Berdichev on the other, in D. Hilman, ed., *Igaroth Ba'al Hatanya Ubnei Doro* (Jerusalem 1953). nos. 58-59, 100, 102. 103.

68 *Likutei Sichot*, II:500*f*.

69 *Zohar* II:162b.

It is not we that count—we with our weaknesses and limited capabilities. It is our will to do a task that we realize is important. Success is not in our hands, it is the Lord's. But we have to will to do what He demands of us, and in that will all our weaknesses and insufficiencies wane and become insignificant.[70]

Tradition 13:1 (summer 1972), pp. 18–35
Reprinted with permission of the publisher

TO IGNITE THE SOUL

AMBASSADOR YEHUDA AVNER

As previously arranged, after the White House talks, I returned to New York to call upon the Lubavitcher Rebbe, and report to him how we had fared. There, at 770 Eastern Parkway, I found myself settled with the sage in his unadorned wood-paneled chamber, where he greeted me with a beaming smile. Dog-eared Talmudic tomes and other heavy, well-thumbed volumes line his bookshelves, representing centuries of scholarship and disputation.

We spoke in Hebrew; the Rebbe's classic, mine modern. What lured me most as we talked were the Rebbe's eyes. They were wide apart, sheltering under a heavy brow, but fine eyebrows. Their hue was azure of the deep sea, intense and compelling, although I knew that when the Rebbe's soul turned turbulent, they could dim to an ominous grey, like a leaden sky. They exuded wisdom and, awareness, kindness, and good fellowship; they were the eyes of one who could see mystery in the obvious, poetry in the mundane, and large issues in small things; eyes that captivated believers in gladness, and joy, and sacrifice.

As he dissected my account, his air of authority seemed to deepen. It came of something beyond his knowledge. It was his state of being, something he possessed in his soul which I cannot possibly begin to explain, something given to him under the chestnut and maple trees of Brooklyn rather than under the poplars and pines of Jerusalem to which, mysteriously, he had never journeyed.

I never asked him why, because I felt that he dwelt on an entirely different plane— a profoundly mystical plane, one to which I, a mere diplomat, could never aspire. The Lubavitcher Rebbe was a theologian, not a political Zionist. But if Zionism is an unconditional, passionate devotion to the Land of Israel and to its security and welfare, then Rabbi Menachem Mendel Schneerson was a fanatical Zionist.

My presentation, his interrogation, and his further clarification, took close to three hours. By the time we finished it was nearly two in the morning. I was utterly exhausted, but not the Rebbe. He was full of vim and vigor when he said, "After listening to what you have told me I wish to communicate the following message to Mr. Begin," and he began dictating in a voice that was soft but touched with fire.

"By maintaining your firm stand on Eretz Yisroel in the White House you have given strength to the whole of the Jewish people. You have succeeded in safeguarding the integrity of Eretz Yisroel while avoiding a confrontation with the United States. That is true Jewish statesmanship; forthright, bold, without pretense or apology. Continue to be strong and of good courage."

Then to me:

"What do I mean when I say to Mr. Begin, 'Be strong and of good courage?' I mean that the Jewish people in Eretz Yisroel cannot live by physical power alone. For what is physical power? It is made up of four major components: One- weaponry: do you have the weaponry to assert your physical power? Two- will: do you have the will to employ your weaponry? Three- competence: do you have the competence to employ your weaponry effectively? And four- perception: does the enemy perceive that you have the weaponry, the will and the competence to effectively employ your physical power so as to ensure your deterrent strength?"

70 *Kranzler*, ibid.

And then, gently, "But even if you have all of these, Reb Yehuda, but you are bereft of the spirit of *'Mi hu ze Melech hakavod? Hashem izuz v'gibor, Hashem gibor milchama'* [Who is the King of glory? The L-rd strong and mighty, the L-rd mighty in battle] then all your physical power is doomed to fail, for it has no Jewish moral compass to sustain it."

At this his usually benign features became grim, and his eyes dimmed to an ominous grey when he added, "For in every generation an Amalek rises up against us, but the *Ribono shel Olam* [the Almighty] ensures that every tyrant in every age who seeks our destruction is himself destroyed. *Am Yisrael chai* [the people of Israel lives on] only by virtue of *hashgocho* [divine protection]. Time and again, our brethren in Eretz Yisroel have been threatened with destruction. Time and again, they have floundered and stumbled and been bled. Yet time and again, *b'siyata d'Shamaya* [with the Almighty's help] they have weathered every storm, overcome every hurdle, withstood every test and, at the end of the day, emerged stronger than before. That is *hashgocho.*"

Relaxing, he fixed me with those eyes, and with a surprisingly sweet smile, said, "Now tell me, Reb Yehuda, you visit us so often yet you are not a Lubavitcher. Why?"

Still trying to absorb what he had said, I sat back, stunned at the directness of the question. It was true. This, probably, was my fifth or sixth meeting with the Rebbe. Over the years I had become a sort of unofficial liaison between the various prime ministers I served and the Lubavitch court.

Swallowing thickly, I muttered, "Maybe it is because I have met so many people who ascribe to the Rebbe, powers which the Rebbe does not ascribe to himself."

Even as I said this I realized I had presumed too much, and could hear my voice trailing away as I spoke.

The Rebbe's brows knitted, and his deep blue eyes grayed again, into something between solemnity and sadness, and he said, "*Yesh k'nireh anashim hazekukim l'kobayim* [There are evidently people who are in need of crutches]." The way he said it conveyed infinite compassion.

Then, as if tracking my thoughts, he raised his palm in a gesture of reassurance, and with an encouraging smile, said, "Reb Yehuda, let me tell you what I try to do. Imagine you're looking at a candle. What you are really seeing is a lump of wax with a thread down its middle. So when do the thread and wax become one candle? Or, in other words, when do they fulfill the purpose for which they were created? When you put a flame to the thread, then the wax and the thread become a candle. "

Then his voice flowed into the rhythmic cadence of the Talmud scholar poring over his text, so that what he said next came out as a chant:

"The wax is the body and wick is the soul. Bring the flame of the Torah to the soul, then the body will fulfill the purpose for which it was created. And that, Reb Yehuda, is what I try to do—to ignite the soul of every Jew and Jewess with the fire of our Torah, with the passion of our tradition, and with the sanctity of our heritage, so that each individual will fulfill the real purpose for which he or she was created."

A buzzer had been sounding periodically, indicating that others from around the world were awaiting their turns for an audience. When I rose to bid my farewells, the Rebbe escorted me to the door, and there I asked him, "Has the Rebbe lit my candle?"

"No," he said, clasping my hand. "I have given you the match. Only you can light your own candle."

I all but trembled as I left his presence.

The Prime Ministers [Jerusalem: The Toby Press, 2010], pp. 443–446

WHERE CHANGE BEGINS

GORDON B. ZACKS

In 1969, I was the Chairman of the Young Leadership Cabinet of the national United Jewish Appeal. As such, I was invited to deliver the keynote address to the Council of Jewish Federations and Welfare Funds Annual Conference, being held that year in November in Boston. The theme was "Youth Looks at the Future of the American Jewish Community." I spent six months preparing for this talk. Usually, I speak extemporaneously with at most a one-page outline. This time—because of its importance—I elected to read the entire speech.

In it, I thanked my parents' generation for supporting the creation of the state of Israel and rescuing survivors from the Holocaust. In its aftermath, two million Jews had been delivered through their efforts from lands of oppression and resettled to lands of freedom. Nonetheless, I pointed out that we faced a disaster in the field of Jewish education. We ran the risk of losing more Jews through assimilation than we had saved through affirmation. We needed to address the failure of our Jewish educational system to inspire many young Jews to continue to be Jewish. I recommended that we create a national Jewish research and development venture capital fund to invest risk capital in innovative approaches to make Jewish education relevant to young people and to create an Institute for Jewish Life that would manage the process.

To fund this Institute, I proposed that the Jewish community endow the Institute with $100 million of State of Israel bonds for a period of ten years. The purchasers would receive a tax deduction. At the end of ten years, they would get their principal back. The Institute would get the use of the interest. Annually it would provide about $6 million in revenue. We would have ten years in which to evaluate the results. If the concept didn't produce worthwhile results, that would be the end of the Institute. Ultimately the idea was adopted in an abbreviated form with funding of $3.5 million. In this truncated version, it failed in its mission and was eventually closed. Still, it stimulated a lot of discussion about Jewish education, and placed it right behind rescue as a priority for the American Jewish community.

In December 1969, I received a call from a man named Leibel Alevsky. He was a rabbi with the Lubavitch movement in the Crown Heights section of Brooklyn. He said the Rebbe wanted to meet me. Given the tone of the phone call, I thought I was being invited for a royal audience. I immediately said yes to a date in January, but I didn't even know who the Rebbe was! My rabbi gave me some background and urged me to go ahead with the meeting. On the appointed day in January, Alevsky and I were finishing dinner in his home at 11:15 at night. We got a call that the Rebbe would see me now. I walked with Alevsky to a modest building to find 300 people—from around the world—each waiting at the Rebbe's headquarters, the Chabad Center, in the middle of the night for an audience with the Rebbe!

Later I learned that the Rebbe held these audiences three times each week, lasting from sundown often until the middle of the night.

I went in alone to see the Rebbe. In his office, illuminated by a single ceiling light, books were stacked from the floor to the ceiling. He was a slight man with translucent skin and absolutely clear whites of his eyes—the sclera encircling his sparkling blue irises, his beard outlining an impish grin. The Rebbe was sixty-seven at the time. He looked at me in such a penetrating way that I felt like I was being x-rayed.

"Mr. Zacks, I have read your speech," he began, "and it's clear you have taken good care of your mind. I can look at you, and it's clear you have taken good care of your body. What have you done to take care of your soul?"

No small talk about how I was or if I had a pleasant trip. I was stunned.

"The Jewish house is on fire," he continued. "We have an emergency, and this is not the time to experiment with new ways to put out the fire. Instead, you call the proven and tested fire department. We are that fire department. We—the Lubavitch—don't have drugs or intermarriage problems with our children or kids opting out of Judaism. Our tradition works, and our children are being educated. We have a worldwide outreach program that contacts and impacts non-observant Jews and saves souls. Give us the $100 million, and we will spend it to correct the problems that you are concerned about."

"Rebbe," I asked after pausing for a moment, "what if the house is on fire, but people have forgotten your telephone number?" "G-d will provide," he answered me.

"There are millions of Jews whose houses are on fire," I said to him. "Most of them are Jews who will not call you, either because they have lost your number or they won't accept the lifestyle compromises you expect. They're still worthy of saving in their own way, and they are entitled to a quality Jewish education that makes Judaism relevant to their lives. That's why we need this Institute."

"Do you believe in revelation, Mr. Zacks?" he asked me next.

"I believe in G-d and I believe he inspires... but I don't believe he writes," I answered.

"You mean, Mr. Zacks, that there is this vast structure G-d has created of plants, animals, food chains, stars, and planets. And, that the only creature in all of creation that doesn't understand how to fit in and live their life purposefully is the human?"

I told him yes.

"What about the complexity of the human body? What about the jewel of the human cell? How does the body ingest food and renew itself with absolute consistency?"

I had no answer.

"Why, Mr. Zacks, is the nose always where the nose belongs? Why are the eyes always on the face for generation after generation?"

I could only shrug my shoulders, but my respect for him deepened by the moment.

"And, how can you account for the brain and the mind? How do they steer this remarkable system in a purposeful and precise way? And, what about how we fit into the earth's ecosystem, where we inhale the oxygen that plants so wonderfully manufacture for us? Could this all be accidental?"

How could I answer him?

"And, beyond what happens on earth. What about all the heavenly bodies in the sky that seem to follow such a perfect order and don't collide with each other? Is man the only creature on the planet earth without guidelines for living its life? Should man ignore the Torah given to us by G-d as a roadmap to guide us? This is the missing link which connects us to the complexity of Nature!"

So it went. Comment after comment. More times than not, I could not begin to answer his points.

He quoted Kazantzakis' book Zorba the Greek to me during our conversation. "Do you remember the young man talking with Zorba on the beach, when Zorba asks what the purpose of life is? The young fellow admits he doesn't know. And Zorba comments, 'Well, all those damned books you read—what good are they? Why do you read them?' Zorba's friend says he doesn't know. Zorba can see his friend doesn't have an answer to the most fundamental question. That's the trouble with you. 'A man's head is like a grocer,' Zorba says, 'it keeps accounts.... The head's a careful little shopkeeper; it never risks all it has, always keeps something in reserve. It never breaks the string.' Wise men and grocers weigh everything. They can never cut the cord and be free. Your problem, Mr. Zacks, is that you are trying to find G-d's map through your head. You are unlikely to find it that way. You have to experience before you can truly feel and then be free to learn. Let me send a teacher to live with you for a year and teach you how to be Jewish. You will unleash a whole new dimension to your life. If you really want to change the world, change yourself! It's like dropping a stone into a pool of water and watching the concentric circles radiate to the shore. You will influence all the people around you, and they will influence others in turn. That's how you bring about improvement in the world."

"Rebbe, I'm not ready to do that," I told him. I remained firm despite the incredibly woven tapestry of the universe he presented to me.

"What do you have to lose?" he asked, "One year of your life? What if I'm right? It could gain you an eternity if I'm right, but only cost you one year if I'm wrong."

"I'll think about it," I said as we wrapped up our hour-and-a-half conversation. The normal audience with the Rebbe was thirty seconds to a minute. Three hundred people were still waiting to come in at one in the morning.

The Rebbe took people the way they were. His ultimate goal was to bring you to the ways of Jewish life, but his means were not confrontational and demanding. You could literally feel his warmth and love in addition to the power of his vast intellect. Once he established the Chabad Center at 770 Eastern Parkway in Crown Heights, I don't think he ever left it. Yet he was totally wired into the events of the world. I sensed this in my first meeting with the Rebbe. He radiated compassion, love, and respect for others—a servant leader totally committed to serving G-d through helping others.

The Rebbe wrote me letters encouraging me to devote myself to Jewish education. Over a series of years, I received five letters from him saying that he wanted to send his representative to me to spend a year teaching me how to be Jewish. I responded to each of them and declined.

Beginning in 1986, the Rebbe had a receiving line on Sunday in which he passed out a dollar bill to be given by the recipient as tzedakah to charity. His reasoning: "When two people meet, something good should result for a third." People waited in line for as long as four hours to be greeted by him and receive his blessing and the dollar bill. The Rebbe was eighty-four when he started doing this. An older woman in the line asked him how he could manage to perform this demanding task. "Every soul is a diamond," he answered. "Can one grow tired of counting diamonds?"

In 1987, my youngest daughter, Kim, had just returned from Israel and she wanted to participate in the custom of Sunday Dollars. I said fine I would take her. I neither called nor told anyone who I was when we arrived. I stood in line with her. It had been seventeen years since I had seen the Rebbe and ten years since he wrote me his last letter. When it was our turn to speak with the Rebbe, he looked at me and asked "What are you doing for Jewish education?" His eyes had the same penetrating look that had scanned me seventeen years earlier and asked, "What are you doing to take care of your soul, Mr. Zacks?" It was as though I had just walked back into his office. In truth, hundreds of thousands of people had filed past him over those years.

"You are amazing!" I exclaimed to him.

"What has that to do with saving Jewish lives? What are you doing for Jewish education?" he retorted. He may not have gotten exactly what he wanted from me, but the Rebbe surely taught me the power of changing yourself to influence others. He wanted to enlist me as his fundraiser for Jewish education. While I certainly considered his invitation, I declined it. Still he may have been the most charismatic man I ever met. He had an incredible aura to him, partly because he was such a combination of charisma and pragmatism. This man came out of the scientific community to return to the religious life. Every Israeli prime minister and Israeli chief of staff found his way to the Rebbe's doorstep when they came to the United States. The most amazing thing? The Rebbe saw himself as perfecting G-d's will. He had no power in the sense that a police commissioner, a general, or a tax collector does. He had no one enforcing his decisions. What he did have was the authority of his holiness, which caused others to connect to him. It wasn't his title that gave the Rebbe authority. It was his presence and his profound grasp of bringing the principles of the Torah to life in himself and in others. The Rebbe didn't declare himself a leader. His overpowering presence inspired those around him to declare him their leader and to revere him. Through earning respect and trust, people endowed him with leadership.

About ten years after I first met the Rebbe, I attended a dinner in Cleveland at the home of Leibel Alevsky. At the table with us was the man the Rebbe sent to the Soviet Union to save Jews. When the Rebbe sent him on this mission, he didn't give him a plan or give him money! This was during the Stalin era. The anti-Jewish, anti-Zionist mentality of the Soviets may have been at its very worst. The Rebbe's designate went to the Soviet Union, lived and worked by his wits, and figured out how he could smuggle Jews out to Poland by train. He succeeded. At the same time, he was smuggling in prayer books, religious articles, and calendars for those still in the Soviet Union. And, he set up secret schools to teach Hebrew. The Lubavitchers are incredibly resourceful people, whose outreach is one-on-one.

The Lubavitchers are the essence of true believers. As I traveled abroad, I first noted their presence in Morocco. They ran schools for kids in the ghetto. That may sound noble, but not earth-shattering until you understand the kind of "social security system" that prevailed in Morocco at the time. Children were the system. At birth, many infants—Arabs and Jews both—were maimed and deformed by their parents so the kids could beg more effectively! The Lubavitchers bought the children from their parents for one more dirham than the market value of the child begging on the street for a year, and then they gave the children an education.

You could see the evidence of the Rebbe's positive work all over the world in places like the Soviet Union, Morocco, and Iran. How did these devout Lubavitchers get there? The Rebbe would simply say, "Go to Morocco and save souls." They didn't get a dime or an ounce of organizational help. They saved thousands and thousands of Jews physically, and they spiritually changed many more. The conviction they are doing G-d's work carries them forward. Their passion brings them to college campuses all over the United States. They will send out a representative wearing payos and a black frock coat and open up a Chabad house on campuses like University of California at Berkeley. They get kids off narcotics and give them a spiritual jolt instead of a buzz on drugs. "Get high on G-d!" they preach. Their individual missions are great illustrations of the power of one. The Rebbe's passion for saving Jewish souls lives through them.

Unlike every other Jewish figure in this book, the Rebbe was not a Zionist. Though very supportive of the state of Israel and its defense forces, he felt that redemption would only be ushered in by the Messiah. He also drove home the point that a commitment to the state of Israel does not exempt us from fulfilling age-old Judaic commandments. In fact, it should actually elicit more loyalty to the Torah. The Rebbe was completely devoted to fulfilling G-d's will.

The essence of the Rebbe's teaching is celebration of G-d. The Chabad radiate a wonderful joy of life that is a reverberation of the Rebbe's spirit. I wish I could believe the way they do, with their absolute confidence in their answer. Their sheer love in celebrating the Jewish traditions with singing and dancing is unmatched. Nothing equals the celebration of a Shabbat with a Chabadnik. The food is homemade, delicious—though not necessarily healthy for your arteries—but it's only the beginning of the positive energy that flows in each Shabbat from celebrating the birthday of the world!

Gordon B. Zacks. Chairman of R. G. Barry Corporation, a leading footwear company, was general chairman designate of the National United Jewish Appeal (UJA) and a founding member and chairman of the Young Leadership Cabinet of the UJA. An expert on the Middle East, Zacks advised U.S. presidents and foreign heads of state on international relations and global trade policy. He was involved in the rescue and resettlement of millions of Jews in distress from more than one hundred countries to Israel and other free countries.

Defining Moments: Stories of Character, Courage, and Leadership [New York: Beaufort Books, 2006], pp. 137–148

INTERVIEW WITH THE LUBAVITCHER REBBE

On March 7, 1960, the Rebbe received a group of Jewish college students in a private audience. The Rebbe began with introductory remarks:

This year has special significance, being the 200th anniversary of the *histalkus* of the Baal Shem Tov, the founder of general Chasidism. The word "*histalkus*" does not mean death in the sense of coming to an end but rather an elevation from one level to another on a higher plane. When one has accomplished his mission in life, he is elevated to a higher plane. The significance of this for us is that everyone can now lift himself easier to a higher level by studying the teachings of the Baal Shem Tov and taking an example from his life.

From the very beginning, one of the first things the Baal Shem Tov did[71] was to teach small children simple things, like blessings, and to explain to them how they could be near to G-d Almighty—that G-d was very real for them and close to them and not far-removed in some "seventh heaven." He worked not only with teenagers but even with six- and seven-year-old children, making them understand how G-d Almighty watches over them all the time—not only Sunday, Monday or Tuesday, but all the days of their life, and that by obeying G-d's will they would be assured of a happy and harmonious life, materially and spiritually.

The epoch of the Baal Shem Tov came after the Chmielnitzky pogroms, which left the Jews in a state of dejection and despair. It was the aim of the Baal Shem Tov to encourage the Jews and to show them how they could meet the problems of their day while living a life of Torah and *Mitzvos*.[72]

Our present age is similar in many ways to the times of the Baal Shem Tov. One-third of the Jewish population has perished under Hitler and has been cut off from us. How great, then, is the obligation that lies upon each and every one of us to do as much as is within his power to spread the light of Torah and *Mitzvos* in his own surroundings and throughout the world in general.

At this point the Rebbe paused for questions and asked whether the students preferred to first ask all their questions and then he would answer, or did they want each question answered as it was asked. The latter was decided upon and the students began:

Question: The Rebbe said that one should spread Torah. How and in what manner is this to be done?

Answer: Everyone must do as much as possible in his immediate surroundings by speaking with other people in a way that shows his certainty and confidence in the matter. For confidence is a characteristic of the youth specifically. An older person is often beset with doubts and hesitancies, while the young are sure of themselves. It is this characteristic that we must utilize in spreading Torah and *Mitzvos*, and everyone must work at 100% capacity. Every means must be employed: the newspaper, the radio. But, above all, the most vital is the personal example we set in our everyday living.

Question: There appears to be a contradiction in the view of death as we find it in Job and in Ecclesiastics. In Job it is considered a redemption, but in Ecclesiastics it is thought of as an evil that transforms everything into vanity. What is the view of Chasidus concerning an afterlife?

Answer: As was explained earlier, death is not a cessation of life, but rather, one's spiritual life takes on new dimensions or is, as we said, elevated to a higher plane. This is logical and follows also from the principles of science which are considered to be the "absolute truth." In science, the principle of the conservation of matter states that nothing physical can be annihilated. This table or a piece of iron can be cut up, burned etc., but in no case could the matter of the table or the iron be destroyed. It only takes on a different form.

71 *Likutei Diburim*, vol. 3, pp. 774-5. See also the Rebbe's talk to camp children on the 15th of Tamuz, 5720 (*B'neos Deshe* pp. 109-119).

72 See also *Sefer HaMaamarim* 5663, pp. 142-3.

So likewise, on the spiritual level, our spiritual being—the soul—can never be destroyed. It only changes its form, or is elevated to a different plane.

Question: *The same questioner then asked:* Is the after-life of a soul personal or impersonal?

Answer: In conjunction with what was said before, the soul takes on a new and higher form. In this, the term "after-life" is inappropriate. Rather, it is a continuation of life. Until 120, life is experienced at one level, and at 121, 122 and 123, etc., it is carried on at another level, and thus we go higher and higher in the realm of spirit.

Question: What was the role that the Baal Shem Tov played in the Chasidic movement?

Answer: We can understand what the Baal Shem Tov did by the simile of the relationship of an electric powerhouse with a lamp that is connected to it by a wire. In order to light his lamp, one must find the right switch, or push the correct button. The soul of every Jew is a part of and is connected with G-d Almighty,[73] but in order that one can enjoy the great benefits of it, the correct switch must be found or the proper button pushed. It was the Baal Shem Tov's mission to explain and proclaim that every Jew without exception is connected with "the powerhouse," and every one of them has a switch in his innermost, that will be found if searched for.

So also, every one of us in our own work in strengthening Judaism must try to find the switch in the soul of every Jew. One can never know what will make the connection, perhaps one word. But by this, you open up the well or inner fountain of his soul.

Rabbi Levy, director of the Hillel Foundation at Princeton University, brought greetings to the Rebbe from Kfar Chabad. He had visited there during the summer and related his admiration for the love that is shown the Moroccan children. Never had he seen such love between Jews of such different backgrounds, upbringing, etc.

[73] See *Tanya* ch. 2; 19.

Question: Can Israel exist as a political state?

The Rebbe asked whether the questioner was speaking from an economical, religious, or political point of view. The questioner replied that he meant whether a political and religious state could coexist harmoniously.

Answer: A machine, system, etc., can be used at different degrees of efficiency, for a small job or a big maximum job. The State of Israel can be a state of Jews—another Levantine state, as Syria is the state of Syrians, or it can become something exceptional, unique, namely a Jewish State. But to be a Jewish State it must be run according to the Jewish Torah and tradition. This is not a contradiction to its being a "normal" state with men, women and children, institutions, etc. as any other. But only in this way will it be a Jewish state, exceptional.

Question: What is the difference between Lubavitch and other Chasidic groups?

Answer: Lubavitcher Chasidim are often called Chabad Chasidim, an abbreviation of the Hebrew words *chochmah*, *binah*, and *da'as*, which indicate different aspects of understanding.[74] To serve G-d with the emotions alone or with faith alone or even with intellect alone is not enough, for it would be an incomplete service. Rather, there must be a fusion of all of these elements;[75] the service must permeate the entire being of a Jew and every single day. However, the intellect is the "Ruler" of these elements, and it is this that the Alter Rebbe stressed when he said that a Chasid must use his intellect and not be content with a service of G-d centered only in the emotions or in faith alone.

Question: Can Chasidism bring non-religious Jews back to their Judaism?

Answer: Certainly! Today it is expected that one understands his doing and therefore many Jews can be reached only through their intellect. But in order to reach the intellect of someone else you must use your

[74] See ibid., ch. 3.

[75] See *Zohar* III, p. 224a. *Tanya* ch. 12; 17; 30; 51.

own intellect, for only through your mind can you reach the mind of another.

Question: Why did many Chasidim refuse to leave Jerusalem during the war when their very lives were in danger?

Answer: It was surely because Jerusalem has special holiness and sanctity and therefore living a Jewish life on a high spiritual level is easier there.

The questioner then asked whether it was proper for them to remain there even if it cost them their lives?

Answer: No. They probably hoped to be taken prisoner and later released.

Question: Why is Chabad so successful in its activities?

Answer: Today everyone tries to understand before he does something. I am not discussing whether this is good or bad, but only stating a fact. Everyone requires proofs and understanding. Chabad Chasidus provides it. It explains aspects of Judaism so that they can be understood by the intellect.

As a Chabad Chasid I have a more categorical answer: I have no doubt that Chabad Chasidus is the Truth and Truth must be successful.

Question: What is the function of a Rebbe?

Answer: As was said earlier, to find the switch in every Jew and help him become connected with the power house.

Question: What is the Jewish attitude towards conversion?

Answer: Never were Torah Jews enthused about conversion.[76] A Jew should be a good Jew and a gentile should be a good gentile. There is for us enough to do in just seeing that Jews are good Jews. Every limb of a body has its particular function. Each limb has its activity to which it is fitted. Likewise, every created thing has its particular function. The Jew has his and the gentile has his.[77]

Question: This afternoon we heard a lecture by Dr. Block in which he explained that a Jew has a Divine spark. He didn't say explicitly, but he intimated that only a Jew has this Divine spark but a non-Jew does not. Is this so?

Answer: A non-Jew, and every created thing, does have a Divine spark, but it is not the same kind of the Divine spark that a Jew has. To illustrate from the body again, each part has its own function: the brain to think, the heart to feel, and the legs to carry one about. So the mission of a Jew in life is to transform the physicality of the world into spiritual, divine. The non-Jew has a different purpose and therefore the two do not have the same Divine spark.

Question: I understand that Chasidism elevates the woman to a state higher than she had before in Judaism. Could you explain this?

Answer: Traditionally, women were not taught Torah except those laws that were directly relevant to herself and her duties. Chasidus however, teaches and demands of every one, man or woman, that the *Mitzvos*, all of them, must be done with joy and inspiration, not automatically. But we cannot expect someone to be inspired unless he understands or feels. The woman has a right, more—must know of the individual providence, of the omnipresence of G-d Almighty that He created not only the heavens but also the home and the kitchen, and then she can be inspired by the mitzvah to make the home and kitchen a Jewish home and kitchen. We must explain to her in detail the teachings of the Jewish religion and the reasons why of Judaism.[78] Especially as the woman has a great effect on her children and her husband. It is necessary, then, that she be taught the basic ideas of Chasidus.

76 See Talmud *Yevamos* 47a-b. Rambam, *Mishneh Torah*, Laws of Isurei Biah 13:14. *Tur* and *Shulchan Aruch Yoreh De'ah*, Section 268.

77 See also *Igros Kodesh* of the Rebbe, vol. 19, p. 492.

78 See also Reshimot #30 and references noted there.

Question: Can a Jew be a Chasid even though it is necessary for him to work on Shabbos, especially in the case of a physician?

Answer: You mean he thinks it is necessary for him to work on Shabbos. Really, it cannot be that it is impossible for a Jew to keep Shabbos. For G-d would not have commanded us to do something and then have put us in a position where it would be impossible to perform.

The questioner continued and asked what a physician should do if a life is in danger?

Answer: Under ordinary conditions, a physician must not desecrate Shabbos, and his entire life must be as holy and Jewish as of every Jew. However, when an emergency arises and a life is at stake, it is not only not a desecration but it is a mitzvah. One is commanded to save the person. And it states (in the Jewish code[79]) if one is a גדול (*gadol*)—if one is very pious, and a *talmid chocham*, the mitzvah should not be given to another but he himself must save the person.

Question: How far does the power of the Rebbe extend in natural law? Does the Rebbe have preferred status as regards prayer? *At this point someone added that what is meant is whether the Rebbe can perform miracles.*

Answer: This world is not separate from the higher worlds but is another step, the last one, in a long chain of worlds. Everything in this world comes from and is influenced by the higher ones. A miracle is something that happens which you could not have calculated. When a Jew connects himself through his Divine spark with G-d through fervent prayer, Torah, and *Mitzvos*, he can affect things in this physical world "from above" —that means by a way which is beyond calculation. This power is not the prerogative of one Jew but of every Jew.

At this point, Rabbi Gurewitz, of the Brooklyn Hillel Foundation, thanked the Rebbe for the interview and started to leave, but then the Rebbe said:

Now I want to ask you a question, and at the same time try to perform a miracle. Everything has a purpose. What was the purpose of our coming together here tonight? Certainly it was not merely to ask questions and receive answers, good or bad. Rather it was to achieve something.

All of us here are young, myself included, and have tens of years yet before us. Since six million of our people in Russia, Poland and Hungary have been lost to us through Hitler, we have a special task to accomplish—the work that they could have done, at least a major part of it. Everyone counts. No Jew is expendable. We all must work to the fullest capacity, every one of us. In our day-to-day life we must use our full strength to add to the side of good, and by this we will gain a life of happiness and harmony—and all this can be done only through a life of Torah and *Mitzvos* tested by our 3,500 year history. This obligation lies upon every Jew and G-d has given him the power to carry this through successfully.

And if each of us, beginning tomorrow, should add in his own personal life more Torah and *Mitzvos* and influence the environment in the same direction, if we all will do this, myself included, this indeed will be our miracle.

Interview with the Lubavitcher Rebbe [New York: Vaad Hanochos Hatmimim, 1996], pp. 5–14

79 Rambam, *Mishneh Torah*, Laws of Shabbos 2:3. *Tur* and *Shulchan Aruch Orach Chayim* 328:12. *Shulchan Aruch HaRav*, ibid. 328:13.

THE REBBE AND VIKTOR FRANKL

THE REBBE'S COMMUNIQUÉ TO THE FOUNDER OF LOGOTHERAPY

RABBI JACOB BIDERMAN

I arrived in Vienna—together with my wife, Edla—in 1981, to serve as Chabad-Lubavitch emissaries in Austria. We immediately started serving the local Jewish community by arranging Torah classes for children, programs for adults and youth, and the like.

We were aware that the famous Dr. Viktor Frankl resided in the city, but as he never associated with the Jewish community in Vienna, we did not have the opportunity to make his acquaintance. He certainly never stepped foot in the Chabad center we established.

How surprised we were when Dr. Frankl responded with a contribution to our annual appeal, which we sent out to all the local Jews along with a Jewish calendar in honor of the upcoming High Holidays. He continued this practice every year thereafter—I never met him or spoke to him, but his donation always came.

We did not understand, until one day in 1995 when all became clear. It started with a visit I received from a youthful, energetic 85-year-old woman, who introduced herself as Marguerite Chajes.

"Perhaps you think you are the first emissary of the Lubavitcher Rebbe to Vienna," Marguerite told me, "but that is not entirely the case. You see, I performed an important mission here on the Rebbe's behalf long before you arrived in Austria."

Marguerite Chajes

Her mother's maiden name was Hager. The Hagers were no ordinary Jewish family but relatives of the Rebbes of the famed Vishnitz chassidic dynasty. Marguerite was born in Chernowitz, but spent her childhood in Vienna. Marguerite became an opera singer; she married and had a daughter.

Just a few days before World War II, friends helped her escape, together with her husband and daughter, across the border to Italy, where they made it onto on the last boat to the United States. Marguerite and her family settled in Detroit. Unfortunately, the rest of her family remained behind and perished.

Years passed. Marguerite's daughter grew up and married a doctor, who, in 1959, was honored at the dinner of a Chabad institution. In conjunction with that occasion, Marguerite had an audience with the Lubavitcher Rebbe, Rabbi Menachem Mendel Schneerson, of righteous memory.

"I cannot explain why," Marguerite said, "but while in the Rebbe's room I suddenly broke down in tears. I felt that it was fine to cry. The dam holding back my river of tears gave way. Like many Holocaust survivors, I had never cried before. If I were to start crying, I felt that I might never stop... I always felt that I have to keep my emotions in check in order to be able to function as a human being."

Marguerite told the Rebbe her entire life story. But more than that, a special relationship was born that night in the Rebbe's room in Brooklyn. Marguerite left that audience feeling that she had been given a second father.

A Favor for the Rebbe

Marguerite had also mentioned to the Rebbe that for some time now she had had a yearning to go back and visit her native land. The Rebbe requested that in the event that she would make such a trip, she should come see him again beforehand. Not much thereafter, Marguerite scheduled a trip to Vienna, and, of course, first came to the Rebbe to inform him of her plan.

How surprised Marguerite was when the Rebbe asked her if she could do for him a favor. The Rebbe wanted her to visit two people in Vienna on his behalf. One of them was Dr. Viktor Frankl, who headed the Vienna Policlinic of Neurology.

"Please send Dr. Frankl my regards. And pass the following message on to him: that I said that he should be strong and continue his work, with complete resolve. No matter what, he should not give up. If he remains strong and committed, he will certainly prevail."

Arranging a meeting with Frankl was no simple task. Arriving at the clinic, she was told that the professor hadn't shown up in two weeks. With effort, though, Marguerite found Frankl's home address and made her way there. Marguerite knocked on the door, and it was opened by a woman. The first thing she caught sight of in the home was a cross, hanging prominently on the wall. (In 1947, Frankl married his second wife, Eleonore Katharina Schwindt, a devout Catholic.) Taken aback, and already wondering whether this was a mistake, if perhaps this wasn't the person the Rebbe had wanted her to visit, she nevertheless asked whether there was a Herr Professor Frankl in the house.

Marguerite was asked to wait. Minutes later, a slightly annoyed-looking and apparently uninterested Dr. Frankl appeared. Marguerite, feeling very self-conscious, told him that she had regards for him "from Rabbi Schneerson of Brooklyn, New York."

Marguerite steeled herself and continued: "Rabbi Schneerson, known as the Lubavitcher Rebbe, sent a message for you: Remain strong! Continue your work with complete resolve. Don't give up. Ultimately you will prevail."

The hitherto apathetic doctor suddenly transformed before a shocked Marguerite's eyes. Tears filled his eyes. After composing himself somewhat he thanked Marguerite, and in the course of the ensuing conversation he told her that he had been planning to abandon his efforts to fight on behalf of his theory and philosophy, and actually was considering departing Vienna—but now he would reconsider...

"So Rabbi Biderman," Marguerite concluded, "now you understand what I meant when I said that I served as the Rebbe's emissary to Vienna way before you arrived!"

The Other Side of the Story

All around Frankl were loyal Freudian scholars. He was taunted, and his lectures were shunned. Marguerite's story fascinated me. What had the Rebbe's message meant to Viktor Frankl?

What I had not known beforehand, but what Marguerite now explained, is that Frankl had not always been lauded and respected, as he is today. In his youth, Frankl had been a young colleague of Sigmund Freud and Alfred Adler. But his beliefs challenged their teachings. Whereas the dominant view at the time was that people are driven by the need to gratify physical needs, a "will to pleasure," he saw humankind differently. In Frankl's view, we are unique beings, driven by a "will to meaning," possessing free choice and the capacity for self-transcendence. "Between stimulus and response . . . is our power to choose our response. In our response lies our growth and our freedom."

Frankl had begun to develop these radical ideas before the war and during his time in the Nazi death camps, seeing how some prisoners were able to eke out a sense of purpose and maintain a positive outlook even there, he had solidified them. Now he found himself a lone dissenter. All around him were loyal Freudian scholars. He was taunted, and his lectures were shunned.

Understandably, Frankl experienced incredible emotional turmoil. The pressures were so great that he decided to simply give up. He decided to move to Australia, to join his sister who lived there. He was emotionally spent, and understandably dejected at the prospect of his life's work going to waste.

When Margaret Chajes arrived at Frankl's home, she told me, he had been sitting and drafting his immigration papers. She brought him a message from a Rebbe, a young chassidic master from overseas he'd never heard of before. "Don't give up," she told him. "You will prevail."

Frankl was beyond astonished. How in the world did this Rebbe know about his situation? And why should this chassidic rebbe care about him or the perpetuation of his philosophy?

It was exactly the shot in the arm that Frankl needed, and the timing could not have been better. Instead of joining his sister in Australia, he continued his practice as a psychiatrist and went back to his work, full of renewed motivation, vigor, and optimism.

A Corroborating Conversation

Marguerite's story certainly explained the annual contribution that Frankl would send to support the Rebbe's institutions in Vienna. And hearing the story stirred me to contact Dr. Frankl himself, thinking perhaps he'd have something to add.

A few days later, I called Frankl and asked to meet him

But it was difficult for him to meet me in person. This was 1995, you must understand, and Viktor Frankl was 90 years of age. So we spoke over the phone. "Do you remember Marguerite Chajes?" I asked. Naturally he did; she had become a friend of the family.

Throughout this short conversation, however, Frankl sounded impatient.

"Do you remember a regards she gave you from Rabbi Schneerson in Brooklyn?" I asked him.

A change in his demeanor. Now Frankl responded warmly: "Ah... of course! Can I ever forget it? The Rabbi came to my aid during a very difficult time in my life. I owe him a tremendous debt of gratitude!"

The Pursuit of Meaning Comes into Vogue

What, indeed, was the result of Marguerite's mission?

Well, it was soon after that, in 1959, that Frankl's book, *Man's Search for Meaning*, was translated into English (at first it was translated under a different title), became a bestseller and classic psychiatric text, and propelled him into the international limelight. Frankl became a guest lecturer at universities on five continents. He received honorary doctorates from universities around the world, and national and international awards and medals for his pivotal work in psychotherapy. Before his death in 1997, his magnum opus had been translated into dozens of languages and sold millions of copies.

So many millions of people benefited—directly or indirectly—from the Rebbe's communiqué to Dr. Frankl. His brand of therapy inspired thousands of other books, seminars, workshops, new-age and spiritual groups, all based on Frankl's idea of the human being's unique ability to make choices and pursue his own meaning. From Scot Peck's *Road Less Traveled* to Steven Covey's *Seven Habits*, and hundreds of other bestsellers during the last 30 years, all are variations of Viktor Frankl's perspective.

So many millions of people benefited—directly or indirectly—from the Rebbe's communiqué to Dr. Frankl. I sometimes shudder when I imagine what would have occurred if not for that perfectly-timed message.

More Details Come to Light

Haddon Klingberg, author of *When Life Calls Out To Us: The Love and Lifework of Viktor and Elly Frankl*, the only authorized biography of Viktor and Eleonore ("Elly"), writes:

"...after his death I asked Elly if he actually made these prayers every day. 'Absolutely. He never missed a day. Every morning for more than fifty years. But nobody knew this.' As they traveled the globe Viktor took the phylacteries with them, and everywhere, every morning, he prayed. He uttered memorized words of Jewish prayers and Psalms...

"(After Viktor died I saw his phylacteries for the first time. Elly had placed them in the little cubicle with his few simple possessions...)"

Indeed, Frankl's non-Jewish son-in-law confirmed this fact to me: "My father-in-law would close himself off in a room every day for a little while. Once I opened the door and saw him with black boxes on his head and hand. He was annoyed about my intruding on his privacy. When he was taken to the hospital, however, his practice of putting on *tefillin* became public."

I've often wondered why the Rebbe took an interest in the success of Viktor Frankl, a secular and intermarried Jew, and sought him out to offer encouragement and support. It would seem that the Rebbe did this not only out of personal concern for Frankl's welfare, but also in order to advance a philosophy which he felt ultimately fosters belief in G-d, a spiritual perspective, and good values. The fact that this constitutes the real cure to a suffering soul is something the Rebbe repeatedly taught us.

I can't help but marvel over the Rebbe's wide reach, broad-mindedness, and remarkably visionary approach.

* * *

In a letter dated June 19, 1969 (3rd Tammuz, 5729), the Rebbe writes (free translation):

> ...I would like to take this opportunity to add another point, that the medical condition of..... proves (if proof is needed in this area) the awesome power of faith—especially when applied and expressed in practical action, community work, observance of *mitzvot*, etc.– to fortify a person's emotional tranquility [and to affect the] minimizing and even elimination of inner conflicts, as well as complaints one may have to his surroundings, etc.
>
> This is in spite the theory that faith and religion demand the discipline to restrain and suppress natural instincts and drives, and is, therefore, generally undesirable, and particularly in the case of a person who requires treatment for emotional issues.
>
> I particularly took interest in the writing of Dr. Frankl (from Vienna) in this matter. To my surprise, however, his approach has apparently not been appropriately disseminated and appreciated. Although one can find numerous reasons as to why his ideas are not widely accepted— including the fact that [such treatment] is related to the personal lifestyle exemplified by the treating doctor —nevertheless, the question [as to why it is not appreciated] still remains...

A VISIT WITH THE NEW LUBAVITZER REBBE

GERSHON KRANZLER

It was shortly after the leaders of the world Chabad movement had elected Rabbi Menachem Mendel Schneerson to succeed his late father-in-law, Rabbi Joseph I. Schneerson, as the head of the famous Chassidic school associated with the name of Lubavitz , on the 10th of Shevat of this year.

I was standing in the hallway of the Rebbe's residence in Brooklyn. The Maariv service had just concluded and the Yeshiva bachurim were streaming out of the Beth Hamidrash into the cold winter evening. Released from the strenuous routine of many hours of concentrated study, the young scholars, most of them with beard and peyoth, were chatting freely and loudly, while they put on their coats to leave the building. Suddenly the loud talk ceased and a look of awed respect appeared on the lively faces as the new Rebbe walked through the hall towards the door. Deferentially, they pressed forward to the wall on both sides of the narrow doorway. One young man, flustered, moved from one side of the way to the other, to make more room and stumbled into the path of the Rebbe. Before he had a chance to recover his balance, the Rebbe had taken him by the shoulder and had gently helped him to the side, a smile lighting up his serious face.

Instantly, the embarrassment of the young scholar was gone. The Rebbe's smile reflected in his happy eyes, and the entire atmosphere was suddenly changed. The awe was gone and a warm current of friendly understanding seemed to flow through the young scholars pressed closely into the hallway, brightening the frosty dark of the evening.

This experience of a few fleeting moments, the mute exchange of a smile and glance, answered many a question that had risen in my mind since the passing of the late Lubavitzer Rebbe a year before, and the election of his successor. I had the privilege of knowing Rabbi Menachem Mendel Schneerson before he assumed his new office and I had come to appreciate the young scholar with the serious face and unassuming, almost shy manners. He then directed the educational projects of the Merkos L'Inyonei Chinuch. But now everything was different. This was no longer the "RemaSh", the son-in-law of the Rebbe, respected as a scholar and popular as a friendly advisor and leader and interpreter of the thoughts of Chabad Chassidism. The new burden of office, with its responsibility for the thousands of followers of Chabad the world over, with its exacting demands for attention to the hundreds of visitors seeking aid, advice and inspiration from the Lubavitzer Rebbe day in, day out, would seem to have removed Rabbi Menachem Mendel Schneerson from any close personal association. But the little incident in the hallway taught me better, and I began to appreciate the importance which a Chassidic leader of this type can assume for the future of the Jewish people, even in these days of Twentieth Century culture.

When the opportunity arose to visit the Rebbe and to transmit his views and perspective on the task ahead, I remembered something Rabbi Schneerson had once said when he addressed a gathering of young workers for the furtherance of Jewish education: "It is not we that count, we with our weaknesses and capabilities. It is our will to do a job that we realize is important. Success is not in our hands, it is the Lord's. But we have to will to do what He demands of us, and in that will all our weaknesses and insufficiencies wane and become insignificant."

I could not have searched for a better motto to characterize the message of courage and encouragement which I took with me when I had the privilege to spend some time with the new Lubavitzer Rebbe, and to question him on his views concerning the contemporary Jewish scene.

The familiar pale face, with its deeply searching eyes and frame of black beard, seemed to have taken on added seriousness. The sense of warm understanding and deep responsibility for every word spoken which had always characterized Rabbi Menachem Mendel Schneerson was now still more marked. Still in his forties, he seemed to personify the centuries of Jewish scholarship and Chassidic self-search as he voiced his reflections upon the problems of the day.

Is Dispersion A Catastrophe?

"It is a mistake," said Rabbi Schneerson, "if we conceive of the worldwide dispersion of the Jewish people in Galuth as a catastrophe. As a matter of fact, this very lack of concentration of the remnants of our nation was the source of our salvation throughout the centuries of persecution and pogroms. Hitler was the greatest threat to our national survival because the largest concentration of the masses of Eastern and Central European Jewry had come into his evil grasp. On the other hand, however, concentration of large groups of our people in one country has been the means of creating the spiritual centers from which the rest of the Jewish colonies could draw their inspiration, leadership and material replenishment.

"Our history in Galuth is an unbroken chain of the emergence and disappearance of such centers in country after country, and from one corner of the earth to the next. As the Jewish sun set in one land, it had already begun to rise in another. Now that the great centers of Eastern Europe have been destroyed by Fascism and Communism, America has become the focus and fountainhead of Jewish survival. Providence has prepared a new home for Torah and Yiddishkeit in this country, while the flames devoured the bastions of the strongest and most impregnable Jewish fortresses on the other side of the ocean."

With earnest emphasis, the new Chabad leader continued: "American Jewry must recognize this sacred, historical mission which Divine Providence has entrusted to it at this critical moment of our struggle for survival. The largest concentration of our best elements is in America. We must lead the smaller Jewish communities in other countries and continents, even in Eretz Yisrael, which must lean heavily on American support for its economic and spiritual survival. The very shape which Jewry and Judaism of tomorrow will present depends on the active leadership of each and every Jew in this country.

"Realization of this historical mission," Rabbi Schneerson said, "demands a complete about-face and reevaluation of our spiritual position. America's great genius has been in the development of the individual, of the pioneering and self-made man type. Although this helped in developing our potentialities by demanding every last ounce of ingenuity and perseverance, it has on the other hand focused too much attention upon egoistic aims and interests. Personal goals have dominated. Only in our spare and leisure time, after we have carved our groove in terms of economic or social success, have we dedicated some time and effort to philanthropic and communal affairs. We have been social workers on an amateur, after-working-hours basis. This pattern of life has been no less characteristic of American Jews than of other Americans.

"But it is at this point that there must be a change of basic outlook and concomitant redirection and reorganization of our existence as a community and as individuals. Primarily we must live the life of social beings, with the responsibility and dedication of our best efforts for the 'Klal'. Only then can we afford to invest in our own individual aims and goals."

Situation Demands Change of Tactic

This, Rabbi Schneerson stressed, was his main message to American Jews: "The only way American Jewry can live up to its historic task is by self-sacrificing, self-effacing 'Mesirath Nefesh' for the Jewish 'Klal'. Everyone must subordinate his own selfish interests and become an 'ish klali', a Jewish social being, instead of an 'ish perati', a self-centered individual.

"This, however, demands not only a spiritual redirection, but a total change of tactics. Orthodox Jewry up to this point has unfortunately concentrated upon defensive strategy. We were always worried lest we lose positions and strongholds. And indeed we had all reason for worry. One Jewish bastion and another has fallen into the hands of the non-religious. Had orthodox Jews, instead of waiting to defend, taken the offensive and sought to widen their influence and create more and better bastions for Torah Yiddishkeit, the situation would be quite different, and the non-religious would not, as is now the case, dominate the Jewish communal affairs.

"The lesson to be drawn from this is obvious. To discharge ourselves of our duty, we must take the initiative and wage an offensive. This, of course, takes courage, planning, vision, and the will to carry on despite all odds.

"But that," said the new Rebbe, "has always been the true Jewish approach, the Torah perspective on life and the ways of Divine Providence. If we were to count the odds and weigh the chances, we would be lacking in Bitachon, faith in the ultimate affirmation of the right and justification of the just. Weakness, lack of power and influence, should never deter us from the path prescribed by the Torah. We must not be frightened by the fact that only a minority of the millions of Jews gathered in this country are to be counted as Torah-conscious Jews. We must know only one thing: our task and our will to do it. Success is not up to us; it is in higher hands.

"The thing we have to fear most at this moment is the defeatism and the defection that has gripped some of our best elements in this country in the face of the growing effects of so-called 'interfaith' movements, of the watering down of the very content of our religion to a point where our children will no longer know whether they are Jews or not. This defeatism is even worse than the limitation to defensive tactics. Charity begins at home. We cannot talk of assuming responsibility for the rest of the Jewish world, of building new centers for Torah and Yiddishkeit elsewhere, even in Eretz Yisrael, when right here in our midst our brothers and sisters are being engulfed. More than that, we have no right to teach and lead others if at home we neglect the very thing we want to make others do.

"But," warned the Rebbe with a smile, "I don't want you to convey the impression that I am merely giving Mussar—moral exhortations. It has never been the way of Lubavitz to give Mussar only. Mussar serves us only as a means towards actions. Whatever we say or preach must be geared to some active goal. We ourselves can point to amazing results that draw in ever-widening circles of non-religious as well as religious elements of our people."

In response to the look of surprise in my eyes, the Rebbe continued: "Yes, I mean non-religious circles. You see, it has always been the belief of Chabad that there is not a single Jew, as far as he may seem or thought himself to have drifted from the center of Yiddishkeit, who does not have some good point, some particular mitzvah which by nature or by inclination he may promote. This spark of good in each soul can and must be utilized for the good of the Jewish community and in turn, for the good of the person who does it. For this reason, the late Lubavitzer Rebbe called not only on Orthodox Jews for cooperation in this work after he settled in this country ten years ago, but he drew on all types of Jews who had the power and will to contribute some aspect, some particular skill or capacity towards the offensive for Jewish education and the Torah life."

Can We Bring Back the Strayed?

Rabbi Schneerson paused. For some minutes he remained sunk in reflection, then said: "Let's realize this. The Jewish people has been so heavily decimated in the past decade or two that each of us must be made to count, and to count doubly. And it is for this reason that this call to take the offensive for Torah Judaism is not only directed at the observant. Take for example the danger of mixed marriages. If we can use even those of our people who do not believe in any other of the six hundred and thirteen Mitzvoth than the preservation of the purity of our families, we must definitely call on them in order to be able to stem such defections from our faith and with it from our nation. Not always does it matter who does the doing, as long as it is done. The accomplishment counts for what it achieves objectively and what it does to the one involved. In this respect too, a Mitzvah is its own reward.

"This is perhaps another reason not to give up hope because our forces are relatively small. Actually, they are not so small, and many of those who may think they are lost as 'Epikorsim' are really not, and need only some stimulation, some bridge to find the way back. There was for example, the man who visited the late Lubavitzer Rebbe to ask for his counsel concerning some business matter. After he had answered the question, the Rebbe suggested that he put on Tefillin. The visitor protested, 'What is the sense of talking to me about Tefillin if I do not believe in anything at all. I am an Epikores.'

"'Not so easily does one become an Epikores,' replied the Rebbe. 'One has to know a great deal of the questions and problems and know the answers, and then refuse to accept them, to deserve this title. You first put on Tefillin, and you will discover that you needed only such a bridge to find yourself.'

"This is in general true of the great majority of non-orthodox Jews who merely choose the easy road of avoiding obligations and the burden of duties," said Rabbi Schneerson. "It would serve no purpose to approach them with demands for immediate full ascent to the Torah way of life. But, through a pleasant understanding and helpful approach, a good many of these straying souls can be brought back partially, and gradually even completely.

"But this is possible only if we take the offensive and if we do not fall into the trap of overlooking the trees because of the forest. To us each individual counts because each individual may perhaps become a leader or the father of many generations to be gained for the Torah, or— G-d forbid—to be lost.

"We can see only what is going on right now, in the present, and on the surface. The patterns of Providence are not unveiled to us till later. Our task, and in particular that of Jewish youth, is to do and want to do. The rest is not up to us. But, to cite the late Lubavitzer Rebbe of sainted memory, we have two basic assurances. The first is: every action is worth more than a thousand sighs. And secondly: no action for a good purpose has ever been done in vain. In the long run it will succeed and pay its dividends. These must be our guiding principles."

Before I left, the new Rebbe perhaps sensed some lingering residue of doubt in the possibility of militant strategy on such a large scale with the forces we have at work. "Let me tell you of a little incident that happened to one of our Shelichim (emissaries) doing social work for the needy in North Africa, in a town in French Morocco. While talking to some leaders of the community he found out that all the hundred and twenty children of the Jewish families were attending the government schools on Shabboth.

"'Don't you realize that they are violating a basic law of the Torah?' he asked the people, who considered themselves orthodox. 'The government forces them to attend these schools and we cannot do anything about it. Later on they will do Teshuvah (penitence),' they replied. Naturally, the Sholiach pointed out to these pious Sefardim that Teshuvah must never be left for later, and is certainly not an excuse for Chillul Shabboth. 'May we quote you to this effect?' asked the people eagerly. 'By all means,' the emissary replied. This conversation occurred on a Wednesday. By the following Shabboth all Jewish children were permanently freed from attending government schools on Shabboth. The leaders of the community had gone to the French superintendent of schools and told him that an Ashkenazic Chacham had told them there was no redemption for the desecration of Sabbath for their children, not even doing penitence later on. This argument had succeeded in saving one hundred and twenty children from violating the Sabbath week after week.

"One conversation was able to accomplish so much, mind you," said the Rebbe. What excuse do we have not to take action, even if it helped only a single Jewish soul, not one hundred and twenty?"

As I took leave, overwhelmed by the spiritual experience of the short hour I had been privileged to spend with the new Lubavitzer Rebbe, he stressed again an earlier warning. "Do not talk or write about me. The only purpose of our talk can be to speak about the work which the late Lubavitzer Rebbe has started in this country, and into which he has been able to draw so many varied groups of Jewish people. This work must and will go on, with the help of the Lord. We must all contribute to this historic mission. This is what I want you to convey to your readers. And if it helps to make them realize what our task is, and put their shoulder to the wheel, then our time was well spent indeed."

This is the new Lubavitzer Rebbe. The high office, the admiration of the people, the burden of directing innumerable activities of world-wide organizations, had not marred his modesty. Publicity is generally sought by leaders of such stature, but the new Rebbe is not that kind of leader. As he once told a gathering of his co-workers: "We, ourselves, don't count. It is our task, our sacred mission, that matters. And if we but want to carry it on, our goal will not remain unachieved."

Reprinted from *Jewish Life*, Sept.-Oct., 1951, pp. 54–61

THE LUBAVITCHER MOVEMENT

RABBI HERBERT WEINER

The heavy wooden door of the red brick house at 770 Eastern Parkway has a gothic trim that is carried over into the stained glass windows. The building, both within and without, must have been very impressive at one time. Old residents of the neighborhood recall, with a touch of malice, that it was formerly owned by a doctor about whose practice there had been some lifted eyebrows. People who now see young bearded men in their black hats and coats going in and out are aware that the structure now houses some kind of Jewish religious group, but there cannot be many passersby who know what is really going on, that here is the headquarters of a unique spiritual realm whose authority extends into many lands and whose ruling head exercises an almost absolute control over the lives of tens of thousands of followers.

Menachem Mendel Schneersohn is the name of the man whose office is to the left of the entrance, behind some windows whose shades are always drawn. He is the present Lubavitcher Rebbe and a direct descendant in the seventh generation of Schneur Zalman, the original founder of this Hasidic dynasty. He is also the son-in-law of the previous Rebbe.

To 770 Eastern Parkway have come thousands of visitors, curiosity-seekers, and "fellow travelers" such as Zalman Shazar, the president of Israel, and Jacques Lipshitz, the sculptor. There are also many who come to beseech the Rebbe's intercession for their troubles, for though Menachem Mendel Schneersohn is a man who has studied at the Sorbonne and speaks a dozen languages, he is also a tzaddik (saintly person), looked upon by some of his followers as a miracle worker. Stories of miracles are to be readily heard at 770 Eastern Parkway, but they are of a peculiar Lubavitch flavor, that is, with a rational explanation. An example is the story of the American soldier in Korea who one day wandered off from his squad looking for a stream in which to wash his hands before opening his can of C rations. A shell struck the squad's position, killing every one of his comrades. Today the young veteran vows he owes his life to a visit he had made, just before shipping out to Korea, to the Rebbe of the Lubavitcher movement. The latter had counseled the young man to observe, even while in combat, as much as he could of the Jewish Law, including the commandment to wash one's hands before eating.

There are hundreds of other examples, but the Rebbe and his followers do not like their movement talked about as if it were only a collection of miracle tales. The plain facts of the history of the movement, they point out, are more wonderful than all the stories about the powers of the Lubavitcher Rebbes. Founded about two hundred years ago in northern Russia, it has since been active in many other countries and is today in some ways stronger and more influential than when it first began. Though mysticism lies at its core, the Lubavitcher movement has been blessed with a flair for organization and public relations that has enabled it to strike firm roots in environments as diverse as communist Russia, North Africa, and the United States. As in the past, thousands of Lubavitcher followers continue to accept the Rebbe's word as authoritative, not only in questions of ritual, but in matters of health, livelihood, and, if it comes to it, life itself.

The first of my many visits to Lubavitcher headquarters took place in 1955. I found an office where several men were typing, chattering, or using the telephone. The one girl working in the office had on a plain long-sleeved dress. The steel filing cabinet, the telephones studded with interoffice buttons, the quiet activity, all created a businesslike atmosphere, hardly what I had expected to find at the headquarters of a sect of mystics. I asked where I could find Rabbi Weinberg who, I had been advised, would be a good initial contact.

"Rabbi Weinberg, of course—the globetrotter we call him," one of the men grinned. "I think he's home now between trips, and you can call him for an appointment."

As for an appointment with the Rebbe himself, I was directed to Rabbi Hodakov, the Rebbe's personal secretary, a thin, fair man, who at the moment was using one of the several phones on his desk at the other side of the office. "Incidentally," my informant added, "Rabbi Hodakov was a member of the Latvian government before our Rebbe's predecessor made him his secretary."

When Rabbi Hodakov had finished his phone conversation and finished with two bearded young men who had been waiting to speak to him, I walked over to his desk. He extended a limp hand and asked if I spoke Yiddish. There was a quizzical but good-natured expression in his light blue eyes as I indicated my purpose in seeking an audience with the Rebbe. Rabbi Hodakov turned the pages of a little black book and murmured that the Rebbe's calendar was filled for the next six months but he would see what he could do for me. The Rebbe received people only three times a week, beginning at eight o'clock in the evening.

I asked how long these evening sessions lasted.

"Oh, sometimes till three, sometimes till five o'clock in the morning," he smiled. His smile, charming and rather bashful, showed a trace of pride when he mentioned the Rebbe.

I asked if the Rebbe slept during the day after these meetings.

Rabbi Hodakov raised his brows. "During the day the Rebbe is busy directing the activities of the Lubavitcher movement in every part of the world."

"When does he sleep?"

The answer was another slightly mysterious smile and a shrug. Then he made a note in his black book and told me that I could see the Rebbe four weeks hence at ten o'clock in the evening. "Anybody can get to see him, but, of course, there have to be priorities, and," the bashful smile appeared again, "sometimes people have to wait a long time."

"Incidentally," I asked, "how many followers of the Lubavitcher movement are there in the world?"

"How many Jews are there in the world?" answered Rabbi Hodakov good-naturedly.

Later I learned that Rabbi Hodakov's reply had not been altogether facetious. Lubavitcher Hasidim regard the Rebbe not only as their own leader but also as the spiritual shepherd of all Israel in his generation. "He is to us," one of his closest disciples explained, "what Moses was to Israel in his time. Not that the Rebbe is to be compared to Moses, 'like whom there has been none other since.' But the Rebbe is like a little Moses, like 'a picture whose size has been reduced.'" That is the difference, my informant went on to say, between the Lubavitcher Hasidim and other Hasidic sects. The other Rebbes are interested mainly in their own Hasidim, while the Lubavitcher Rebbe considers himself responsible for the spiritual and bodily welfare of every Jew, no matter where he lives or what he believes. In this respect he follows the first Lubavitcher Rebbe, who taught that "Israel is really one soul with different bodies."

The following week I called Rabbi Weinberg. The genial personality of the globetrotter came though even on the phone, but when I met him, it was still surprising to find such a young man; despite his beard, he did not seem much more than thirty years old. My visit had been arranged for the early evening, and all his children were asleep except for a five-year-old whose head (covered by a yarmulke) kept popping out of the window above while his father and I conversed on the small porch below. "*Gei shlofen, yingele*—go to bed, little boy," Rabbi Weinberg called out to him, and the little head darted in, only to reappear a few seconds later. Rabbi Weinberg's English was touched by the slightest of accents, and I asked him if he always used Yiddish with his children. He told me that Yiddish was still the basic language of the Lubavitcher movement, though his children spoke English. The rebbe delivered his discourses in Yiddish but was fluent in many languages. "He studied science, you know, at the Sorbonne, before being chosen rebbe."

Rabbi Weinberg began to supply me with stories about people who had been helped by the rebbe. A girl from Brazil, for example, had been advised by her doctors to undergo a serious brain operation, but the rebbe had disagreed. "'They make their living by cutting; I make my living not by cutting,' the rebbe likes to say." His opinion had been upheld by a brain specialist, and child was now well.

How could such powers be explained? Rabbi Weinberg admitted it would be hard for someone who had not seen the evidence with his own eyes to believe. Basically, the rebbe had unusual powers because he was a holy man, that is, every limb of his body was sanctified by pure living and by the total observance of God's commandments. This was not an idea peculiar to Hasidism; even Maimonides, the philosopher and rationalist, had asserted that the spirit of prophecy might descend upon anyone who had completely purified his heart and tongue and limbs. In addition, the rebbe, being a direct descendant of Schneur Zalman, the founder of the Lubavitcher movement, had inherited the accrued merit of his ancestry. Of course, to Rabbi Weinberg it was clear that the movement represented the main branch of the Hasidic movement inaugurated by the Baal Shemtov.

I asked him how Lubavitcher Hasidim had been able to escape the degeneration of spirit which had marked other Hasidic sects.

"Mesiras nefesh" he replied quickly, "the willingness to sacrifice oneself. Our rebbes set us an example; they showed us that if something is very important, it can be done. If something matters very much—as much as life itself—you find a way to do it."

Besides, Lubavitch believed that no Jew was ever wholly lost to God. The Alter Rebbe, Schneur Zalman, had taught that within every Jew there was a point of authentic religious faith, an element of pure Jewishness, *"dos pintele yid."* One had to remember that "the soul itself was so much deeper that what appeared to the eye," and hence surface appearances ought never to discourage one from attempting to tap a man's inner capability for faith in and love for Judaism. It was the principle that gave the movement its missionary spirit.

Before I left, Rabbi Weinberg told me that if I wanted to see Lubavitch in action, I could do no better than be present in two weeks' time at the *farbrengung.* This festival was the annual celebration of the release of Rabbi Joseph Isaac (predecessor of the present rebbe) from the Spalerno prison in Leningrad, where he had been held by the communists. Hasidim would be coming from all parts of the world for the occasion, and I would have a chance to hear the rebbe "give Torah."

I spent the next two weeks trying to learn more about the Lubavitcher movement in order to be better prepared for the *farbrengung.* Understanding could not grow without an acquaintance with the movement's history. . . .

The *Farbrengung*

I had been warned to come early to the *farbrengung* if I wanted a sear, but the wooden tables and benches set up in the courtyard adjoining the building were already filled when I arrived. At one end of the courtyard was a long table covered with a white cloth and mounted on a platform. Most of the seats on the dais were still empty, but a row of chairs behind the central table was already occupied by bearded dignitaries of the movement. A microphone had been set up at the center of the table and hooked to loudspeakers at the other end of the courtyard. I saw a few inches of space on one of the rear benches and, following the example of the others, climbed from table to table over the backs of the seated people to reach it—the tables and benches had been packed so closely together there was no aisle space left. It was a humid summer evening, and there were beads of sweat of the faces of many of the Hasidim, who wore full jackets or long black coats along with large-brimmed hats. But nobody seemed to mind the heat, and the crowded courtyard was only further proof to the Hasidim of the greatness of their rebbe.

The person next to me was dressed in a neat business suit and conventional gray hat. He was a Conservative rabbi in Brooklyn who had been raised in the Lubavitcher movement and "would never cut his ties to them." He tried to attend ever "gathering" and despite his own strayings from strict Orthodoxy, was an admirer of the rebbe. I asked him how he felt about the powers which the Hasidim attributed to the rebbe. "Listen," he answered, "I know only this—nobody is more concerned with the fate of Jews—every Jew—than the rebbe." He indicated a man with a black beard sitting near us. "He was raised in Russia in the Lubavitch 'underground.' If you ask him how he was able to maintain his religion at the risk of death, he will tell you it was the inspiration of the rebbe."

My neighbor pointed out some of the important personages in the courtyard. Directly to the right of the rebbe's chair was a red-bearded man, Rabbi Mintlik, who was head of the Eastern Parkway Yeshiva. Seated at one end of the table on the dais was Rabbi Gur Aryeh, the brother-in-law of the rebbe. I tried to get a look at him, for we had already spoken on the phone and arranged an interview. Joseph Isaac had had no sons, but he did have two daughters, and Gur Aryeh had married one of them. But it was the other son-in-law, Menachem Mendel, who had been chosen as rebbe after Joseph Isaac's death. I wondered on what grounds the choice had been made.

At about nine-thirty the yard suddenly became quiet. There was that sound of the scraping of chairs and benches as people tried to stand, all eyes turned to the door which led from the courtyard into the main building. Into the yard with quick step walked the seventh rebbe of the Lubavitcher movement, son-in-law of Joseph Isaac and a direct descendant on his father's side of the Alter rebbe.

Rabbi Menachem Mendel turned out to be a man of average height and build. The most striking feature of his well-formed face was his deep, gentle blue eyes, in which there was little of the *malchus*—imperial sternness—of his predecessor. His complexion was pale, contrasting with his short black beard in which streaks of gray were beginning to appear. His frock coat, hat, and tie were all black and neatly tailored. The brim of his hat was just a bit larger than a conventional brim, but smaller than that of the Orthodox Hasid. I had heard that when Menachem Mendel was studying in Paris, he had refused to wear the long black coat which was customary in Hasidic circles. Now he alludes jokingly to his former habit of dress as a device that gave him more hours for study—"Hasidism didn't come to me when I wore a short coat."

There must have been considerable discussion when the question of elevating Menachem Mendel to the spiritual throne of Lubavitch arose; Lubavitcher rebbes had never approved of secular studies, and some of the elders of the movement must have wondered whether a Paris gentleman could ever be a rebbe. Nevertheless, it was apparent to all who knew him that Menachem Mendel was suited by birth, by marriage, and by his own intellectual and spiritual gifts to be the leader of the Lubavitcher movement. For his part Menachem Mendel was genuinely reluctant to assume the leadership. He had taken courses in electrical engineering in Paris, while his wife was studying architecture, and they had planned to earn their living in these professions. It required two years to persuade him to accept the position of rebbe.

All this, however, was past. As he mounted the dais now and took his chair, Rabbi Menachem Mendel seemed very much at ease in his role. The audience rose when he entered and remained standing until he sat down. Once seated, he turned to receive a bottle of whiskey which he passed over the table to some outstretched hand below. As if by prearranged signal, little paper cups and bottle of whiskey appeared on all tables in the yard.

The students on the bench in front began clapping hands and swaying back and forth in rhythmic accompaniment to a song. Everyone, including the rebbe, participated in the singing. In the middle of one particularly animated melody, the rebbe leaned forward and began beating out a rhythm on the table with his fists, at which the singing of the Hasidim immediately mounted in volume and intensity. The rebbe, a slight smile on his lips, began to sway from side to side and rose from his chair. An almost physical current of excitement ran through the audience and the singing reached a fever pitch. Near a fan in the back of the courtyard a man wearing a hat which came down to his ears was jumping up and down, clapping his hands, his eyes closed as if hypnotized. Behind the rebbe, an elderly man with a long white beard was hopping from leg to leg, waving his arms about. Then the rebbe sat down, and at once the current of excitement subsided.

Rabbi Menachem Mendel cleared his throat and reached for the microphone. The courtyard grew quiet as the rebbe called out several names. One of those called was sitting near me. He leaped to his feet, his face flushed and his hands trembling as he raised his cup to the rebbe and said, "*L'chaim*, to life!" The rebbe, with a faint smile, vigorously nodded his head in return and moved his lips in an answering "*Lchaim.*" After all those he had singled out by name had offered toasts in this fashion others in the room began to rise from their seats , and as soon as they had succeeded in catching the rebbe's eye they too called out, "To life!" Near me, a youngster was unable to hide a grimace of distaste as he downed his cup of strong liquor. These exchanges between the rebbe and his Hasidim continued for about an hour, and then they began singing a slow melody with Yiddish words that sounded like "*Essen est zisch, shlofen shloft zich, ober davenin davent zich nisht*" ("Eating and drinking take care of themselves, but not prayer").

Only one person in the room seemed not to be singing, and that was the red-bearded rabbi standing at the rebbe's right. He stood immobilized, staring fixedly at a spot on the table before the rebbe. I was told that this was Rabbi Mintlik who had the honor of being the rabbi's cup-bearer; his feeling for the rebbe was so intense that it had reached the level of *hitbatlut,* self-extinction. The act of extinguishing oneself before the rebbe was evidently considered one of the summits of Hasidic devotion.

After the singing was over, the rebbe reached for the microphone and cleared his throat with a nervous little cough. As one, the *farbrengung* rose, and my neighbor informed me that we were about to be instructed in Torah. . . .

At about two A.M. I left the *farbrengung,* which showed no signs of ending, and walked toward my car trying to sum up my feelings. It had been an interesting evening, and yet frustrating. There was no question about the genuineness of faith in that courtyard, but it was a faith that seemed completely beyond the comprehension of most people in the twentieth century.

Perhaps the rebbe, who I recalled, had studied science at the Sorbonne, would be able to resolve some of the questions I still had.

Alone with the Rebbe

I arrived for my appointment with the rebbe at 10 P.M., but was still waiting after midnight when a young student ran into the outer office to announce that the "case" from California, a man who had flown in to consult with the Lubavitcher rebbe about a business problem, had just left. That meant it was my turn, and clutching my notebook, I hurried past several people in the hallways whose appointments with the rebbe would be even later. Remembering that there are thousands who depend on the rebbe for major and even minor decisions in their lives, and that a worldwide spiritual network, including schools and charities and publications, waited on the personal attention of this one man, I made a resolution not to stay long.

Rabbi Menachem Mendel Schneersohn, the seventh Lubavitcher rebbe, was folding some papers at a desk in the far corner of a large, rather bare room. His fedora hat, neatly tailored frock coat, and carefully arranged tie, all black, set off the pallor of his face. The brim of his hat was bent, casting a shadow over his deep blue eyes, which looked up with a direct but good-humored expression. I extended my hand, forgetting for the moment that the Hasidim do not offer their hands to the rebbe, who is to them a holy vessel and not to be touched casually. But Rabbi Menachem Mendel didn't seem to mind the impropriety; he shook my hand and motioned gently toward the chair by his desk, suggesting in a soft voice that I address him in English, although he would reply in Yiddish.

Before I could begin my inquiries, he asked me what kind of work I was engaged in and what I had studied. My notebook with its proposed questions remained closed, and I found myself chatting freely about matters I had not expected to discuss. The rebbe listened, nodding his head from time to time to indicate understanding, and gradually the sense of urgent haste I had felt in the hallway began to ebb away. . . .

Suddenly a buzzer sounded, a signal from Rabbi Hodakov, the rebbe's secretary, that almost a full hour had passed since my interview began. Hastily I turned to my prepared questions and asked how Lubavitcher Hasidism, a mystical movement, had become so skillful in worldly matters like public relations and methods of business efficiency. The rebbe folded his hands on his desk and in a measured voice outlined his answer, which was punctuated by an occasional mild cough.

Lubavitch's interest in public relations is simply a practical extension of its special interpretation of the oneness of God. God is in everything, and therefore evil has no real existence. But it must appear to have real existence, so that man might have freedom of choice. It might seem to us an evil thing for one man to cut another with a knife, yet there are occasions, as for example a medical operation, when a good and not an evil purpose is served by the cutting of a man. So also, what appears evil in our sight is, in the light of a higher wisdom, really good. To believe otherwise, to believe that evil has a positive existence, is to be driven in the end to the conviction that there are two divine powers rather than one. The oneness of God implies that everything is ultimately justified. . . .

Again the buzzer sounded, but the rebbe indicated that I needn't hurry. I turned to my central question: how could the rebbe assume responsibility for giving advice to his Hasidim not only on religious matters, but on medical problems or business affairs, especially when he knew that his advice was binding?

Menachem Mendel did not seem offended. "To begin with, it is always pleasant to run away from responsibility. But what if running might destroy the congregation, and suppose" —the good-humored smile in the rebbe's eyes stronger—"they put the key into your pocket and walk away? What can you do then—permit the books to be stolen?"

I was surprised to hear him hint at the well-known fact that it had taken the Hasidim more than a year to persuade Rabbi Menachem Mendel to become the seventh rebbe of the Lubavitcher movement. But this wasn't the answer to my question, which I tried to press by leafing through a copy of the Tanya (a collection of the writings of the first Lubavitcher rebbe, Schneur Zalman) to find a letter in which the Alter rebbe tells his Hasidim that they must not ask him for help in non-spiritual matters. The rebbe interrupted my search to say that I was probably looking for Letter 22. "That letter," he pointed out quietly, "was printed after Schneur Zalman's death, and besides," he smiled, "despite the letter, he did give advice in material matters."

Sensing after a moment that his explanation did not satisfy me, the rebbe cleared his throat and continued. "When a man comes with a problem, there are only two alternatives—either send him away, or try to help him. A man knows his own problem best, so one must try to unite oneself with him and become *batel*, as dissociated as possible from one's own ego. Then, in concert with the other person, one tries to understand the rule of Divine Providence in this particular case. And, of course, if the man who comes to you shares your ideas and faith, there is immediate empathy" (he used the English word).

But didn't the power of the Lubavitcher movement stem directly from this faith of the Hasid in his rebbe? Rabbi Menachem Mendel demurred gently, "I'm not so sure."

The buzzer rang again, and I looked at the rebbe to see if my interview was over. Instead of sending me away, however, he began talking about Conservative and Reform Judaism. His voice remained soft, but the opinions were firm. "The great fault of Conservative and Reform Judaism is not that they compromise, but that they sanctify the compromise, still the conscience, and leave no possibility for return." The rebbe went on to explain that though the Lubavitcher movement encourages every Jew to observe as many of the commandments as he could, even if only a few, it insists that the Jewish religion as such should be identified exclusively with the Orthodox tradition; otherwise, a repentant Jew who wants to "return" would not know what there was to return to.

When the buzzer rang once again, I rose to leave, but Rabbi Menachem Mendel stopped me: "Wait—now I would like to ask you a question," he said, and I sat down again. "How is it that you are not Orthodox?" Surprised, I offered something about not being able to believe that the whole of the Torah was given by God.

"Yet you believe in the oneness of God," the rebbe pressed. "And if you follow out the implication of that belief logically, then you must come to the *mitzvot*, the commandments, as surely as theorems follow from axioms." Again the rebbe used English words. I remained silent, and after a moment he leaned back in his chair and spoke as if answering himself, "But I guess in America people don't feel the need for a full logical *shitah*, system of belief, as they do in Europe."

For the fifth time the buzzer rang and, disturbed at the thought of all those people waiting outside, I made a determined effort to leave. But as I stood up the rebbe stopped me again. "You haven't asked, but probably you'd like to know, what Hasidim think about miracles?" I remained standing while Rabbi Menachem Mendel asserted that even science recognizes all "laws" as mere probabilities and that there is no way to foretell every event in nature with certainty. He cited the throwing of dice as an example, a strange *mashal* (illustration), I thought to myself, for a Hasid to use.

After he had finished expounding the Hasidic view of miracles, I asked him if it would be possible to see him again when I had become more familiar with the Lubavitcher movement. "Gladly," he smiled, "but not until after the High Holy days" which were only a month away. . . .

The Second Private Audience with the Rebbe

My appointment was again for ten P.M. I came on time, though knowing by now that with respect to appointments, Lubavitch followed the dictum of another rebbe, the Kotsker, who maintained, "Where there is a soul, there cannot be a clock." On arrival, I found a group of Hasidim in the study hall, listening to one of their comrades who reputedly had a gift for remembering every word of the rebbe's discourses. Several weeks ago the rebbe had spoken Torah, and since then the Hasidim had been gathering to hear this man with the photographic memory "repeat the Torah."

Noticing that the phones in the office were quiet, I approached Rabbi Hodakov's desk, and requested a few minutes of his time. The rebbe's secretary shrugged his thin shoulders and invited me to take a seat. "Rabbi Hodakov," I asked, "could you tell me briefly what Lubavitch offers people?"

Rabbi Hodakov sat straight in his chair and his eyes brightened. Then he spoke so forcefully that a student standing over in a corner of the office looked up in surprise. "I can tell you in one word —*leben,* life." He paused for a moment. "There are other kinds of death besides the one of the grave. What is life for one creature on earth need not be life for another. A monkey may act like a man, and I don't know how he feels then—but if a man acts like a monkey, he stops being a man—he stops living."

"What is it that makes life?" Rabbi Hodakov's voice grew stronger as he continued to speak. "It is the fulfillment of a mission and a purpose. In nature, we have different classes—mineral, vegetable, animal, and then Jew. The Jew has his purpose like every other species, but what is this purpose?"

A few more students had entered the office and were now listening openly to our discussion.

Rabbi Hodakov went on passionately, "We would not have known the purpose if God had not done us a *chesed,* a gracious favor. He gave us Torah."

The room has become quiet. The boys edged close and I think Rabbi Hodakov was aware that he had an audience. I too felt self-conscious. All were waiting for my next question. Through the slight haze of my fever, an appalling thought suddenly penetrated to my mind. This was not just a conversation. It was going to become a *vikuach,* a religious disputation, similar to those held in the Middle Ages between the "believer" and the "heretic." I, of course, was cast in the role of the heretic, and the boys in the room who had gathered to listen were convinced that, like all heretics, I was about to be annihilated by the logic and spiritual power of the truth. But dabbing my watery eyes and running nose with a handkerchief, and feeling somewhat like a lamb stretching out its neck to the knife, I offered the question that I knew was expected of me. "But how do we know that God gave us the Torah?"

Rabbi Hodakov's eyes glinted; the knife was lifted. "When was the constitution written?"

I mumbled a date, hoping that it was correct.

But Rabbi Hodakov was not interested in my knowledge of American History. "How do you know?" he demanded.

Witnesses and correlating documents, I ventured, adding a protest to the effect that the Constitution did not purport to be more than a human document. I remember using the word "witness" deliberately because I felt that he would want to seize on it in answering me.

"Ah-ha," Rabbi Hodakov sat up in his chair to deliver the *coup de grace*. "If witnesses are to be believed about a human document, then how much more difficult would be to find real witnesses for a divine document? Wouldn't it be even more difficult to forge such testimony?"

Actually I wasn't sure that I followed his logic, but I blamed that on myself or on the fever which was blurring my mind. Besides, I had come across the same line of argument before; it was made use of in the twelfth century by Judah Halevi in his *Sefer ha-Kuzari*. Six hundred thousand witnesses, says Judah Halevi, saw the Torah given by God to Moses. The event has been related by father to son in an unbroken chain of testimony. How could the claim that a whole generation had witnessed the giving of the Torah possibly have been invented in some later age? The elders would deny having heard of the event from their fathers and the claim would fall to the ground. Consequently, concludes Judah Halevi, revelation must be as credible a fact as any recorded event in history.

This argument had never impressed me before, but it now occurred to my feverish mind that it was very sensible, and I wondered why I hadn't understood it on the other occasions. I was reaching for my handkerchief again when the buzzer rang. The rebbe was waiting. I grabbed my notebook and escaped into the hallway.

The quiet of the rebbe's office and his soft-spoken greeting were like balm after the "disputation."

"*Shalom aleichem*, Rabbi Weiner," Rabbi Menachem Mendel smiled, extending his hand.

I protested that, after a year of visiting 770 Eastern Parkway, I knew that a good Hasid should not take the rebbe's hand.

"We don't have to begin that way," he said, beckoning me toward a chair. He looked a bit paler than when I had first seen him a year ago and there was more gray in his black beard, but the same grave smile played in his deep blue eyes.

I opened my notebook and sat back in the chair, again conscious of how comfortable and relaxing it was in the rebbe's office. Then I remembered that this was my last chance and resolved to ask even the most embarrassing questions in an effort to solve the enigma of Lubavitch. I explained to the rebbe that more than a year had passed since I began trying to understand the movement, and that I had come to him now with a confession: I did not understand. Would he mind if I started this interview by asking him about the character of a Hasid?

Rabbi Menachem Mendel smiled and told me to go ahead; as before I could speak English but he would answer in Yiddish.

"Isn't the fact that Hasidim turn to the rebbe for almost every decision in their lives—isn't this a sign of weakness, a repudiation of the very thing that makes a man human, his b'chirah, freedom of will?"

The rebbe's answer came without hesitation, as if he had dealt with the question before. "A weak person is usually overcome by the environment in which he finds himself. But our Hasidim can be sent into any environment, no matter how strange or hostile, and they maintain themselves within it. So how can we say that it is weakness which characterizes a Hasid?"

I pressed my question from another angle and told him that I sensed a desire in Chabad to oversimplify, to strip ideas of their complexity merely for the sake of a superficial clarity. As a matter of fact, I blurted out, all his Hasidim seemed to have one thing in common: a sort of open and naive look in their eyes that a sympathetic observer might call t'mimut (purity) but that might less kindly be interpreted as emptiness or simple-mindedness, the absence of inner struggle.

I found myself taken aback by my own boldness, but the rebbe showed no resentment. He leaned forward. "What you see missing from their eyes is a *kera*!"

"A what?" I asked.

"Yes, a *kera*," he repeated quietly, "a split." The rebbe hesitated for a moment. "I hope you will not take offense, but something tells me you don't sleep well at night, and this is not good for 'length of days.' Perhaps if you had been raised wholly in one world or in another, it might be different. But this split is what comes from trying to live in two worlds."

The rebbe's ad hominem answer encouraged me to be personal in return. "But you too have studied in two worlds, and your Hasidim are rather proud of the fact that you once attended the Sorbonne. Why then do you discourage them from studying in the 'other world'?"

"Precisely because I have studied, and I know what the value of that study is," the rebbe replied quickly. "I recognized its usefulness. If there are people who think they can help G-d sustain the world, I have no objection. We need engineers and chemists, but engineering and chemistry are not the most important things. Besides, to study does not mean only to learn facts. It means exposure to certain circles and activities which conflict with a believer's values and faith. It's like taking a person from a warm environment and throwing him into a cold water shock-treatment several times a day. How long can he stand it? In addition, studies in college take place at an age when a man's character is not yet crystallized, usually before the age of thirty. Exposure then is dangerous."

There was a slight pause, and then I asked the rebbe if he would object to being questioned about himself. He shrugged smilingly. Well, then, I said: the boys at 770 Eastern Parkway claimed that the rebbe was able to see things they could not see and that he was not mere flesh and blood. He himself, in our last interview, had given me a rather more rational explanation of the powers of the rebbe, saying that they were a matter of empathy. But I wanted to know whether he regarded himself and his six predecessors as mere flesh and blood.

For the first time he hesitated over his answer. "Are you asking me to tell you about myself?" he smiled. "I don't think you should write about me and my beliefs. But I can tell you what the position of the rebbe is in Hasidism. We are, of course, all of us only flesh and blood, and I'm not responsible for all the stories you may hear. But you must approach the facts of the case without preconceived theories. Science, after all, means the willingness to observe facts and follow them to whatever conclusions they will lead not to try to push the facts into a desired pattern."

"Do you believe, then, that the rebbe has special insight and can see things and know things beyond the comprehension of ordinary people?" I still wanted a clear answer.

"Yes," said the rebbe.

"And is this power given only to the rebbe, or to other men also?"

"As a believer," replied the rebbe, "I am convinced that it can only be given to a 'keeper of Torah and mitzvot.'"

At that moment, a question I had not planned to ask came to my lips. "What is a *b'rachah*?"

"What?" asked the rebbe, slightly startled.

"What does it mean when somebody comes to ask you for a blessing?"

"Are you asking me what I mean by a *b'rachah*?" the rebbe deflected the question. "Better that I tell you what Hasidism means by it. A man is affected by many levels, higher and lower. It is possible for the *tsaddik*, the rebbe, to awaken powers slumbering within a man. It is also possible to bring him into contact with a higher level of powers outside his own soul. A person lives on one floor of a building and needs help from the floor above; if he can't walk up himself, someone else must help him get that help."

"Does that mean that the rebbe can help a man up to a higher spiritual plane?"

"That's the hardest way," answered the rebbe. "The easier way is to bring these powers down upon him."

I asked about miracles, and this time the rebbe replied immediately. "To believe in the Creator, and to believe that there is a continuous relationship between the Creator and the creation, is necessarily to believe that the Creator can do anything with His creation."

We spoke about religious faith and I suggested that many people would like to believe but found it hard. Rabbi Menachem Mendel disagreed. "It's not so hard for people to believe. There are millions who believed in Gandhi and millions who believe in the Pope, and even atheists when pressed to a corner come up with belief."

When I protested that in most cases doubt seems to overwhelm faith, the rebbe nodded. "There can be doubts. To question God, however, is the first indication that one believes in something. You have to know something about God even to question Him. But we must try to overcome doubts by a constant feeding of the spirit. Just as a body that has been kept healthy can overcome a crisis, so a soul can defeat its crises and its doubts if it is constantly kept healthy."

"In that case, why are there so many without faith?"

The rebbe looked at me directly. "They are afraid of their faith. They are afraid of following out the consequences of the faith which they would arrive at by honest observation of the facts. They are afraid that they might have to abandon some of their comfort or give up cherished ideas. They are afraid of changing their lives."

I brought up another problem. Several weeks before I had heard him say that America, rather than Israel, was the place where Jewish life could flourish best. How did he reconcile this attitude with the commandment to leave the *galut*, the Diaspora?

"What is *galut*? *Galut* means the estrangement of a person from his essential self. If a person moves from an environment where he observed the commandments and had a Jewish soul and comes to America where he forsakes the Torah while growing rich, free, and comfortable, he has nevertheless gone into exile, because he has left himself. It's not just assimilation, it's worse, it's what we call in English an inferiority complex. It is the admission that one's own values are inferior to the values of those around one. In Israel, too, it may be possible to go into *galut*, to forsake the Torah and lose the spirit which is our essential nature, to be 'like unto all the nations.' In addition," the rebbe said quietly, "America has not only the largest Jewish population in the world, but great material resources. Even as the spiritual can affect the material, so with material resources one can do things for the spirit."

The buzzer at the rebbe's desk sounded. Rabbi Hodakov was reminding us that others were waiting. I decided to ask a final question. "Many Jews today are searching," I said to the rebbe, "they want to return. What would you say to them to help them find their way?"

The rebbe paused for a moment. "I would say that the most important thing is 'no compromise.' I would send to them the words spoken by the prophet Elijah: 'How long halt ye between two opinions? If the Lord be God, follow Him; but if Baal, follow him.' Compromise is dangerous, because it sickens both the body and the soul. A compromiser who tries to mediate between religion and the environment is unable to go in either direction and unable to distinguish the truth."

But would not people reject such rigid alternatives?

"This is the contribution of Chabad Hasidism," the rebbe pointed out. "It's important to know that one must do everything, but at the same time we welcome the doing of even a part. If all we can accomplish is to save only one limb, we save that. Then we worry about saving another."

The buzzer rang again, and I rose, but the rebbe motioned for me to wait. To my surprise, he informed me that he had carefully read some articles about religion in Israel which I had published in *Commen-*

tary (July and August, 1955). Another hour passed as Menachem Mendel Schneersohn gently but firmly offered his criticism of the pieces. It was after three o'clock in the morning when I left the rebbe's office and guiltily passed a bearded young man who was still waiting for his appointment. The secretary's office was closed, but from the street through a window I could see the Rabbi Hodakov was bent over his desk, his head buried in his arms.

The next morning when I returned to retrieve a briefcase I had left in the office, Rabbi Hodakov was still at his desk. His eyes were red and the phylacteries were on his head and arm. While he recited the morning prayers, one of the boys attended to his busy telephone. Two of the older students came up to me as I was leaving the office. They had heard that I had spent almost three hours with the rebbe early that morning, and they wanted to know what I thought now about their rebbe. Their eyes shone with pride as they awaited my reply. I remembered that the rebbe had said that the open look in a Hasid's eyes was not naiveté but the absence of a *kera*, a split.

Indeed, I thought, there is no split at Lubavitch. It offered its followers a world in which the mind was never confused by contradictions; where life was not compartmentalized; where the tensions between heart and mind flesh and soul, God and His creation were all dissolved in the unity of a higher plan. And any doubt or confusion that arose might be clarified by making oneself "as nothing" before the rebbe, who in turn made himself "as nothing" before the will of G-d.

No, there was no *kera* in the eyes of the Hasidim who awaited my answer. They nodded their heads enthusiastically as I expressed my admiration for their rebbe. I confessed to them that before leaving early that morning, I had asked the rebbe for his personal blessing. What was more, my cold of last night was much better. They shook my hand as if I were paying them a personal compliment, for, after all, in this respect too there is no split in Lubavitch, where the Hasidim "are only the branches and the rebbe is the root."

There is something immensely attractive in a "way" which provides answers for all questions, whether they be details of personal life or problems of cosmic significance. It is reassuring to have a logical explanation for chaos and to learn that God is most revealed where He seems to be most absent. It is heartening to believe that what seems like meaningless accident is actually the revelation of God's most hidden essence and that pain is the chastisement of love; but not all souls are able to turn darkness into light with the help of such a clear system. There are many individuals whose struggle with darkness is more agonized and torturous, because they themselves are deeply touched and at times almost overcome by this darkness. Such individuals may be drawn to another rabbi who called himself a "moon man," one whose strength and even faith was subject to periods of waxing and waning.

9½ Mystics: The Kabbalah Today [New York: Holt, Rinehart & Winston, 1969], pp. 157–196

Excerpted and reprinted with permission of the author

THE REBBE AND THE TEENAGER

RABBI SHMUEL KAPLAN

For two years after my marriage, I attended a post-rabbinical college for Torah study, known as a Kollel. About three months into my studies, I was summoned by Rabbi Chaim Mordechai Aizik Hodakov, the Rebbe's personal secretary and also the director of the Kollel. Rabbi Hodakov told me that he had a special mission for me, one that should take precedence over everything else I was doing. He instructed me to take as much time off from my studies as necessary.

What was this important mission, which justified my absence from the Kollel? There was a young girl, a seventeen year old, who was going through some serious emotional difficulties: teenage angst, rebelliousness, religious confusion, family issues—the typical teenage issues but unusually severe. The Rebbe had taken an extraordinary personal interest in helping this girl through this stage in her life.

And so I was recruited to be the one to do whatever necessary to guide her through her difficulties. For about three months, I spent half of my time working on this issue. I didn't do a single thing without consultation with Rabbi Hodakov. He would often consult with the Rebbe and relay the Rebbe's instructions on how to deal with each particular situation.

This young girl regularly wrote letters to the Rebbe with various questions. The Rebbe would respond to each of her letters within a couple hours, or, at the latest, the next day, and instructed me to discuss his responses with her.

At one point, she had written a letter of several pages to the Rebbe, in which she described her inner turmoil and anguish. The Rebbe responded to her letter and wrote, among other things, that he feels her pain.

So she wrote back a letter and said, "Rebbe, I don't believe you. How can you feel my pain? You're not going through what I'm going through. What do you mean that you feel my pain?"

Within two hours the Rebbe answered, and this was the gist of the response:

"When you will merit to grow up and marry, and, G-d willing, you will have a child, the nature of things are that during the child's first year, he or she will begin to teethe. The teething is painful and the child cries. And a mother feels that pain as if it were her own." He then concluded the letter with these words: "This is how I feel your pain."

This had a very strong impact on her. We discussed it and she began to realize that the Rebbe was indeed feeling what she was going through and that the Rebbe was trying to help her. Slowly she began to respond to it. She made progress, she matured, and things turned out well for her.

I feel very privileged to have experienced firsthand the Rebbe's intervention in the fate of a child. I was struck by how he put himself into it with such intensity—answering her letters back and forth, again and again, over weeks and months. I could not imagine how a scholar and world leader of the Rebbe's magnitude would take such a personal interest, make the time and pour out his heart to ensure the wellbeing of a single teenager.

Printed with permission of JEM's *My Encounter with the Rebbe* oral history project

THE REBBE SAID THANK YOU

RABBI YANKI TAUBER

When Joseph Cabiliv—today a successful real estate developer—regained consciousness in the Rambam Hospital in Haifa, he remembered nothing of the circumstances that had brought him there. He felt an excruciating pain in his legs. The discovery that followed was far more horrendous: glancing under the sheet, he saw that both his legs had been amputated, the right leg at the knee, the left at mid-thigh.

The day before, Joseph, who was serving on reserve duty in Zahal (the Israeli Defense Forces), was patrolling the Golan Heights with several other soldiers when their jeep hit an old Syrian land mine. Two of his comrades were killed on the spot. Another three suffered serious injury. Joseph's legs were so severely crushed that the doctors had no choice but to amputate them.

Aside from the pain and disability, Joseph was confronted with society's incapacity to deal with the handicapped. "My friends would come to visit," he recalls, "sustain fifteen minutes of artificial cheer, and depart without once meeting my eye. My mother would come and cry, and it was I, who so desperately needed consolation, who had to do the consoling. My father would come and sit by my bedside in silence—I don't know which was worse, my mother's tears or my father's silence.

"Returning to my civilian profession as a welder was, of course, impossible, and while people were quick to offer charity, no one had a job for a man without legs. When I ventured out in my wheelchair, people kept their distance, so that a large empty space opened up around me on the busiest street corner."

When Joseph met with other disabled veterans he found that they all shared his experience: they had given their very bodies in defense of the nation, but the nation lacked the spiritual strength to confront their sacrifice.

"In the summer of 1976," Joseph tells, "Zahal sponsored a tour of the United States for a large group of disabled veterans. While we were in New York, a Lubavitcher chassid came to our hotel and suggested that we meet with the Lubavitcher Rebbe. Most of us did not know what to make of the invitation, but a few members of our group had heard about the Rebbe and convinced the rest of us to accept.

"As soon as they heard we were coming, the Chabadniks sprang into action, organizing the whole thing with the precision of a military campaign. Ten large commercial vans pulled up to our hotel to transport us and our wheelchairs to the Lubavitch headquarters in Brooklyn. Soon we found ourselves in the famous large synagogue in the basement of 770 Eastern Parkway.

"Ten minutes later, a white-bearded man of about 70 entered the room, followed by two secretaries. As if by a common signal, absolute silence pervaded the room. There was no mistaking the authority he radiated. We had all stood in the presence of military commanders and prime ministers, but this was unlike anything we had ever encountered. This must have been what people felt in the presence of royalty. An identical thought passed through all our minds: Here walks a leader, a prince.

"He passed between us, resting his glance on each one of us and lifting his hand in greeting, and then seated himself opposite us. Again he looked at each of us in turn. From that terrible day on which I had woken without my legs in the Rambam Hospital, I have seen all sorts of things in the eyes of those who looked at me: pain, pity, revulsion, anger. But this was the first time in all those years that I encountered true empathy. With that glance that scarcely lasted a second and the faint smile on his lips, the Rebbe conveyed to me that he is with me—utterly and exclusively with me.

"The Rebbe then began to speak, after apologizing for his Ashkenazic-accented Hebrew. He spoke about our 'disability,' saying that he objected to the use of the term. 'If a person has been deprived of a limb or a faculty,' he told, 'this itself indicates that G-d has given him special powers to overcome the limitations this entails, and to surpass the achievements of ordinary people. You are not "disabled" or "handicapped," but special and unique, as you possess potentials that the rest of us do not.

"'I therefore suggest,' he continued, adding with a smile 'of course it is none of my business, but Jews are famous for voicing opinions on matters that do not concern them—that you should no longer be called *nechei Yisrael* ("the disabled of Israel," our designation in the Zahal bureaucracy) but *metzuyanei Yisrael* ("the special of Israel").' He spoke for several minutes more, and everything he said—and more importantly, the way in which he said it—addressed what had been churning within me since my injury.

"In parting, he gave each of us a dollar bill, in order—he explained—that we give it to charity in his behalf, making us partners in the fulfillment of a mitzvah. He walked from wheelchair to wheelchair, shaking our hands, giving each a dollar, and adding a personal word or two. When my turn came, I saw his face up close and I felt like a child. He gazed deeply into my eyes, took my hand between his own, pressed it firmly, and said 'Thank you' with a slight nod of his head.

"I later learned that he had said something different to each one of us. To me he said 'Thank you'—somehow he sensed that that was exactly what I needed to hear. With those two words, the Rebbe erased all the bitterness and despair that had accumulated in my heart. I carried the Rebbe's 'thank you' back to Israel, and I carry it with me to this very day."

WHAT IS A REBBE?

RABBI TZVI FREEMAN

Rabbi Moshe Yitzchak Hecht had been the Chabad presence in New Haven, Connecticut, since 1941. The demands on him grew year by year, with a synagogue, a school, a yeshiva and many other responsibilities that required a staff several times that which he could afford.

In 1974, he wrote to the Rebbe complaining that in 33 years of work he felt he was back at the same place as when he started and that he simply could not continue.

He signed off the letter with a heart-rending plea that "the Rebbe should help and do all he can."

The Rebbe responded—not with counsel, but with light:

> *I've already followed your advice. I've sent there Rabbi Moshe Yitzchak Hecht. But it appears from your letter and from those preceding it that you still are not familiar with him and with the capabilities with which this person is endowed.*
>
> *Whatever the case, you should get to know him now. Immediately, everything will change—your mood, your trust in G-d, everyday happiness, etc., etc.*

Who Is a Rebbe?

Rebbe means "my master" or "my teacher." Whether you are a small child learning alef-bet, or an expert scholar sailing the seas of the Talmud, you call your teacher, "rebbe."

There's another meaning to the title rebbe, one especially associated with a rabbi they called the Baal Shem Tov. The Baal Shem Tov was a teacher who touched not only your mind and heart, but could reach into your essential being and guide you to find yourself there.

A rebbe then is a guide to your true self. Which means that before you can understand "What is a rebbe?" and "Who is a rebbe?" you must first ask "What am I" and "Who am I?"

Who Needs a Rebbe?

Imagine a rebbe as a ray of light. Light is not a thing for itself. Light is only light when it illuminates. Think of the space beyond our planet's atmosphere; between the brilliant sun and the glowing earth is only darkness. For light to be light, you must provide something for it to enlighten.

If your major concern is getting from today to tomorrow, there is nothing to enlighten. If you consider yourself nothing more than a two-legged creature with an excess of neurons, Wikipedia and TED may be all you need.

But if you seek that which transcends physical sensation and satisfaction, if you feel a need to make sense of life, if you have ever asked yourself, "What am I doing here?" and you are looking for something deep inside yourself—then you need a rebbe to get you in touch with that inner self.

Context and Liberation

How does a rebbe do that? How could he show you something about you that you yourself could not discover?[1]

Because as soon as you are connected to a rebbe, you are connected to a higher, wider context. A context in which you are no longer a lonely speck of dust in the vast, empty space, but a vital part of a greater whole.

[1] The following is based on Rabbi Schneur Zalman of Liadi, *Tanya*, chapter 2.

There, within that context, you discover where you are needed, what you are here to accomplish, and how you have the powers to fulfill that mission.

Context is everything. A sentence fallen out of a book can never make sense of itself without its story. Out of context, all meaning is distorted—often into its opposite. A precious ring in the snout of a boar, King Solomon the Wise tells us, just renders the beast yet more beastly. A swan out of context is an ugly duckling.

Life out of context is called exile. Without your context, it's not just that your place is missing. Without knowing your place, you cannot find your center, the very core of who you are.

Connecting to a rebbe connects you to the whole. And within that whole, you are liberated from exile.

Nucleus and Bonding

A rebbe is capable of doing that because he himself stands at the nucleus of that context.

All beauty in our universe begins with a nucleus. For a crystal to form, whether it be a snowflake or a diamond, a tiny nucleus of molecules must first become the basic structure from which a marvelous symmetry may extend. The same with life—whether it be a single cell, an entire tree or a human being—all begins with a tiny seed carrying the information that will unfold to form the limbs and organs of a mature organism.

And we all form a single organism. Our bodies may be separate, but our souls are one. What makes them one? That they have a single nucleus. In that nucleus, all of us find our origin, and from it, we continue to be nurtured. Nurtured and bonded in a perfect union with one another and with the origin of all things. For that nucleus is the place where G-d enters His universe. It is the place of a rebbe's soul, and from there he invites you to join him.

We and G-d

After all, what is a soul? It is G-d breathing inside you; it is the divine presence invested within your physical body. It is what we call a neshamah—meaning a breath, as in the story of the creation of the first human being, "And G-d blew into his nostrils the breath of life." At every moment, G-d breathes within us, and through that breath we are one with Him and He is one with us. In that breath, we are our Creator.

G-d is one, and so He is found in our oneness. Not as individuals, but as a whole; a singularity. Not as I, but as we. As a harmony of multifarious parts becoming one.

Which means that to find that oneness, that place inside you in which you are one with your G-d, you must first connect your soul with other souls, which connect with yet more networks of souls, all forming a single cell around a single nucleus. That nucleus, in turn, is the nodal point at which G-d's breath enters. It is where all things become one.

In that nucleus, a rebbe stands, and from there he brings us together as one, to feel one another, to know us, to know ourselves, and to know our center, our core, the place where G-d enters each of our souls. A rebbe connects us with our G-d—and then gets out of the way.

Heads and Heads

Rebbe, they say, stands for rosh b'nei Yisrael. That means "A head of the Jewish People."

Most of us think of a head as a control center. The head tells the heart, the lungs, the stomach, the fingers and toes what to do. Certainly, I am not interested in handing myself over to one who controls me. G-d gave me my life to be me, not to be controlled by someone else.

But if you think of your own head, it is certainly not like that. That is, unless you are the philosopher who complained at the end of his days, "My whole problem, it turns out, is that I have no body, only a head."

The head we are talking about here is not a philosopher's head, or an artificial head. It is the head of an organism, a body. Which means that before it is a head, it is first a part of this body. And so, the head is not concerned with consuming all other body parts into the head's agenda. The head is concerned with the heart being a healthy heart, the stomach being a healthy stomach, the fingers doing what fingers are supposed to do and the toes keeping well within their own domain as well. The head is concerned with each body part fulfilling its own agenda.

So too, a rebbe is firstly a servant of his people.

Knowing Your Name

Jerry Levine was an anchorman for Miami's Channel 10 News, and a good one. He had won an Emmy for producing programs encouraging Floridians to participate in regular medical examinations. But in 1989, Rabbi Sholom Lipskar asked him to work for his organization, Aleph, assisting Jewish prisoners and military personnel and their families.

Jerry was young and thought, "Hey, here's a great opportunity to try something new and different. And I can always get back into the news business if it doesn't work out."

So, at Rabbi Lipskar's suggestion, Jerry wrote to the Rebbe to ask his advice, providing many details about himself and his personal goals.

The Rebbe's response? A fax arrived on Rabbi Lipskar's desk: "Tell me all his names."

Jerry thought he had told the Rebbe all his names: Yosef ben Hirsch Leib ha'Levi. But when he went to talk with his mother about it, she told him it was Yosef Mordechai ben Hirsch Leib ha'Levi.

So he wrote again, this time with his full name. The Rebbe responded, telling him to ask the advice of a good friend.

"What I got from that," Jerry says, "is that this is a different sort of leader."

Any other leader would have been concerned with "What can this person provide my organization? How can he get us better media exposure?"

The Rebbe's concern, in Jerry's words, was that a Jewish boy didn't know his own name. How did he know that? How did he recognize something was missing?

Why shouldn't he? As a brain knows what the stomach needs, so a rebbe knows a Jew better than the Jew knows his own self.

But it is not the knowing that is relevant here. It is the caring. That was the Rebbe's first concern, because that is the job of a rebbe—to help you find your name, your true self, and where you belong.

Nothing for Yourself

Freddy Hager, came as a young man to see the Rebbe. He showed the Rebbe a picture of his grandfather, who had been a chassidic rebbe in Galicia.

The Rebbe asked him, "Do you know what it means to be a rebbe?" But Freddy didn't respond. So the Rebbe answered.

"The Baal Shem Tov was the first rebbe. He would not go to sleep at night as long as he had anything of value left in his house. Whatever he had, he gave away to those who needed it."

"That's what it means to be a rebbe," concluded the Rebbe. "Whatever you have, you have for others."

GLOSSARY

Adam. Man.

Adamah. Earth.

Adar. Twelfth month in the Jewish calendar; the month in which Purim is celebrated.

Admor. Acronym for "*adoneinu moreinu verabeinu*"—"Our master, teacher and rebbe"; generally used as a reference to the rebbes of Chasidic sects.

Ahavat Yisrael (Ahavas Yisroel). Love for a fellow Jew; as enjoined by the biblical precept "Love your fellow like yourself" (Leviticus 19:18).

Alef. First letter of the Hebrew alphabet, with a numerical value of one.

Alter Rebbe. (lit. "Old Rebbe") Rabbi Schne'ur Zalman of Liadi, 1745–1812, founder and first Rebbe of the Chabad branch of Chasidism.

Aluf. Master.

Am Yisrael chai. The Jewish nation lives on.

Amal. Toil.

Amalek. Legendary foe of the Jewish people; the first nation to attack the Jewish people after the Exodus from Egypt.

Amoraim. (lit. "those who tell over"); Post-Mishnaic authorities cited in the Talmud.

Ani vahu. He and I.

Av. The fifth month of the Jewish year, corresponding to July-August; the month in which both Temples were destroyed; also called Menachem Av.

Avodah beko'ach atsmo. Working with one's own strength.

B'chirah. Choice; free choice.

B'rachah. (a) Ritual blessing recited before eating, the performance of certain *mitzvot*, and at certain other occasions; (b) a blessing shared with another for good health, etc.

B'siyata d'shmaya. With the help of God.

Ba'al Shem Tov. (lit. "Master of the Good Name"); Rabbi Yisrael ben Eliezer (1698–1760), founder of Chasidism.

Ba'al teshuvah. (lit. "master of return"); a person who returns to God in repentance.

Bachur (pl. bachurim). (lit. "young man"); often used in reference to a yeshivah student.

Batel. Self-nullified in the presence of God.

Beit cholim. (lit. "house of the sick"); hospital.

Beit refuah. House of healing.

Beit. The second letter of the Hebrew alphabet, with a numerical value of two.

Beth hamidrash. Study hall.

Beth Hamikdosh (Beit Hamikdash). The Holy Temple in Jerusalem.

Binah. (lit. "comprehension"); the second of the ten *sefirot*; the second stage of the intellectual process of Chabad that develops abstract conceptions, giving it breadth and depth.

Bitachon. Trust in God.

Chabadnik. (colloq.) adherent of Chabad.

Chacham. Sage.

Chanukah. Eight-day festival beginning on 25 Kislev, celebrating the Maccabees' recapture of the second Temple from the Syrian Greeks, and its rededication, marked by the kindling of the menorah.

Chassid, Hasid (pl. chassidim). (lit. "pious"); (a) One who goes beyond the letter of the law; (b) a member of a Chasidic community.

Chassidut. Chasidic philosophy.

Chayei Sarah. (lit. "life of Sarah"); the fifth Torah portion in the book of Genesis.

Cheder. (lit. "room"); Jewish school for young children.

Chesed. (lit. "kindness"); fourth of the ten *sefirot*; the divine attribute associated with the dispersion of Godly light and energy to lower levels of existence.

Chillul shabboth. Transgression of the laws of Shabbat.

Chochmah. (lit. "wisdom"); in Kabbalistic-Chasidic terminology, refers to the first of the ten sefirot, and the first of the intellectual powers of the soul.

Chol. A supernatural bird mentioned in Job 29:18, often identified with the Greek phoenix.

Chumash. The Pentateuch.

Da'at. (lit. "knowledge"); the third of the ten *sefirot*; the third stage of the intellectual process, which guides emotion.

Di Yiddishe Heim. (Yiddish: lit. "The Jewish Home"); a magazine published by Nshei U'bnos Chabad, half in English and half in Yiddish.

Dikdukei Mitzvoth. Details of the *mitzvot*.

Dirah betachtonim. (lit. "a dwelling in the lowly realms"); the concept that God desired to create a reality that obscures His truth, in order that it be transformed into an environment that is hospitable to, subservient to, and expressive of His essence.

Dos pintele yid. (Yiddish) The spark of Jewishness.

Dvar (pl. dvarim). Thing; word.

Edameh. I will liken.

Epikores (pl. epikorsim). A heretic.

Eretz Heifetz. A land of delight; a land of treasure (Malachi 3:12).

Eretz Yisroel/Yisrael. The Land of Israel.

Essen est zich, shlofen shloft zich, ober davenin davent zich nisht. (Yiddish) Eating takes care of itself, sleeping takes care of itself, but prayer doesn't take care of itself.

Farblonged. (Yiddish) Lost.

Farbrengen (pl. farbrengens), farbrengung. (Yiddish) A gathering of Chasidim characterized by singing and inspiring talk.

Gadol. Great.

Galut (Galuth). Exile.

Gei shlofen, yingele. (Yiddish) Go to sleep, little boy.

Geulah (Geulo). Redemption.

Gibborim. Strong ones.

Gimel. The third letter of the Hebrew alphabet, pronounced as a hard "g," with a numerical value of three.

Golah. Exile.

Halacha. Jewish law.

Hashgocho. Divine providence.

Hatzlocho. Success.

Ha'yah tehei shnat arenu nifla'ot. It shall be a year in which I will reveal wonders to them.

Ha'yah tehei shnat nisim. It shall be a year of miracles.

Hefech ha-chayyim. Opposite of life.

Hefech ha-kedushah. Opposite of holiness.

Hefech ha-seichel. Opposite of wisdom.

Hefech ha-tov. Opposite of good.

Histalkus. Passing of a righteous individual.

Hitbatlut. Self-nullification in the presence of something much greater.

Inyanah shel Torat Hachassidut. An essay published the Rebbe explaining the essence of *Chasidut*.

Ish klali. An individual who is concerned with communal affairs.

Ish perati. An individual who is concerned with personal affairs.

Kabbalah. (lit. "received tradition"); the body of Jewish mystical teachings.

Kabbalist. An expert in the Kabbalah.

Kedushah. Holiness.

Kera. Split.

Kinus Hashluchot. Annual conference of the Rebbe's female emissaries.

Klal. The general populace.

Kollel. Advanced Torah study program, usually for married people.

Lashon hara. Derogatory speech about another person.

Le'chaim (l'chaim, lechayim). (lit. "To life!"); a toast or blessing, often exchanged over wine or other drink.

Leben. (Yiddish) Life.

Letaken olam bemalchut shadai. To rectify the world with the kingship of God.

Lulav. Palm branch used during the festival of Sukot as one of the four species.

Maariv. The evening prayer service.

Maggid. Teacher or preacher; when capitalized, often refers specifically to Rabbi Dovber of Mezeritch.

Mailin bakodesh, v'ein moreidin. We ascend in holiness; we do not descend.

Malchut. Royalty; the last of the ten *sefirot*.

Mamash. Literally.

Mashal. Analogy.

Mashiach. Messiah.

Megilah. (lit. "scroll"); usually a reference to the biblical book of Esther, which is read on Purim and chronicles the story of the holiday.

Mekarev. Bring close.

Menorah. (a) A branched candelabrum lit during the eight-day holiday of Chanukah; (b) the branched candelabrum that was present in the Tabernacle and Holy Temple.

Mesirat nefesh (mesiras nefesh). (lit. "giving of the soul"); self-sacrifice.

Metzuyanei yisrael. The exceptional ones of Israel.

Mezuzah (pl. mezuzot). A parchment scroll affixed to the doorposts of a Jewish home or business, containing biblical passages.

Midrash. (a) The classical collection of the sages' homiletic teachings on the Torah; (b) any one such teaching.

Misnaged (pl. misnagdim). Opponent of Chasidism.

Moshiach (Mashiach). (lit. "the anointed one"); the Messiah.

Moshiach Tzidkeinu. Our righteous Messiah.

Mosif veholech. Ever-increasing.

Motza'ei Shabbat. Saturday night, after the conclusion of Shabbat.

Mussar. (a) Jewish works dealing with personal conduct and character; (b) harsh and critical speech.

N'shei Chabad. Lubavitch Women's Organization

Naaseh. We will do.

Nechei yisrael. The disabled ones of Israel.

Negev. The south [of Israel].

Nes. Miracle.

Neshamah. Soul.

Nesi'ey Yisrael. Leaders of Israel.

Netzutzot kedusha. Sparks of holiness.

Niggun (pl. niggunim). Chassidic melody, often wordless.

Nisan. The Hebrew month in which Passover falls.

Nukvah. Feminine.

Nu. A Yiddish interjection with multiple meanings, including, "okay," and "so what?"

Nun (pl. nuns). The fourteenth letter of the Hebrew alphabet, pronounced "n," with a numerical value of 50.

Parashat Noach. The second Torah portion in the book of Genesis.

Parashat Vayikra. The first Torah portion in the book of Leviticus.

Payos (peyoth). Sidelocks.

Pikuach nefashot. Preservation of life.

Pnimiyut. The internal.

Purim. (lit. "lots"); the holiday that commemorates the Jews' salvation from Haman's plot to annihilate them, as related in the biblical book of Esther.

Ra'atan. A contagious disease with extremely repugnant symptoms, discussed in the Talmud.

Rasha. A wicked individual; anyone attached to sin.

Rebbeim. Plural of rebbe.

Ribono shel olam. Master of the world.

Rosh B'nei Yisrael. Head of the Jewish people. The first letters of these words spells, in Hebrew, Rebbe.

Rosh Chodesh. One or two semi-festive days marking the beginning of the Jewish month.

Rosh Hashanah. The Jewish new-year holiday.

Rov (rav). Rabbi; halachic authority; spiritual mentor.

S'iz gut tzu zein a Yid. (Yiddish) It's good to be a Jew.

S'iz shver tzu zein a Yid. (Yiddish) It's hard to be a Jew.

Sanhedrin. The rabbinical courts of ancient Israel, the most supreme of which was composed of 71 sages.

Seder (pl. sedarim). (lit. "order"); the order of service observed on the first two nights of Passover.

Sefirah (pl. sefirot). Divine attributes, or emanations, which are the source of the corresponding faculties of the human soul.

Shabbat Hagadol. (lit. "the great Shabbat"); the Shabbat preceding Passover.

Shalom Aleichem. (lit. "peace upon you"); a common greeting.

Shechinah. The manifestation of the divine presence; God's feminine manifestation.

Shelita. An acronym for the Hebrew words meaning, "May he live a long and good life."

Sheva mitzvoth b'nai Noach. The seven Noahide laws.

Shitah. A system of logic or belief.

Shiva. (lit. "seven"); the seven-day mourning period following the burial of a deceased next of kin.

Shliach/ Shaliach/ Sholiach, (pl. shluchim/ shelichim). (lit. "emissaries"); commonly denoting emissaries of the Lubavitcher Rebbe.

Shlichut. Mission.

Shluchah. Feminine form of "shliach."

Shofar. Ram's horn sounded during the month of Elul, on Rosh Hashanah, and at the close of Yom Kippur.

Sholom U'Brocho. Peace and blessings.

Sichah (pl. sichot). (lit. "a talk"); a Torah discourse delivered by the Rebbe.

Siddur. (lit. "ordered"); Jewish prayer book.

Sidra. The weekly Torah portion.

Simcha shel mitzvah. The joy of a mitzvah.

Sivan. Hebrew month corresponding to May-June in which the festival of Shavu'ot is celebrated.

Smicha. Rabbinic ordination.

Sukkah. A hut or booth roofed with vegetation in which the festival of Sukot is observed.

Sur mera. Turning away from evil.

T'mimut. Earnestness; simplicity; wholeness.

Talmid chochom. Torah scholar.

Tammuz. Hebrew month corresponding to June-July.

Tefillin. Small black leather cubes containing parchment scrolls inscribed with biblical passages, wrapped on the arm and head of adult Jewish men during weekday morning prayers.

Teshuvah (teshuvo). (lit. "return"); repentance; returning to one's essence.

Tikkun olam. Rectification of the world.

Tisha be'Av. (lit. "ninth of Av"); day of fasting and mourning commemorating the destruction of the first and the second Temples.

Torat Chayim. A living Torah.

Torat Emet. A Torah of truth.

Tracht gut un vet zein gut. Think good and it will be good.

Tsadik (tzaddik). A righteous person. In Chabad literature, those who have defeated their animalistic impulses and are filled entirely with love and reverence for God.

Tzadik yichyeh. A righteous person will live.

Tzarikh lihiot gam na'arah. There also must be a girl.

Tzdodim lekan u'lekan. There are considerations for pro and con.

Tzedakah (tsedakah). (lit. "righteousness"); charity.

Tzemach Tzedek. Rabbi Menachem Mendel of Lubavitch, third leader of Chabad (1789–1866).

Tzitzit. Four-cornered garment adorned with fringes.

Tzivos Hashem. (lit. "The army of God"); a Jewish children's club established by the Rebbe.

U'lemata me-assarah tefachim, b'karov mamash. Here in this realm, immediately.

Unetaneh Tokef. Part of the Rosh Hashana and Yom Kippur liturgy, describing the importance of the day.

V'Nishma. And we will understand (hear).

Ve'anvehu. And I will exalt him.

Vikuach. Debate.

Yarmulke. (Yiddish) Skullcap. The head covering worn by Jewish men.

Yechayeh. Will enliven.

Yehidut (yechidus). Private audience with the Rebbe.

Yeshiva (pl. yeshivas). Academies of Torah learning.

Yesod. (lit. "foundation"); the sixth of the ten *sefirot*.

Yetzer Hora. Evil inclination.

Yiddishkeit. (Yiddish) Judaism.

Zahal. The Israel Defense Force.

Zechus. Merit.

Zechuso yagen aleinu. (lit. "may his merit shield us"); term used in reference to a departed righteous person.

Zog. (Yiddish) Say.

Zohar (Zoharic). The classic text of the Kabbalah.

ACKNOWLEDGEMENTS

> The Zohar states that when a *tsadik* passes on, he is present in all the worlds more so than during his lifetime. This means that he is more present even in this world, the world of physical deed, because the *tsadik's* deeds and their effects continue growing and expanding.
>
> —Rabbi Shne'ur Zalman of Liadi, *Tanya*

Over the past fifteen years, the Rohr Jewish Learning Institute (JLI) has become the premier provider of adult Jewish education, offering courses on a wide range of topics at 960 chapters worldwide, with locations spanning six continents. The success and continued growth of JLI is attributed, in large measure, to the hundreds of devoted instructors who operate JLI chapters. The tireless devotion of these extraordinary men and women knows no bounds; they spare no effort in their endeavor to reach out with love and warmth to each and every Jew in an effort to teach Torah and nurture Jewish identity and observance. These JLI instructors are inspired by the call of the **Lubavitcher Rebbe**, of righteous memory.

This course, *Paradigm Shift: Transformational Life Teachings of the Lubavitcher Rebbe*, is being released in conjunction with the 20th anniversary of the Rebbe's passing (3 Tamuz 5774 - July 1, 2014). This course attempts to present the Rebbe's philosophy and worldview, and showcases the Rebbe's insights into life and his profound and resonant messages for humankind. This course also provides participants with a glimpse into the hearts and minds of their instructors, allowing participants to understand what motivates them to selflessly dedicate their lives to helping their fellows, spiritually, emotionally, and materially.

Considering the magnitude of distilling and applying the Rebbe's intellectual and spiritual legacy, contained in hundreds of volumes of his published works, the JLI editorial team set out to listen to and learn from tens of scholars and teachers who have studied the Rebbe's life, philosophy, and unique leadership style. The team spent much time interviewing the individuals charged with transcribing and disseminating the Rebbe's talks and discourses (*chozrim*), the Rebbe's personal aides and secretaries, as well as individuals who hold key positions in the Chabad leadership. These gripping and thought-provoking interviews, conducted over a period of twelve months, provided JLI with an enormous amount of material that was then distilled into the six lessons of this course. We are extremely grateful to all these individuals—a list of whom follows these acknowledgments—who graciously shared of their time and wisdom to help shape this course.

We extend our appreciation to **Rabbis Mordechai Dinerman** and **Naftali Silberberg,** who capably direct the JLI Curriculum Department and the Flagship editorial team, and to **Rabbis Eli Raksin** and **Yanky Raskin** for their extensive and meticulous research and editorial suggestions. Rabbi Raskin also coordinated and conducted many of the interviews for the course. Special thanks to **Rabbi Shmuel Klatzkin** for his help with translations, and to **Mrs. Rochel Holzkenner** for her pedagogic suggestions.

We acknowledge **Nechama (Fridman) Ioffe** and **Zeldy Nemanov** for their assistance in managing the various components of the course production. We extend a warm mazal tov to Nechama Ioffe on her recent marriage; in the merit of her important work, may she and her husband be showered with much blessing and happiness.

The JLI editorial board provided many useful suggestions to enhance the course and ensure its suitability for a wide range of students. Many thanks to Rabbis **Chaim Block**, **Yossi Groner**, **Mendy Herson**, **Yehuda Shemtov**, **Avrohom Sternberg**, and **Mrs. Rivkah Slonim**. We are also indebted to **Rabbi Dovid Olidort** for his editorial suggestions and his overall assistance with this course.

Many of the videos for this course have been supplied by Jewish Educational Media (JEM). Special thanks to **Rabbi Elkanah Shmotkin**, executive director of JEM, and to **Rabbi Mendel Gourarie** for their help in facilitating this partnership and for working closely with JLI's multimedia team, which is ably headed by **Rivkah Dubov**. We also thank Rabbi Shmotkin for his review of the lessons and his insightful comments.

Our devoted copyediting team, **Naomi Saul, Esther Tauber,** and **Rachel Witty,** enhanced the quality and professionalism of the course. **Mendel Schtroks** designed the textbooks with taste and eloquence.

We acknowledge the hard work and efforts of JLI's support staff and administration, whose contributions to this course were critical, but whose names are too many to enumerate.

We are immensely grateful for the encouragement of JLI's visionary chairman and vice-chairman of Merkos L'inyonei Chinuch—Lubavitch World Headquarters, **Rabbi Moshe Kotlarsky**. We are blessed to have the unwavering support of JLI's principal benefactor, **Mr. George Rohr,** who is fully invested in our work and has been and continues to be instrumental in achieving the monumental expansion of the organization.

JLI's dedicated executive board—**Rabbis Chaim Block, Hesh Epstein, Ronnie Fine, Yosef Gansburg, Shmuel Kaplan, Yisrael Rice,** and **Avrohom Sternberg**—devote countless hours to the development of JLI. Their commitment and sage direction help JLI continue to grow and flourish.

Finally, as mentioned, JLI represents an incredible partnership of more than 350 *shluchim,* who give of their time and talent to further Jewish adult education, who have devoted their days and years to sharing with their communities the beauty of their Jewish heritage and "the transformational life teachings of the Lubavitcher Rebbe." We thank them for generously sharing their feedback, offering advice, and making suggestions that steer JLI's development and growth. They are our most valuable critics and our most cherished contributors.

Inspired by the call of the Rebbe, it is the mandate of the Rohr JLI to encourage all Jews throughout the world to experience and take part in the Torah learning that is their heritage. May this course succeed in fulfilling this sacred charge.

On behalf of the Rohr Jewish Learning Institute,

Rabbi Efraim Mintz, Executive Director
Rabbi Yisrael Rice, Chairman, Editorial Board

11 Nissan, 5774

SPECIAL THANKS

The following individuals graciously agreed to be interviewed by the editorial team of the Rohr Jewish Learning Institute. These interviews assisted us tremendously in developing the ideas and insights of this course, and we thank them warmly for sharing their wisdom. Of course, any inadequacies of this course or errors that might be found within its materials are the responsibility of JLI alone.

Rabbi Yehudah Leib Altein
Director, Heichal Menachem
Transcriber of the Rebbe's talks
Brooklyn, NY

Rabbi Chaim Shaul Brook
Director, Va'ad Hanachos Lahak
(a publishing arm of the Rebbe's teachings)
Brooklyn, NY

Rabbi Sholom Charitonow
Mashpia, Oholei Torah Talmudic Seminary
Editorial team, *Sefer Ha'erchim Chabad* (Chabad Encyclopedia)
Brooklyn, NY

Rabbi Shlomo Cunin
Regional director, Chabad-Lubavitch of California
Member, Agudas Chassidei Chabad - Lubavitch World Headquarters
Los Angeles, CA

Rabbi Yisrael Deren
Regional director, Chabad of Western and Southern New England
Member of the board, Merkos L'inyonei Chinuch - Lubavitch World Headquarters
Stamford, CT

Rabbi Adin Even-Yisrael Steinsaltz
Founder of Shefa and the Israel Institute for Talmudic Publications
Author, *My Rebbe*
Jerusalem, Israel

Rabbi Dovid Feldman
Editor in chief, Va'ad Hanachos Lahak,
(a publishing arm of the Rebbe's teachings)
Brooklyn, NY

Rabbi Moshe Feller
Regional director, Chabad-Lubavitch of the Upper Midwest
Member of the board, Merkos L'inyonei Chinuch - Lubavitch World Headquarters
S. Paul, MN

Rabbi Tzvi Freeman
Senior editor, Chabad.org
Toronto, Canada

Rabbi Manis Friedman
Founder, Bais Chana Institute of Jewish Studies
Translator of the Rebbe's telecasts into English
S. Paul, MN

Rabbi Yehudah Leib Groner
Secretariat of the Rebbe
Brooklyn, NY

Rabbi Tzvi Grunblatt
Regional director, Chabad-Lubavitch of Argentina
Buenos Aires, Argentina

Rabbi Simon Jacobson
Transcriber of the Rebbe's talks
Director, Meaningful Life Center
Brooklyn, NY

Rabbi Yosef Yitzchak Jacobson
Rosh yeshivah, theyeshiva.net
Brooklyn, NY

Rabbi Yoel Kahn
Chief transcriber of the Rebbe's talks
Senior mashpia, Central Lubavitch Yeshivah
Editor in chief, *Sefer Ha'erchim Chabad* (Chabad Encyclopedia)
Brooklyn, NY

Rabbi Shmuel Kaplan
Regional director, Chabad-Lubavitch of Maryland
Member of the board and executive committee,
Merkos L'inyonei Chinuch - Lubavitch World Headquarters
Baltimore, MD

Rabbi Binyomin Klein
Secretariat of the Rebbe
Brooklyn, NY

Rabbi Moshe Kotlarsky
Vice-chairman, Merkos L'inyonei Chinuch - Lubavitch World Headquarters
Chairman, International Conference of Shluchim
Brooklyn, NY

Rabbi Chaim Yehudah Krinsky
Chairman, Merkos L'inyonei Chinuch - Lubavitch World Headquarters
Secretariat of the Rebbe
Brooklyn, NY

Rabbi Shmuel Lew
Director, Lubavitch Senior Girls School
London, England

Rabbi Sholom Dovber Lipskar
Founder and spiritual leader, "The Shul"
Founder, Aleph Institute
Bal Harbor, FL

Mrs. Sara Lieberman
Teacher, Beth Rivkah Division of Higher Learning
Brooklyn, NY

Dr. Naftali Loewenthal
Lecturer, University College London
London, England

Mrs. Baila Olidort
Editor in chief, Lubavitch.com
Brooklyn, NY

Rabbi Dovid Olidort
Editor in chief, Kehot Publication Society
Transcriber of the Rebbe's discourses
Brooklyn, NY

Rabbi Abba Paltiel
Mashpia
Brookyn, NY

Rabbi Yosef Yitzchak Paltiel
Mashpia, Central Lubavitch Yeshiva
Founder, InsideChassidus.org
Brooklyn, NY

Rabbi Ezra Binyomin Schochet
Dean, Yeshivas Ohr Elchonon Chabad
Member, Central Committee of Chabad Lubavitch Rabbis
Los Angeles, CA

Dr. Don Seeman
Associate professor, Tam Institute for Jewish Studies
Emory University
Atlanta, GA

Rabbi Avraham Shemtov
Chairman, executive committee,
Agudas Chassidei Chabad - Lubavitch World Headquarters
Regional director, Lubavitch of Pennsylvania
Chairman, American Friends of Lubavitch, Washington DC
Philadelphia, PA

Rabbi Yisroel Shmotkin
Regional director, Lubavitch of Wisconsin
Member of the board and executive committee,
Agudas Chassidei Chabad - Lubavitch World Headquarters
Milwaukee, WI

Mrs. Rivka Slonim
Education director, Chabad Center for Jewish Student Life at Binghamton University
Binghamton, NY

Rabbi Avrohom Sternberg
Director, Chabad of Eastern Connecticut
Rabbi, Congregation Ahavath Chesed
New London, CT

Rabbi Shlomo Sternberg
Mashpia, Oholei Torah Talmudic Seminary
Brooklyn, NY

Rabbi Shais Taub
Author, *God of Our Understanding* and JLI's *Soul Maps*
Pittsburgh, PA

Rabbi Yanki Tauber
Editor in chief, Chabad.org
Woodmere, NY

Rabbi Joseph Telushkin
Author, *Rebbe: The Life and Teachings of Menachem M. Schneerson, the Most Influential Rabbi in Modern History*
New York, NY

Mrs. Shimona Tzukernik
Founder and director, Omek
Brooklyn, NY

Rabbi Avraham Menachem Mendel Vechter
Head of Kollel
Nachalat Har Chabad, Israel

The **Rohr Jewish Learning Institute**

An affiliate of
Merkos L'Inyonei Chinuch
The Educational Arm of
The Chabad Lubavitch Movement
822 Eastern Parkway, Brooklyn, NY 11213

Rabbi Yossi Nemes
Metairie, LA

Rabbi Reuven New
Boca Raton, FL

Rabbi Dr. Shlomo Pereira
Richmond, VA

Rabbi Shalom Raichik
Gaithersburg, MD

Rabbi Nochum Schapiro
Sydney, AU

Rabbi Shraga Sherman
Merion Station, PA

Rabbi Avraham Steinmetz
S. Paulo, BR

Rabbi Avrohom Sternberg
New London, CT

Rabbi Aryeh Weinstein
Newtown, PA

Rabbi Motti Wilhelm
Portland, OR

Multimedia Development

Rivkah Dubov
Director

Mrs. Neria Ben Avi
Mrs. Mushka Lisker
Mrs. Rivkah Rapoport
Mrs. Chava Shapiro
Rabbi Chesky Edelman
Getzy Raskin
Moshe Raskin
Rabbi Yisroel Silman

Administration

Mrs. Chana Dechter

Affiliate Support

Rabbi Mendel Sirota
Mrs. Fraydee Kessler
Mrs. Mindy Wallach

Online Division

Dovid Ciment
Rabbi Mendy Elishevitz
Zalman Margolin

Marketing and Branding

Rabbi Zalman Abraham
Director

Shevi Rosenberg
Graphic Design

Rabbi Yossi Klein
Marketing for Results

Rabbi Shmuel Loebenstein
Writer

Marketing Committee

Rabbi Simcha Backman
Glendale, CA

Rabbi Ronnie Fine
Montreal, QC

Rabbi Ovadia Goldman
Oklahoma City, OK

Rabbi Mendy Halberstam
Miami Beach, FL

Rabbi Reuven New
Boca Raton, FL

Rabbi Yehuda Shemtov
Yardley, PA

Marketing Consultants

JJ Gross
New York, NY

Warren Modlin
MednetPro, Inc.
Alpharetta, GA

Alan Rosenspan
Alan Rosenspan & Associates
Sharon, MA

Gary Wexler
Passion Marketing
Los Angeles, CA

Publication Design

Rabbi Zalman Abraham
Mendel Schtroks

Printing

Shimon Leib Jacobs
Point One Communications
Montreal, QC

Shipping

Mary Stevens
Nixa, MO

Accounting

Musie Karp
Mrs. Shaina B. Mintz
Mrs. Shulamis Nadler

JLI Departments

Rabbi Levi Kaplan
Director of Operations

Rabbi Dubi Rabinowitz
Administrator

JLI Flagship

Rabbi Yisrael Rice
Chairman
S. Rafael, CA

Rabbi Mordechai Dinerman
Rabbi Naftali Silberberg
Editors-in-Chief

Rabbi Dr. Shmuel Klatzkin
Senior Editor
Dayton, OH

Rabbi Eli Raksin
Rabbi Yanky Raskin
Associate Editors

Zeldy Nemanow
Administrative Assistant

Rabbi Mendel Sirota
Production Manager

Mrs. Miriam Levy-Haim
Copy Editor

Mrs. Naomi Saul
Mrs. Rachel Witty
Proofreaders

Department of Continuing Education

Mrs. Mindy Wallach
Director

Musie Karp
Registrar

Mrs. Shulamis Nadler
Service and Support

Dr. Michael Akerman, MD
Consultant
Continuing Medical Education
Associate Professor of Medicine,
SUNY–Downstate Medical Center

JLI International Desk

Rabbi Avrohom Sternberg
Chairman
New London, CT

Rabbi Dubi Rabinowitz
Director
Brooklyn, NY

Mendel Schtroks
Content Manager

Rabbi Yossi Baitsh
Administrator, JLI Israel
In Partnership with
Tzeirei Agudat Chabad

Rabbi Eli Wolf
Administrator, JLI in the CIS
In Partnership with the Federation of Jewish
Communities of the CIS

Rabbi Avraham Golovacheov
Regional Respresentative
German Division

Rabbi Nochum Schapiro
Regional Respresentative
Australia

Rabbi Hirshel Hendel
Regional Representative
Spanish Division

Beis Medrosh L'Shluchim

in partnership with
Shluchim Exchange

Rabbi Mendy Yusewitz
Director

Rabbi Mendel Margolin
Producer

Steering Committee

Rabbi Simcha Backman
Rabbi Mendy Kotlarsky
Rabbi Efraim Mintz

JLI Academy

Rabbi Hesh Epstein
Chairman

Rabbi Yossi Klein
Director

Steering Committee

Rabbi Yoel Caroline
Rabbi Mordechai Grossbaum
Rabbi Levi Mendelow

JLI Teens

in partnership with
CTeeN: Chabad Teen Network

Rabbi Chaim Block
Chairman
San Antonio, TX

Rabbi Michoel Shapiro
Director

Mrs. Nechi Gudelsky
Raizel Schapiro
Program Administrators

Advisory Board

Rabbi Mendy Cohen
Merion Station, PA

Rabbi Yitzi Hein
Pittsford, NY

Rabbi Zalman Marcus
Mission Viejo, CA

Machon Shmuel

The Sami Rohr Research Institute

Rabbi Avrohom Bergstein
Dean

Rabbi Chaim Rapoport
Rabbi Levi Yitzchak Raskin
Rabbi Mordechai Farkash
Rabbi Moshe Miller
Rabbi Yossi Yaffe
Senior Contributing Scholars

Rabbi Yehudah Altein
Rabbi Binyomin Bitton
Rabbi Yaakov Gershon
Rabbi Moshe Gourarie
Rabbi Elchonon Kazen
Rabbi Zalman Korf
Rabbi Levi New
Rabbi Mendel Zirkind
Rabbi Eliezer Raksin
Rabbi Nesanel Loeb
Rabbi Shraga Homnick
Research Fellows

Mishnah Project

Rabbi Elya Silfen
Director

myShiur:

Advanced Learning Initiative

Rabbi Shmuel Kaplan
Chairman
Potomac, MD

Rabbi Levi Kaplan
Director

National Jewish Retreat

Rabbi Hesh Epstein
Chairman
Columbia, SC

Bruce Backman
Coordinator

Mrs. Shaina B. Mintz
Administrator

Rabbi Mendy Weg
Founding Director

Rochelle Katzman
Program Coordinator

Rabbi Shmuel Karp
Shluchim Liaison

Liz Halpern
Development

Rosh Chodesh Society

Rabbi Shmuel Kaplan
Chairman
Potomac, MD

Mrs. Shaindy Jacobson
Director

Mrs. Chava Shapiro
Associate Director

Mrs. Fraydee Kessler
Administrator

Steering Committee

Mrs. Shula Bryski
Mrs. Rochel Holzkenner
Mrs. Devorah Kornfeld
Mrs. Chana Lipskar
Mrs. Ahuva New
Mrs. Binie Tenenbaum

Sinai Scholars Society

in partnership with Chabad on Campus

Rabbi Menachem Schmidt
Chairman
Philadelphia, PA

Rabbi Dubi Rabinowitz
Director

Devorah Balarsky
Administrator

Devorah Leah Notik
Coordinator

Executive Committee

Rabbi Moshe Chaim Dubrowski
Rabbi Yossy Gordon
Rabbi Efraim Mintz
Rabbi Menachem Schmidt
Rabbi Nechemia Vogel
Rabbi Eitan Webb
Rabbi Avi Weinstein
Dr. Chana Silberstein

Curriculum Committee

Rabbi Zalman Bluming
Rabbi Shlomie Chein
Rabbi Shlomo Rothstien

Steering Committee

Rabbi Shlomie Chein
Rabbi Moshe Laib Gray
Rabbi Dovid Gurevitch
Rabbi Mendel Matusof
Rabbi Yisroel Wilhelm

TorahCafe.com

Online Learning

Rabbi Levi Kaplan
Director

Rabbi Simcha Backman
Consultant

Rabbi Mendy Elishevitz
Rabbi Elchonon Korenblit
Website Development

Mrs. Esty Perman
Administrator

Rabbi Yisroel Silman
Director of Development

Rabbi Mendel Katzman
Marketing Director

Rabbi Elya Silfen
Director of Communications

Mendel Serebryanski
Content Manager

Avrohom Shimon Ezagui
Raphael Roston
Yossi Rubin
Filming Crew

Torah Studies

Rabbi Yosef Gansburg
Chairman
Toronto, ON

Rabbi Meir Hecht
Founding Director

Rabbi Moshe Teldon
Administrator

Rabbi Ahrele Loschak
Managing Editor

Steering Committee

Rabbi Levi Fogelman
Rabbi Yaacov Halperin
Rabbi Nechemia Schusterman
Rabbi Ari Sollish

JLI Central

Founding Department Heads

Rabbi Mendel Bell
Brooklyn, NY

Rabbi Zalman Charytan
Acworth, GA

Rabbi Mendel Druk
Cancun, Mexico

Rabbi Menachem Gansburg
Toronto, ON

Rabbi Yoni Katz
Brooklyn, NY

Rabbi Chaim Zalman Levy
New Rochelle, NY

Rabbi Benny Rapoport
Clarks Summit, PA

Dr. Chana Silberstein
Ithaca, NY

Rabbi Elchonon Tenenbaum
Napa Valley, CA

Rohr JLI Affiliates

Share the **Rohr JLI** experience with friends and relatives worldwide

ALABAMA

BIRMINGHAM
Rabbi Yossi Friedman
205.970.0100

ARIZONA

CHANDLER
Rabbi Mendel Deitsch
480.855.4333

FLAGSTAFF
Rabbi Dovie Shapiro
928.255.5756

PHOENIX
Rabbi Zalman Levertov
Rabbi Yossi Friedman
602.944.2753

SCOTTSDALE
Rabbi Yossi Levertov
480.998.1410

ARKANSAS

LITTLE ROCK
Rabbi Pinchus Ciment
501.217.0053

CALIFORNIA

AGOURA HILLS
Rabbi Moshe Bryski
Rabbi Shlomo Bistritsky
818.991.0991

BAKERSFIELD
Rabbi Shmuli Schlanger
661.835.8381

BEL AIR
Rabbi Chaim Mentz
310.475.5311

BEVERLY HILLS
Rabbi Chaim I. Sperlin
310.734.9079

BRENTWOOD
Rabbi Boruch Hecht
Rabbi Mordechai Zaetz
310.826.4453

BURBANK
Rabbi Shmuly Kornfeld
818.954.0070

CARLSBAD
Rabbi Yeruchem Eilfort
Mrs. Nechama Eilfort
760.943.8891

CHATSWORTH
Rabbi Yossi Spritzer
818.718.0777

CONTRA COSTA
Rabbi Yaakov Kagan
Rabbi Dovber Berkowitz
925.937.4101

CORONADO
Rabbi Eli Fradkin
619.365.4728

ENCINO
Rabbi Joshua Gordon
Rabbi Aryeh Herzog
818-784-9986

FOLSOM
Rabbi Yossi Grossbaum
916.608.9811

GLENDALE
Rabbi Simcha Backman
818.240.2750

HUNTINGTON BEACH
Rabbi Aron Berkowitz
714.846.2285

IRVINE
Rabbi Alter Tenenbaum
Rabbi Elly Andrusier
949.786.5000

LA JOLLA
Rabbi Baruch Shalom Ezagui
858.455.5433

LAGUNA BEACH
Rabbi Elimelech Gurevitch
949.499.0770

LOMITA
Rabbi Eli Hecht
Rabbi Sholom Pinson
310.326.8234

LONG BEACH
Rabbi Abba Perelmuter
562.621.9828

LOS ANGELES
Rabbi Leibel Korf
323.660.5177

MARINA DEL REY
Rabbi Danny Yiftach-Hashem
Rabbi Mendy Avtzon
310.859.0770

MILL VALLEY
Rabbi Hillel Scop
415.336.3055

NEWPORT BEACH
Rabbi Reuven Mintz
949.721.9800

NORTH HOLLYWOOD
Rabbi Nachman Abend
818.989.9539

NORTHRIDGE
Rabbi Eli Rivkin
818.368.3937

PACIFIC PALISADES
Rabbi Zushe Cunin
310.454.7783

PALO ALTO
Rabbi Menachem Landa
CLASSES IN HEBREW
650.322.1708

PASADENA
Rabbi Chaim Hanoka
626.564.8820

RANCHO CUCAMONGA
Rabbi Sholom B. Harlig
909.949.4553

RANCHO PALOS VERDES
Rabbi Yitzchok Magalnic
310.544.5544

RANCHO S. FE
Rabbi Levi Raskin
858.756.7571

REDONDO BEACH
Rabbi Yossi Mintz
Rabbi Zalman Gordon
310.214.4999

SACRAMENTO
Rabbi Mendy Cohen
916.455.1400

S. BARBARA
Rabbi Yosef Loschak
805.683.1544

S. CLEMENTE
Rabbi Menachem M. Slavin
949.489.0723

S. DIEGO
Rabbi Motte Fradkin
858.547.0076

S. DIEGO-UNIVERSITY CITY
Rabbi Yudell Reiz
619.723.2439

S. FRANCISCO
Rabbi Shlomo Zarchi
415.752.2866

Rabbi Peretz Mochkin
415.571.8770

S. LUIS OBISPO
Rabbi Chaim Leib Hille
805.706.0256

S. MATEO
Rabbi Yossi Marcus
Rabbi Moishe Weinbaum
650.341.4510

S. MONICA
Rabbi Boruch Rabinowitz
310.394.5699

S. RAFAEL
Rabbi Yisrael Rice
415.492.1666

S. ROSA
Rabbi Mendel Wolvovsky
707.577.0277

SOUTH BAY
Rabbi Yosef Levin
Rabbi Ber Rosenblatt
650.424.9800

Stockton
Rabbi Avremel Brod
209.952.2081

Studio City
Rabbi Yossi Baitelman
818.508.6633

Temecula
Rabbi Yitzchok Hurwitz
951.303.9576

Thousand Oaks
Rabbi Chaim Bryski
805.493.7776

Tustin
Rabbi Yehoshua Eliezrie
714.508.2150

Ventura
Rabbi Yakov Latowicz
Mrs. Sarah Latowicz
805.658.7441

West Hills
Rabbi Avrahom Yitzchak Rabin
818.337.4544

Yorba Linda
Rabbi Dovid Eliezrie
714.693.0770

COLORADO

Aspen
Rabbi Mendel Mintz
970.544.3770

Denver
Rabbi Mendel Popack
720 515 4337

Rabbi Yossi Serebryanski
303.744.9699

Highlands Ranch
Rabbi Avraham Mintz
303.694.9119

Longmont
Rabbi Yakov Dovid Borenstein
303.678.7595

Vail
Rabbi Dovid Mintz
970.476.7887

Westminster
Rabbi Benjy Brackman
303.429.5177

CONNECTICUT

Guilford
Rabbi Yossi Yaffe
203.453.5580

Greenwich
Rabbi Yossi Deren
Rabbi Menachem Feldman
203.629.9059

New Haven
Rabbi Yosef Y. Hodakov
203.795.5261

New London
Rabbi Avrohom Sternberg
860.437.8000

Orange
Rabbi Sheya Hecht
203.795.5261

Stamford
Rabbi Yisrael Deren
Rabbi Levi Mendelow
203.3.CHABAD

West Hartford
Rabbi Yosef Gopin
Rabbi Shaya Gopin
860.659.2422

Westport
Rabbi Yehuda L. Kantor
Mrs. Dina Kantor
203.226.8584

DELAWARE

Wilmington
Rabbi Chuni Vogel
302.529.9900

FLORIDA

Aventura
Rabbi Laivi Forta
Rabbi Yakov Garfinkel
305.933.0770

Bal Harbour
Rabbi Dov Schochet
305.868.1411

Boca Raton
Rabbi Moishe Denberg
Rabbi Zalman Bukiet
561.417.7797

Boynton Beach
Rabbi Yosef Yitzchok Raichik
561.732.4633

Bradenton
Rabbi Menachem Bukiet
941.388.9656

Coconut creek
Rabbi Yossi Gansburg
954.427.7788

Coral Gables
Rabbi Avrohom Stolik
305.490.7572

Coral Springs
Rabbi Yankie Denburg
954.471.8646

Delray Beach
Rabbi Sholom Ber Korf
561.496.6228

East Boca Raton
Rabbi Ruvi New
561.417.7797

Fisher island
Rabbi Efraim Brody
347.325.1913

Fort Lauderdale
Rabbi Yitzchok Naparstek
954.568.1190

Fort Myers
Rabbi Yitzchok Minkowicz
Mrs. Nechama Minkowicz
239.433.7708

Hollywood
Rabbi Leizer Barash
954.965.9933

Kendall
Rabbi Yossi Harlig
305.234.5654

Key Biscayne
Rabbi Yoel Caroline
305.365.6744

Lake Mary
Rabbi Yanky Majesky
407.878.3011

Miami Beach
Rabbi Shragi Mann
786.264.1111

Miami–Midtown
Rabbi Shmuel Gopin
305.573.9995

Ocala
Rabbi Yossi Hecht
352.291.2218

Orlando
Rabbi Yosef Konikov
407.354.3660

Palm Beach Gardens
Rabbi Dovid Vigler
561.624.2223

Palmetto Bay
Rabbi Zalman Gansburg
786.282.0413

Parkland
Rabbi Mendy Gutnik
954.796.7330

Plantation
Rabbi Pinchas Taylor
954.644.9177

Ponte Vedra Beach
Rabbi Nochum Kurinsky
904.543.9301

Sarasota
Rabbi Chaim Shaul Steinmetz
941.925.0770

Satellite Beach
Rabbi Zvi Konikov
321.777.2770

South Palm Beach
Rabbi Leibel Stolik
561.889.3499

South Tampa
Rabbi Mendy Dubrowski
813.287.1795

Sunny Isles Beach
Rabbi Alexander Kaller
305.803.5315

Weston
Rabbi Yisroel Spalter
954.349.6565

West Palm Beach
Rabbi Yoel Gancz
561.659.7770

Venice
Rabbi Sholom Ber Schmerling
941.493.2770

GEORGIA

ALPHARETTA
Rabbi Hirshy Minkowicz
770.410.9000

ATLANTA
Rabbi Yossi New
Rabbi Isser New
404.843.2464

ATLANTA: INTOWN
Rabbi Eliyahu Schusterman
Rabbi Ari Sollish
404.898.0434

GWINNETT
Rabbi Yossi Lerman
678.595.0196

MARIETTA
Rabbi Ephraim Silverman
Rabbi Zalman Charytan
770.565.4412

IDAHO

BOISE
Rabbi Mendel Lifshitz
208.853.9200

ILLINOIS

CHAMPAIGN
Rabbi Dovid Tiechtel
217.355.8672

CHICAGO
Rabbi Meir Hecht
312.714.4655

CHICAGO-HYDE PARK
Rabbi Yossi Brackman
773.955.8672

GLENVIEW
Rabbi Yishaya Benjaminson
847.998.9896

HIGHLAND PARK
Mrs. Michla Schanowitz
847.266.0770

NAPERVILLE
Rabbi Mendy Goldstein
630.778.9770

NORTHBROOK
Rabbi Meir Moscowitz
847.564.8770

Rabbi Menachem Slavaticki
CLASSES IN HEBREW
847.350.9770

OAK PARK
Rabbi Yitzchok Bergstein
708.524.1530

PEORIA
Rabbi Eli Langsam
309.692.2250

ROCKFORD
Rabbi Yecheskel Rothman
815.596.0032

SKOKIE
Rabbi Yochanan Posner
847.677.1770

WILMETTE
Rabbi Dovid Flinkenstein
847.251.7707

INDIANA

INDIANAPOLIS
Rabbi Mendel Schusterman
317.251.5573

KANSAS

OVERLAND PARK
Rabbi Mendy Wineberg
913.649.4852

LOUISIANA

METAIRIE
Rabbi Yossi Nemes
504.454.2910

MARYLAND

BALTIMORE
Rabbi Elchonon Lisbon
410.358.4787

Rabbi Velvel Belinsky
CLASSES IN RUSSIAN
410.764.5000

BETHESDA
Rabbi Bentzion Geisinsky
Rabbi Sender Geisinsky
301.913.9777

COLUMBIA
Rabbi Hillel Baron
Rabbi Yosef Chaim Sufrin
410.740.2424

FREDERICK
Rabbi Boruch Labkowski
301.996.3659

GAITHERSBURG
Rabbi Sholom Raichik
301.926.3632

OWINGS MILLS
Rabbi Nochum H. Katsenelenbogen
410.356.5156

POTOMAC
Rabbi Mendel Bluming
301.983.4200

Rabbi Mendel Kaplan
301.983.1485

ROCKVILLE
Rabbi Moishe Kavka
301.836.1242

SILVER SPRING
Rabbi Berel Wolvovsky
301.593.1117

MASSACHUSETTS

ANDOVER
Rabbi Asher Bronstein
Rabbi Zalman Borenstein
978.470.2288

CAPE COD
Rabbi Yekusiel Alperowitz
508.775.2324

CHESTNUT HILL
Rabbi Mendy Uminer
617.738.9770

LONGMEADOW
Rabbi Yakov Wolff
413.567.8665

SUDBURY
Rabbi Yisroel Freeman
978.443.3691

SWAMPSCOTT
Mrs. Layah Lipsker
781.581.3833

MICHIGAN

ANN ARBOR
Rabbi Aharon Goldstein
734.995.3276

GRAND RAPIDS
Rabbi Mordechai Haller
616.957.0770

WEST BLOOMFIELD
Rabbi Kasriel Shemtov
248.788.4000

Rabbi Elimelech Silberberg
248.855 .6170

MINNESOTA

MINNETONKA
Rabbi Mordechai Grossbaum
952.929.9922

ROCHESTER
Rabbi Dovid Greene
507.288.7500

S. PAUL
Rabbi Shneur Zalman Bendet
651.278.8401

MISSOURI

S. LOUIS
Rabbi Yosef Landa
314.725.0400

MONTANA

BOZEMAN
Rabbi Chaim Shaul Bruk
406.585.8770

NEVADA

HENDERSON
Rabbi Mendy Harlig
Rabbi Tzvi Bronchtain
702.617.0770

SUMMERLIN
Rabbi Yisroel Schanowitz
Rabbi Tzvi Bronchtain
702.855.0770

NEW JERSEY

BASKING RIDGE
Rabbi Mendy Herson
908.604.8844

Cherry Hill
Rabbi Mendy Mangel
856.874.1500

Clinton
Rabbi Eli Kornfeld
908.623.7000

Fair Lawn
Rabbi Avrohom Bergstein
718.839.5296

Fanwood
Rabbi Avrohom Blesofsky
908.790.0008

Fort Lee
Rabbi Meir Konikov
201.886.1238

Franklin Lakes
Rabbi Chanoch Kaplan
201.848.0449

Haskell
Rabbi Mendy Gurkov
201.696.7609

Hillsborough
Rabbi Shmaya Krinsky
908.874.0444

Holmdel
Rabbi Shmaya Galperin
732.772.1998

Madison
Rabbi Shalom Lubin
973.377.0707

Manalapan
Rabbi Boruch Chazanow
Rabbi Levi Wolosow
732.972.3687

Medford
Rabbi Yitzchok Kahan
609.953.3150

Mountain Lakes
Rabbi Levi Dubinsky
973.551.1898

North Brunswick
Rabbi Levi Azimov
732.398.9492

Old Tappan
Rabbi Mendy Lewis
201.767.4008

Rockaway
Rabbi Asher Herson
Rabbi Mordechai Baumgarten
973.625.1525

Teaneck
Rabbi Ephraim Simon
201.907.0686

Tenafly
Rabbi Mordechai Shain
Rabbi Yitzchak Gershovitz
201.871.1152

Toms River
Rabbi Moshe Gourarie
732.349.4199

West Orange
Rabbi Mendy Kasowitz
973.486.2362

Woodcliff Lake
Rabbi Dov Drizin
201.476.0157

NEW MEXICO

S. Fe
Rabbi Berel Levertov
505.983.2000

NEW YORK

Bedford
Rabbi Arik Wolf
914.666.6065

Binghamton
Mrs. Rivkah Slonim
607.797.0015

Brighton Beach
Rabbi Zushe Winner
Rabbi Moshe Winner
718.946.9833

Bronxville
Rabbi Sruli Deitsch
917.755.0078

Brooklyn
Rabbi Moishe Dovid Winner
718.946.9833

Brooklyn Heights
Rabbi Mendy Hecht
Rabbi Ari Raskin
347.378.2641

Cedarhurst
Rabbi Zalman Wolowik
516.295.2478

Chestnut Ridge
Rabbi Chaim Tzvi Ehrenreich
845.356.6686

Dix Hills
Rabbi Yaakov Saacks
Rabbi Avraham Lehr
631.351.8672

Dobbs Ferry
Rabbi Benjy Silverman
914.693.6100

East Hampton
Rabbi Leibel Baumgarten
Rabbi Mendy Goldberg
631.329.5800

Great Neck
Rabbi Yoseph Geisinsky
516.487.4554

Ithaca
Rabbi Eli Silberstein
607.257.7379

Kingston
Rabbi Yitzchok Hecht
845.334.9044

Larchmont
Rabbi Mendel Silberstein
914.834.4321

Long Beach
Rabbi Eli Goodman
516.897.2473

NYC Kehilath Jeshurun
Rabbi Elie Weinstock
212.774.5636

NYC Tribeca
Rabbi S. Zalman Paris
646.510.3109

NYC West Side
Rabbi Yisrael Kugel
212.799.0809

Ossining
Rabbi Dovid Labkowski
914.923.2522

Port Washington
Rabbi Shalom Paltiel
516.767.8672

Riverdale
Rabbi Levi Shemtov
718.549.1100

Rochester
Rabbi Nechemia Vogel
585.271.0330

Roslyn
Rabbi Yaakov Reiter
516.484.8185

Sea Gate
Rabbi Chaim Brikman
718.266.1736

Rabbi Nachman Segal
Classes in Hebrew
718. 761.4483

Stony Brook
Rabbi Shalom Ber Cohen
631.585.0521

Suffern
Rabbi Shmuel Gancz
845.368.1889

West Hempstead
Rabbi Yossi Lieberman
Rabbi Mordechai Dinerman
516.596.8691

NORTH CAROLINA

Caryy
Rabbi Yisroel Cotlar
919.651.9710

Charlotte
Rabbi Yossi Groner
Rabbi Shlomo Cohen
704.366.3984

Greensboro
Rabbi Yosef Plotkin
336 617 8120

Raleigh
Rabbi Pinchas Herman
Rabbi Lev Cotlar
919.637.6950

Wilmington
Rabbi Moshe Lieblich
910.763.4770

OHIO

Beachwood
Rabbi Shmuli Friedman
216.370.2887

Blue Ash
Rabbi Yisroel Mangel
513.793.5200

Columbus
Rabbi Areyah Kaltmann
Rabbi Levi Andrusier
614.294.3296

Toledo
Rabbi Yossi Shemtov
419.843.9393

OKLAHOMA

Oklahoma City
Rabbi Ovadia Goldman
405.524.4800

Tulsa
Rabbi Yehuda Weg
918.492.4499

OREGON

Portland
Rabbi Moshe Wilhelm
Rabbi Mordechai Wilhelm
503.977.9947

Salem
Rabbi Avrohom Yitzchok Perlstein
503.383.9569

PENNSYLVANIA

Ambler
Rabbi Shaya Deitsch
215.591.9310

Bala Cynwyd
Rabbi Shraga Sherman
610.660.9192

Clarks Summit
Rabbi Benny Rapoport
570.587.3300

Devon
Rabbi Yossi Kaplan
610.971.9977

Fox Chapel
Rabbi Aaron Herman
Rabbi Ely Rosenfeld
412.781.1800

Lafayette Hill
Rabbi Yisroel Kotlarsky
347.526.1430

Lancaster
Rabbi Elazar Green
717.368.6565

Media
Rabbi Eli Dovid Strasberg
610.543.5095

Newtown
Rabbi Aryeh Weinstein
215.497.9925

Philadelphia: Center City
Rabbi Yochonon Goldman
215.238.2100

Pittsburgh
Rabbi Yisroel Altein
412.422.7300 ext. 269

Pittsburgh: South Hills
Rabbi Mendy Rosenblum
412.278.3693

Rydal
Rabbi Zushe Gurevitz
215.572.1511

Wynnewood
Rabbi Moishe Brennan
610.529.9011

RHODE ISLAND

Warwick
Rabbi Yossi Laufer
401.884.7888

SOUTH CAROLINA

Columbia
Rabbi Hesh Epstein
803.782.1831

TENNESSEE

Chattanooga
Rabbi Shaul Perlstein
423.490.1106

Knoxville
Rabbi Yossi Wilhelm
865.588.8584

Memphis
Rabbi Levi Klein
901.766.1800

Nashville
Rabbi Yitzchok Tiechtel
615.646.5750

TEXAS

Arlington
Rabbi Levi Gurevitch
817.451.1171

Dallas
Rabbi Peretz Shapiro
Rabbi Moshe Naparstek
972.818.0770

Fort Worth
Rabbi Dov Mandel
817.263.7701

Houston
Rabbi Moishe Traxler
713.774.0300

Houston: Rice University Area
Rabbi Eliezer Lazaroff
Rabbi Yitzchok Schmukler
713.522.2004

League City
Rabbi Yitzchok Schmukler
713.398.2460

Plano
Rabbi Mendel Block
Rabbi Yehudah Horowitz
972.596.8270

S. Antonio
Rabbi Chaim Block
Rabbi Yossi Marrus
210.492.1085

The Woodlands
Rabbi Mendel Blecher
281.719.5213

U.S. VIRGIN ISLANDS

S. Thomas
Rabbi Asher Federman
340.998.8889

UTAH

Salt Lake City
Rabbi Benny Zippel
801.467.7777

VERMONT

Burlington
Rabbi Yitzchok Raskin
802.658.5770

VIRGINIA

Alexandria/Arlington
Rabbi Mordechai Newman
703.370.2774

Fairfax
Rabbi Leibel Fajnland
703.426.1980

Norfolk
Rabbi Aaron Margolin
Rabbi Levi Brashevitzky
757.616.0770

Tysons Corner
Chapter founded by
Rabbi Levi Deitsch, OBM
Rabbi Chezzy Deitsch
703.829.5770

WASHINGTON

Olympia
Rabbi Cheski Edelman
360.584-4306

Seattle
Rabbi Elazar Bogomilsky
206.527.1411

Spokane County
Rabbi Yisroel Hahn
509.443.0770

WISCONSIN

Madison
Rabbi Avremel Matusof
608.231.3450

Mequon
Rabbi Menachem Rapoport
262.242.2235

Milwaukee
Rabbi Mendel Shmotkin
414.961.6100

PUERTO RICO

Carolina
Rabbi Mendel Zarchi
787.253.0894

ARGENTINA

BUENOS AIRES
BELGRANO-OLLEROS
Rabbi Mendy Birman
54.11.4774.5071

BUENOS AIRES
Rabbi Mendel Levy
Rabbi Shlomo Levy
54-11-4807-2223

CAPITAL FEDERAL
Rabbi Mendy Gurevitch
54.11.4545.7771

PALERMO NUEVO
Rabbi Mendy Grunblatt
54.11.4772.1024

RECOLETA
Rabbi Hirshel Hendel
54.11.4807.7073

VILLA DEL PARQUE
Rabbi Yosef Itzjok Levy
54.11.4504.1908

AUSTRALIA

NEW SOUTH WALES
BONDI
Rabbi Pinchas Feldman
Rabbi Eli Feldman
Rabbi Robert Kremnizer
612.9387.3822

Mrs. Shterna Althaus
614.0861.3770

DOUBLE BAY
Rabbi Yanky Berger
Rabbi Yisroel Dolnikov
612.9327.1644

DOVER HEIGHTS
Rabbi Motti Feldman
612.9387.3822

NORTH SHORE
Rabbi Nochum Schapiro
Mrs. Fruma Schapiro
612.9488.9548

RANDWICK
Rabbi Aryeh Leib Solomon
613.9375.1600

SOUTH HEAD
Rabbi Benzion Milecki
612.9337.6775

QUEENSLAND
BRISBANE
Rabbi Levi Jaffe
617.3843.6770

VICTORIA
MALVERN
Rabbi Zev Slavin
614.0476.6759

Rabbi Shimshon Yurkowicz
613.9822.3600

SOUTH YARRA
Rabbi Yehuda Hoch
03.9613.0738

BELARUS

GRODNO
Rabbi Yitzchak Kofman
375.29.644.3690

BELGIUM

ANTWERP
Rabbi Mendel Gurary
Rabbi Shabtai Slavaticki
32.3.218.4196

BRAZIL

S. PAULO
Rabbi Avraham Steinmetz
55.11.3081.3081

CANADA

ALBERTA
CALGARY
Rabbi Mordechai Groner
403.238.4880

EDMONTON
Rabbi Ari Drelich
Rabbi Mendy Blachman
780.851.1515

BRITISH COLUMBIA
RICHMOND
Rabbi Yechiel Baitelman
604.277.6427

VANCOUVER
Rabbi Yitzchok Wineberg
604.266.1313

VICTORIA
Rabbi Meir Kaplan
250.595.7656

MANITOBA
WINNIPEG
Rabbi Avrohom Altein
Rabbi Shmuel Altein
204.339.8737

NOVA SCOTIA
HALIFAX
Rabbi Mendel Feldman
902.422.4222

ONTARIO
HAMILTON
Rabbi Chanoch Rosenfeld
905.529.7458

LAWRENCE/EGLINTON
Rabbi Menachem Gansburg
416.546.8770

LONDON
Rabbi Eliezer Gurkow
519.434.3962

MISSISSAUGA
Rabbi Yitzchok Slavin
905.820.4432

NIAGARA FALLS
Rabbi Zalman Zaltzman
905.356.7200

OTTAWA
Rabbi Menachem M. Blum
613.823.0866

RICHMOND HILL
Rabbi Mendel Bernstein
905.770.7700

Rabbi Yossi Hecht
905.773.6477

TORONTO AREA BJL
Rabbi Leib Chaiken
416.916.7202

GREATER TORONTO
REGIONAL OFFICE & THORNHILL
Rabbi Yossi Gansburg
905.731.7000

YORK MILLS
Rabbi Levi Gansburg
647.345.3800

WATERLOO
Rabbi Moshe Goldman
226.338.7770

WHITBY
Rabbi Tzali Borenstein
905.493.9007

QUEBEC
MONTREAL
Rabbi Ronnie Fine
Rabbi Pesach Nussbaum
514.342.3.JLI

Rabbi Levi Y New
514.739.0770

TOWN OF MOUNT ROYAL
Rabbi Moshe Krasnanski
Rabbi Shneur Zalman Rader
514.739.0770

VILLE S. LAURENT
Rabbi Schneur Zalmen Silberstein
514.808.1418

COLOMBIA

BOGOTA
Rabbi Yehoshua B. Rosenfeld
Rabbi Chanoch Piekarski
571.635.8251

DENMARK

COPENHAGEN
Rabbi Yitzchok Lowenthal
45.3316.1850

ESTONIA

TALLINN
Rabbi Shmuel Kot
372.662.30.50

GEORGIA

TBILISI
Rabbi Meir Kozlovsky
995.593.23.91.15

GERMANY

BERLIN
Rabbi Yehuda Tiechtel
49.30.2128.0830

Cologne
Rabbi Mendel Schtroks
49.22.1240.3902

Dusseldorf
Rabbi Chaim Barkahn
49.21.1420.9693

Hamburg
Rabbi Shlomo Bistriztsky
49.40.4142.4190

Munich
Rabbi Yochonon Gordon
49.89.4190.2812

GREECE

Athens
Rabbi Mendel Hendel
30.210.520.2880

GUATEMALA

Guatemala City
Rabbi Shalom Pelman
502.2485.0770

ISRAEL

Ashkelon
Rabbi Shneor Lieberman
054.977.0512

Balfurya
Rabbi Noam Bar-Tov
054.580.4770

Caesarea
Rabbi Chaim Meir Lieberman
054.621.2586

Even Yehuda
Rabbi Menachem Noyman
054.777.0707

Ganei Tikva
Rabbi Gershon Shnur
054.524.2358

Giv'atayim
Rabbi Pinchus Bitton
052.643.8770

Haifa
Rabbi Yehuda Dunin
054.426.3763

Jerusalem
Rabbi Eliyahu Canterman
Classes in English
054.682.3737

Karmiel
Rabbi Mendy Elishevitz
054.521.3073

Kfar Sabba
Rabbi Yossi Baitch
054.445.5020

Kiryat Bialik
Rabbi Pinny Marton
050.661.1768

Kiryat Motzkin
Rabbi Shimon Eizenbach
050.902.0770

Kochav Yair
Rabbi Dovi Greenberg
054.332.6244

Maccabim Re'ut
Rabbi Yosef Yitzchak Noiman
054.977.0549

Modiin
Rabbi Boruch Slonim
054.300.1770

Nes Ziyona
Rabbi Menachem Feldman
054.497.7092

Netanya
Rabbi Schneur Brod
054.579.7572

Ramat Gan-Krinitzi
Rabbi Yisroel Gurevitz
052.743.2814

Ramat Gan-Marom Nave
Rabbi Binyamin Meir Kali
050.476.0770

Ramat Yishai
Rabbi Shneor Zalman Wolosow
052.324.5475

Rishon Lezion
Rabbi Uri Keshet
050.722.4593

Rosh Pina
Rabbi Sholom Ber Hertzel
052.458.7600

Yehud
Rabbi Shmuel Wolf
053.536.1479

KAZAKHSTAN

Almaty
Rabbi Shevach Zlatopolsky
7.7272.77.59.77

LATVIA

Riga
Rabbi Shneur Zalman Kot
371.6733.1520

NETHERLANDS

Den Haag
Rabbi Shmuel Katzman
31.70.347.0222

Noord-Holland
Amsterdam
Rabbi Yanki Jacobs
31 6 44988627

PANAMA

Panama City
Rabbi Ari Laine
Rabbi Gabriel Benayon
507.223.3383

RUSSIA

Astrakhan
Rabbi Yisroel Melamed
7.851.239.28.24

Bryansk
Rabbi Menachem Mendel Zaklas
7.483.264.55.15

Chelyabinsk
Rabbi Meir Kirsh
7.351.263.24.68

Moscow-Marina Rosha
Rabbi Mordechai Weisberg
7.495.645.50.00

Moscow-Sokolniki
Rabbi Avraham Bekerman
7.495.660.07.70

Nizhny Novgorod
Rabbi Shimon Bergman
7.920.253.47.70

Omsk
Rabbi Osher Krichevsky
7.381.231.33.07

Perm
Rabbi Zalman Deutch
7.342.212.47.32

Samara
Rabbi Shlomo Deutch
7.846.333.40.64

Saratov
Rabbi Yaakov Kubitshek
7.8452.21.58.00

S. Petersburg
Rabbi Zvi Pinsky
7.812.713.62.09

Rostov
Rabbi Chaim Danziger
7.8632.99.02.68

Togliatti
Rabbi Meier Fischer
7.848.273.02.84

Ufa
Rabbi Dan Krichevsky
7.347.244.55.33

Voronezh
Rabbi Levi Stiefel
7.473.252.96.99

SINGAPORE

Singapore
Rabbi Mordechai Abergel
656.337.2189

Rabbi Netanel Rivni
Classes in Hebrew
656.336.2127

SOUTH AFRICA

Cape Town
Rabbi Mendel Popack
Rabbi Pinchas Hecht
27.21.434.3740

Johannesburg
Rabbi Dovid Hazdan
Rabbi Shmuel Simpson
27.11.728.8152

Rabbi Dovid Masinter
Rabbi Ari Kievman
27.11.440.6600

SPAIN
Barcelona
Rabbi Dovid Libersohn
34.93.410.0685

SWEDEN
Stockholm
Rabbi Chaim Greisman
468.679.7067

SWITZERLAND
Basel
Rabbi Zalman Wishedski
41.76.559.9236

Lugano
Rabbi Yaakov Tzvi Kantor
41.91.921.3720

Luzern
Rabbi Chaim Drukman
41.41.361.1770

UKRAINE
Cherkassy
Rabbi Dov Axelrod
380.472.45.7080

Dnepropetrovsk
Rabbi Dan Makagon
380.504.51.13.18

Nikolayev
Rabbi Sholom Gotlieb
380.512.37.37.71

Zhitomir
Rabbi Shlomo Wilhelm
380.504.63.01.32

Odessa
Rabbi Avraham Wolf
Rabbi Yaakov Neiman
38.048.728.0770 ext. 280

UNITED KINGDOM
Edgeware
Rabbi Leivi Sudak
Rabbi Yaron Jacobs
44.208.905.4141

Leeds
Rabbi Eli Pink
44.113.266.3311

London
Rabbi Gershon Overlander
Rabbi Dovid Katz
44.208.202.1600

Rabbi Nissan D. Dubov
44.20.8944.1581

URUGUAY
Montevideo
Rabbi Eliezer Shemtov
598.2.709.3444

VENEZUELA
Caracas
Rabbi Yehoshua Rosenblum
58.212.264.7011

NOTES

NOTES

NOTES

NOTES

NOTES

NOTES

NOTES

NOTES

NOTES

NOTES

NOTES

NOTES

The Jewish Learning Multiplex

Brought to you by the Rohr Jewish Learning Institute

In fulfillment of the mandate of the Lubavitcher Rebbe, of blessed memory, whose leadership guides every step of our work, the mission of the Rohr Jewish Learning Institute is to transform Jewish life and the greater community through the study of Torah, connecting each Jew to our shared heritage of Jewish learning.

While our flagship program remains the cornerstone of our organization, JLI is proud to feature additional divisions catering to specific populations, in order to meet a wide array of educational needs.

THE ROHR JEWISH LEARNING INSTITUTE,
a subsidiary of *Merkos L'Inyonei Chinuch*,
is the adult education arm of the Chabad-Lubavitch Movement.